# Peace Processes

# Peace Processes

## A Sociological Approach

John D. Brewer

polity

First published in 2010 by Polity Press

Polity Press
65 Bridge Street
Cambridge CB2 1UR, UK

Polity Press
350 Main Street
Malden, MA 02148, USA

ISBN-13: 978-0-7456-4776-0
ISBN-13: 978-0-7456-4777-7(paperback)

A catalogue record for this book is available from the British Library.

Typeset in 10 on 11.5pt Utopia
by Servis Filmsetting Ltd, Stockport, Cheshire
Printed and bound in Great Britain by MPG Books Group, UK

The publisher has used its best endeavours to ensure that the URLs for external websites referred to in this book are correct and active at the time of going to press. However, the publisher has no responsibility for the websites and can make no guarantee that a site will remain live or that the content is or will remain appropriate.

Every effort has been made to trace all copyright holders, but if any have been inadvertently overlooked the publisher will be pleased to include any necessary credits in any subsequent reprint or edition.

For further information on Polity, visit our website: www.politybooks.com

For my father, Charles Benjamin Brewer, who died in a mining accident when I was too young to know him, and for my adult children, Bronwen and Gwyn, in thanks for the memories we have.

# Contents

# Acknowledgements

Three different sorts of colleague ignited my interest in the sociology of peace processes. First, were Tom Bamat and Mary Ann Cejka, from Maryknoll Missionary Research Center New York, when, on the basis of my writings on religion as a site of conflict, they asked me in 1998 to participate in research on religion as a site of reconciliation. Regular visits to Maryknoll enabled me to meet and become friends with the second significant group of colleagues. Shirley Wijesinghe, Deepthi Silva and, later, Jude Fernando, from Sri Lanka, introduced me over two visits to the beauty of the island and the pains of its conflict. Third was Jack Spence, formerly of the Royal Institute of International Studies, and now retired to the wilds of wonderful Shropshire, when, for a conference in Dublin in 1998, he asked me to reflect as a sociologist on the occurrence of the peace processes in Northern Ireland and South Africa. From there it has been a series of easy – and inevitable – steps to look at peace processes in general.

But the stimulus has not been solely intellectual, for there is a biographical referent to this book that connects my life and work. I lived for twenty-three years in Northern Ireland amidst on-going conflict and some of the worst years of 'the Troubles'; my son Gwyn was born in Belfast at the height of the Hunger Strikes, and my daughter Bronwen in South Africa four years earlier, in the troubled aftermath of Steve Biko's death. Family and personal life demanded more than passing interest in peace and stability. Through my relationship with the Revd Ken Newell, and via him with members of the Faith in a Brighter Future Group of ecumenical churchmen and women in Northern Ireland, Francis Teeney and I became activists in Northern Ireland's peace processes, small-scale though our involvement was. Gareth Higgins inspired me to this as well; and that Francis and Gareth are former Ph.D. students of mine illustrates how much I have learned from them.

I have many other debts. I am grateful to colleagues at the University of Aberdeen who have helped to make academic life congenial, especially Bernie Hayes. Cohorts of students in my fourth-year sociology option course, on the sociology of peace processes, warrant special respect for listening to my draft ideas. Some of the research for this book was undertaken while a Visiting Fellow in the Research School of Social Sciences at the Australian National University and I am particularly grateful to my sponsors on that occasion: Ian McAllister, John Braithwaite and Clifford Shearing. An extra-special debt is owed to the following colleagues for reading the manuscript in its entirety: John Brown Childs, Gerard Delanty, John A. Hall and Clifford Shearing. John Brown Childs is another Maryknoll friend and I am grateful for all I have learned from him. The following people kindly read parts of the manuscript: Jude Lal Fernando, Gareth Higgins, Myra Hird, Shadd Maruna, Tim Strangleman, Francis Teeney and Iain Wilkinson. All are excused responsibility for its continuing faults. I am also grateful to Patricia Lundy for sight of her unpublished research report to the British Academy on the operation of the Historical Enquiries Team of the Police Service of Northern Ireland, and to Gerard Delanty for pre-publication access to the Summer 2008 special issue of the *European Journal of Social Theory* on emotions in post-trauma societies. I am especially grateful to the Leverhulme Trust for awarding me a Research Fellowship for 2007–8, which enabled me to complete the writing of this book.

Last – but by no means least – I owe very much to Caitríona and Fiachra for keeping me sane over many years; they deserve far more than this inadequate acknowledgement can convey, but, being a creature of habit, I end this acknowledgement, as every other before, in expressing my love for Bronwen and Gwyn, no less now than that for Caitríona and Fiachra.

John D. Brewer
Belfast, 16 April 2009

# Introduction
# War, peace and communal violence

## Introduction

I have two purposes in writing this book: to highlight sociology's contribution to our understanding of peace processes and the factors that help stabilize them; and to introduce specialists in peace processes to sociology and some of its special debates and concerns. I hope to inform sociologists about peace processes and enlighten experts in peace processes from other disciplines about sociology. The field indicates they know little of each other, suggesting this book may prove useful to both. I offer a sustained intellectual justification for the contribution of sociology not only for the analysis of peace processes but also for the stability and quality of peace processes themselves, making the book an unremitting defence of public sociology.

I have been interested in 'the sociological imagination' as a life's work and have applied it in the past in ways that bring sociology's insights to areas relatively neglected by the discipline, as a way of drawing attention to its role in analysing public issues. None can be more topical than the concern with war and peace. As Cortright (2008) explains in his history of peace movements, peace is an old idea and modern forms of violence attest to its enduring relevance (the idea of 'perpetual peace' was used by Kant in 1795; for another history of the durability of peace see Adolf, 2009). If new kinds of war help to define global society, as so many social scientists claim (see in particular Kaldor, 1999), late modernity is also marked by new kinds of peacemaking. It is ironic, therefore, that most of the attention in social science has been on the changing character of organized violence rather than the impact of globalization on peace. This book addresses peace processes from a sociological perspective and seeks to correct the weaknesses in the current literature in the belief that sociology can disclose some of the better ways to manage the after-effects of communal violence. There can be no single definitive 'sociology of peace processes' but I hope to illustrate how useful the sociological imagination can be.

---

### Vignette: Sociology and 'the moral imagination' for peace

I seek here to illustrate sociology's potential to unlock hidden features of peace processes by using the example of the 'moral imagination', a term associated with John Paul Lederach (2005), Professor of International Peacebuilding at the Joan B. Kroc Institute of International Peace Studies at the University of Notre Dame, and a leading peace studies teacher, trainer, practitioner and researcher. Lederach is a Mennonite Christian and sociologist whose religious convictions infuse his many writings on peace (notably Lederach, 1997). The idea of the 'moral imagination' became popular in peace studies very quickly. Etymology suggests that Christianity gives meaning to what is 'moral' in this idea, and cognitive and artistic ability supplies the 'imagination'. Peace builders are therefore urged to conceive of their work as akin to an artistic process. Unfettering their imagination enables them to recognize turning points, venture down unknown paths, transcend orthodox conflict resolution strategies by new forms of thinking and act anew to create the peace process, thereby 'linking unlike-minded people', as Lederach puts it (2005: 13). However, peace processes require soul as well as art, and the steps that peacemakers are enjoined to take can only really be understood in terms of the moral values that encourage and motivate activists, for peacemakers have to imagine themselves in a web of relationships that include even their enemies, embrace complexity and diversity without further schism, and accept the risks involved (Lederach, 2005: 5). Without this moral framework, giving free rein to peacemakers' curiosity, creativity and risk-taking could harm rather than transform social relationships. Thus, without acknowledging it, Lederach is forced to draw on his Christianity to describe the moral precepts peace builders use as a resource when 'moving parties toward a relationship of love rather than fear' and developing 'relationships of love characterized by openness, mutual respect, and dignity' (2005: 57).

In truth, the moral imagination is another in a series of ideas within peace studies that deploy quasi-religious discourse. Peace unavoidably encourages the re-enchantment of our vocabulary by references to healing, reconciliation, forgiveness, redemption, hope, 'truth', restoration, love and the like, all of which have a Judeo-

Christian resonance. Peace processes do require eschatology, the sense of a better, longed-for future society without violence, but this ought to be secular. Many conflicts are about religion, or involve religious protagonists, making Christian eschatology divisive, and some have involved the Christian Church taking the side of the dominant group and state. Secularization is another reason why religious eschatology is problematic. Peace processes are, as Lederach rightly contends, too focused on reaching a political agreement rather than healing damaged relationships. Peaceful transformation involves on-going changes to social relationships and constructive engagements between people who have been historically divided, but placing social change within Christian eschatology seriously limits the purpose.

The other major weakness of the term is its restriction to professional peacemakers. It describes the moral precepts and behavioural and cognitive challenges of activists engaged in mediation, negotiations and conflict resolution. Their work might well benefit from being rethought as both art and morality, but peace processes require that lay people are addressed as well. Part of the fragility of peace processes is that reconciliation is professionalized – sometimes to outside third parties – and not taken ownership of by society at large. Bystanders, victims and ex-combatants also need to rethink and reformulate, to risk-take and develop a new set of moral precepts for living together with their former enemies. The moral imagination seems a quality necessary for everyone. Indeed, this is its greatest contribution.

Sociology helps us significantly at this point by supplying a secular eschatology within which the moral landscape of post-violence societies as a whole can be discussed without recourse to religion. Reconstructing the moral landscape becomes possible in a peace process once space has been opened up by the negotiated accord; and a specialism within sociology gives an account of what this morality might look like. The sociology of citizenship is an area of sociology quite comfortable with normative vocabulary and with advocating a particular set of moral values. Its depiction of cosmopolitan virtues – trust, tolerance, respect, civic responsibility, duty, altruism, empathy and the like – makes this a suitable moral code to underpin peace processes.

Citizenship is an inter-disciplinary field but what distinguishes sociology's focus is the connection it makes between citizenship and societal solidarity, as Turner (1990: 189) put it, making citizenship a moral as well as legal category. Sociology speaks less about the formal legal rights and entitlements that define citizenship, addressing instead how citizenship is conferred by social membership rather than law. In rendering citizenship as a moral category, it becomes a normative term bound up with society's values, and invokes moral (as well as legal) responsibilities. The difficult questions for the sociology of citizenship, however, are two-fold: what are the specific moral injunctions in a situation of changing or diverse moral codes, competing sets of values and different normative systems?; and how does moral diversity affect conceptions of the obligations of citizens?

The literature on this is interesting and we can have a brief taster. Couching the discussion of citizenship in terms of obligations rather than rights has led some to argue that we have, for example, an obligation to work (Becker, 1980; Mead, 1986), a public responsibility akin to paying taxes and obeying the law. Neo-conservative approaches such as this tend to prioritize citizens' economic obligations. In assessing such a view, Goodin (2002) encouraged its advocates to consider 'mutual obligations', 'fair play', 'reciprocity', and to broaden out from focusing on the economy, although, as Scholz and Pinney (1995) argued, ordinary people nonetheless comply with tax and financial laws through a sense of duty rather than fear. Duty is commented on also by Conover, Leonard and Searing (1993: 161–2), whose focus group interviews picked up people for whom the notion was 'a four-letter word' but also others who experienced it as an obligation. It was noticeable, however, that the latter grounded their responsibilities more in terms of social roles than as citizens, feeling duties toward children, parents, grandparents, friends and the local community and neighbourhood. This tends to reinforce the ideas of the communitarians and civil society theorists, who see citizenship obligations in terms of the moral injunction to promote public-spiritedness, civic responsibilities and a just and ethical society (see Dagger, 1997: 6), based on both the filial and intimate connections associated with social roles and wider notions of 'civic citizenship' (on which, see also Janoski, 1998).

One of the most interesting dimensions of the debate about the moral underpinning to citizenship obligations is the emphasis on virtue. This is expressed overtly in the outline of what is called 'cosmopolitan virtue' (thus giving us 'cosmopolitan citizenship'; H. Smith, 2007), but is also evident in the emphasis placed on specific cosmopolitan virtues, notably tolerance and trust. The return of virtue is remarkable, since it was only in 1981 that a leading moral philosopher entitled his review of modern thought *After Virtue* (MacIntyre, 1981). Its re-emergence, however, has paralleled the rediscovery of citizenship. Its rediscovery by academic writers on citizenship is echoed in the voluntary sector by the 'Virtues Project' (see www.virtuesproject.com/). This was set up in 1991 and addresses 'spiritual and moral virtues' through leadership training and programmes of activities for secular and religious youth groups. The project emphasizes that it is about virtues not values: about character rather than beliefs. This is not the sense in which it is used in the academic literature. In the latter, virtue does not mean virtuousness, the moral excellence of a person's behaviour, as it tends to do in the several world faiths that identify specific virtues as part of their scriptures, but the classic civic humanist sense of the social traits, habits and values that promote the public good, such as tolerance, respect, sociability, duty, loyalty, trust and the like. This was such a motif of eighteenth-century thought that Hont and Ignatieff entitled their account of it *Wealth and Virtue* (1983), and Pocock *Virtue, Commerce and History* (1985). This is the sense in which it is used, for example, in Dagger's (1997) reference to the 'civic virtues' of citizenship, such as public-spiritedness and active engagement in community affairs, and by Bryan Turner (2002), when he outlines 'cosmopolitan virtues' as the specifically cultural obligations that accrue from cultural citizenship (see also Turner, 2000). In Turner's accounts, cosmopolitan virtue involves respect for other cultures and an 'ironic' attitude toward one's own. Dobson (2003) has referred to our obligations to protect the environment as part of cosmopolitan virtue, in what he calls 'ecological citizenship'.

The use of cosmopolitanism to flesh out the morality that is required under conditions of culturally plural citizenship after conflict, where groups bear rights to cultural citizenship, is not without its critics in sociology (see Nash, 2008) and needs some justification given cosmopolitanism's association with individualism. Atack (2005: 40–1) emphasizes that cosmopolitanism normally refers to the view that all individuals are part of one universal moral community, so that rights are grounded in egalitarianism, universalism and individualism. The respect is for persons not cultures, individuals not groups. Therefore, the deployment of cosmopolitanism to understand the virtues necessary for cultural citizenship requires revision to the grounds on which these values are invoked and of the moral entities to which they accord recognition. It can be argued that community membership, not individualism, is the dynamic. Citizens apply these moral notions as members of a particular community in order to give recognition to members of other groups, in realization that it is the best way to live harmoniously in societies where there is deep diversity. The values are grounded in community membership and accorded to all communities for the purpose of managing multiculturalism. While cosmopolitan virtues are still universal, their application in particular settings recognizes that in some locations people happen to live their lives in groups, that group membership in these settings frames their notions of morality, and that moral codes are needed there to structure the relationship between groups. The discourse of rights in these societies is about groups not individuals (on group rights, see Baubock, 1999).

Dobson (2006) refers to this as 'thick cosmopolitanism', which he contrasts with the thin veneer of group protection in individualism. There is something of this in Appiah's (2007) contention that cosmopolitanism provides an ethic for living amidst strangers, an idea directly opposed to Bauman's (1998) sociology of modernity, where we are supposedly cast adrift morally and project our ontological fears onto the strange 'other'. There are also parallels in Kaldor's (1999: 68) idea of 'cosmopolitanism from below', a respect for universal values that is grounded in the concerns of particular civil society groups, and in what Erskine (2000: 582) calls 'embedded cosmopolitanism', which portrays people as being morally obligated to each other as a result of the community networks to which they belong (see also Atack, 2005: 52–5). Hampson's (2002: 58) notion of 'civil society cosmopolitanism' captures this in the clearest terms. This is the version of cosmopolitanism that gives meaning to the moral code best suited for citizenship in post-violence societies.

In these writings sociology does not shrink from discussions of morality and it does not automatically endorse moral relativism (Lukes, 2009). Nussbaum (1996), for example, has argued that compassion is the basic social emotion and is a leading advocate of the use of citizenship education to encourage cosmopolitan virtues in our global age (Nussbaum, 2002). Waghid (2004) argued from a South African perspective that encouraging people to take seriously the suffering of others ought to be the outcome of that country's citizenship education curriculum, as well as peace and democracy. And Ure (2008: 290–1) and Frost (2008) have argued that post-conflict societies ought to be rebuilt on the basis of compassion and empathy, emotions cultivated through collective senses of tragedy. This argument represents an example of the general idea that emotions can be constructed through the 'education of emotion' (a term I owe to Iain Wilkinson). There is potential for particular types of emotion to be actively cultivated and the principal cultural means by which this can be achieved is through schools, civil society associations and grassroots groups, International Non-Governmental Organizations (INGOs), governments and the like, using school curricula, adult education workshops, voluntary-sector courses, training programmes, forms of popular culture and the media to encourage the positive emotions that are needed to undergird a peace process, such as compassion for others' suffering, empathy with victims, forgiveness for perpetrators, toleration of difference and tolerance towards others' identity and culture, hope in the future, and courage to take the 'leap of trust' (Mollering, 2001) in relationships with erstwhile enemies. Thus sociology enables us to use Delanty's (2006) notion of the 'cosmopolitan imagination' as an alternative to Lederach's 'moral imagination' when referring to the moral landscape necessary for successful peace processes.

Johan Galtung, the principal founder of the discipline of peace studies, is a Norwegian sociologist but the new subject is primarily located within political science; Evangelista's (2005) multi-volume collection of classic readings in peace studies is sub-titled *Critical Concepts in Political Science*. Galtung's (1996: 3ff.) pioneering distinction between negative and positive peace – the former being the absence of violence, the latter the achievement of fairness, justice and social redistribution – finds empathy with Wolterstorff's (1983) suggestion that peace incorporates feelings of well-being and a sense of flourishing and Sen's idea that socio-economic development is freedom (1999). As Wolterstorff notes, peace is often perceived in negative terms as the absence of something (violence) rather than as an affirmation (of justice, fairness and the like). No author, however, locates positive peace sociologically. Wolterstorff draws on Augustinian philosophy and Galtung stresses its political, military, economic and cultural dimensions. The distinction between negative and positive peace, however, has lasting relevance to a sociological approach to peace, as will become clear throughout these pages (for a modern discussion of the distinction, see Barash and Webel, 2009: 3–12).

There is, however, a small literature within sociology on aspects of peace processes that suggests there is value in a broader treatment. Jon Elster (2004) analysed 'transitional justice', by which demands for retribution and reparation are handled; some sociological literature focuses on the principles and practices surrounding reconciliation as a normative value, addressing the interpersonal and even spiritual grounds (for example Lederach, 1997) on which co-existence is feasible (for example Kriesberg, 2003; Weiner, 1998). There is also research by sociologists on conflict resolution and mediation techniques, such as John Brown Child's notion of 'transcommunality' (2003a), which is based on indigenous North American mediation procedures. Sociologists, amongst others, have contributed substantially to our understanding of the 'truth' recovery procedures. Other sociological analyses have taken a case study approach, looking at specific peace processes (J.D. Brewer, 2003a; Knox and Quirk, 2000; Oberschall, 2007).

In what follows I offer an analysis of the different types of post-violence society and the various ways in which peace can be achieved. There are all sorts of ways in which communal conflicts and wars come to an end, such as partition (and repartition), cultural absorption or annihilation, third-party intervention, United Nations' peacekeeping, and negotiated peace settlements in which parties give up their preferred options for a second-best compromise. It is the latter that forms the focus here. I explore the array of social issues that negotiated peace accords throw up: questions like globalization, civil society, religion, women's victim experiences, the problem of violent masculinities amongst ex-combatants, emotions, the management of shame–guilt, the garnering of hope and forgiveness, restorative justice, memory, 'truth' recovery and victimhood. As a piece of sociology itself, this volume tends to concentrate on the general analytical features of negotiated peace processes but it draws eclectically on empirical examples to illustrate the arguments and I include in-depth case studies and shorter vignettes.

At first sight these issues do not appear to be exclusively sociological ones, but they represent what the art historian Griselda Pollock once called 'travelling concepts' – ideas which pass through various disciplines, taking on different dimensions and nuances as they journey. While they are not the sole provenance of sociology, this study suggests they coalesce to make an important sociological dynamic in peace processes, the resolution of which is vital to the success of post-violence adjustments. Societies like Northern Ireland, South Africa, Rwanda, the Sudan, the Philippines, Sierra Leone, Liberia, Sri Lanka and various South American countries will be used for illustration, giving us an expansive geographic range. Some obvious cases are missing from this list because the conflict was resolved by partition or repartition (the Balkans, Cyprus), cultural annihilation (Australian treatment of aboriginal peoples and indigenous Americans in North America) or continued third-party ring-keeping (Afghanistan, Iraq). Some have simply not yet stopped the killing and have no peace process (Somalia, Democratic Republic of Congo, Israel–Palestine). Negotiated compromise peace deals based on consensus form the cases tackled here since they involve societies having to find ways of internally managing the social cleavages that once provoked conflict in non-violent ways, whilst maintaining their territorial integrity.

## Sociology, war and peace

Sociology's contribution to understanding the globalization of war (for example Martin Shaw, 2003, 2007) has been immense. However, the sociological study of war necessitates a corresponding approach to peace. War and peace are implied by each other, for no war is irresolvable and no peace secure from renewed conflict. They implicate each other in another sense for the nature of the conflict often shapes the potential for peacemaking. They are two sides of the same Janus face, above all because the globalization of war has impacted on the globalization of peace, producing new forms of peacemaking. If war is no longer a matter just for the protagonists, neither is peace; peacemaking is as much a global process as war. Peacemakers have learned from warmakers how to mobilize global networks and in the process mediate the very global structures that constitute the new forms of peacemaking in the modern world. If globalization has resulted in new forms of war, as many contend, it has also transformed peacemaking.

So implicated are war and peace in each other that it is first necessary to provide context to our discussion of peace processes by briefly exploring the globalization of organized violence. In a penetrating account of the impact of globalization on 'new wars', Kaldor (1999) argues that it has eroded the autonomy of the state, even facilitated the disintegration of the state, lost the state its monopoly of organized violence, encouraged a more dangerous kind of 'identity politics' that is easily mobilized by modern means of electronic media and slips readily into organized killings that do not protect the immunity of non-combatants, and has disseminated the means of mass killing to groups less easily regulated and controlled by international norms (1999: 4–7).

We can begin to understand these processes by making the common distinction between 'global militarization' and 'military globalization' (see Held et al., 1999: 88ff.). The former refers to the global military build-up under the arms race, to the point where very localized wars can involve the use of very sophisticated weaponry; the latter to the military connectedness between the world's major regions as localized wars impact on the geo-political order and reinforce the necessity for the geo-governance of war. War, communal violence and rapidly expanding military technologies have been amongst the most important processes that are reconstituting the world into a single strategic geo-space. This time–space compression in turn has increased the potential for war, as well as its destructive consequences and its capability to disrupt relations well beyond the site of conflict. These are not the only reasons why globalization is said to have resulted in new kinds of war. The reassertion of regional and local interstate rivalry has intensified with the ending of the Cold War and the fragmentation that has accompanied globalization has witnessed the resurgence of nationalist, religious, ethnic and communal conflicts. The intensity with which 'local traditions' (Giddens, 1996: 15) are upheld in moments of transition or as a reaction to globalization often results in old identities assuming significance, thus perpetuating old divisions and sometimes turning them violent. Bauman (1998) argues that the human consequences of globalization encourage us to feel secure only in collective identities and to project risk onto the stranger in our midst. Democracy itself is increasingly perceived to have a 'darker side' (Mann, 2004) by permitting people to mobilize openly around cleavages that can become divisive and encouraging people to feel that that their particular religious, ethnic or communal values *must* be represented politically, sometimes at the cost of other people's. Whilst this increases the potential for conflict in global society, ironically, changing technologies of warfare permit the prosecution of war without the total mobilization of societies. This tends to make war several steps removed from many people's direct experience, at least in the global First World (which causes British generals, for example, to complain that the public does not understand what the army is going through in Iraq and Afghanistan), which can assist in public acquiescence in war. These separate processes make for both more war and changed forms of war.

But it is also the case that lying within the globalization of war are increased opportunities for peacemaking and new forms of peace work. The development of regional security blocs contributes both to fragmentation and to centripetal processes at the same time, for these networks can encourage co-operation over defence and security arrangements as much as rivalry. Their interconnectedness makes us all vulnerable to conflicts in distant parts of the globe and can heighten our mutual interest in peaceful intervention. The rising density of economic connections between states and regional security blocs means that nations no longer see threats to national security just in military terms, but also as economic threats, so that intervention is more readily contemplated. The development of extensive diaspora networks gives nations a cultural connectedness with distant others that may also motivate peacekeeping as diaspora and other filial connections increase the pressure on governments to do something. New technologies and effective use of the Internet can mobilize for peace (and bring to world attention various atrocities), as evidenced in the Burmese case in 2007 and Tibet in 2008.

The growth of humanitarian cosmopolitanism also affects peacemaking. Military globalization inevitably involves new forms of geo-governance that monitor the means and conduct of organized violence. The development of cosmopolitan humanitarian law to regulate conflict (see Atack, 2005; Hirsh, 2003; Woodiwiss, 2002), to limit use of instruments of war and to hold people to account for war crimes constitutes a moral justification for peacekeeping and legal support for the interventions of the United Nations (UN). The UN Charter provides for the body to intervene to restore peace, and it has increasingly done so after its security function became real with the ending of the Cold War. The human rights discourse that affects so much of geo-politics is in essence a language of peace by constituting a powerful deterrent to the violation of human rights. It has furnished a monitoring regime of numerous INGOs that operate transnationally, bypassing governments to establish a global network of peace activists. This network allows

INGOs to play an international role as peace campaigners, which gives peace a global voice. There are many weaknesses in the enforcement of human rights and in the geo-governance regulation of warfare, but peace has become a universal principle that is mediated by global networks – noted at present for its breaching as much as its practice, but an international principle nonetheless.

The impact of this global network is enhanced by the co-operation between human rights INGOs and a plethora of global networks mobilizing around gender, violence against women, the environment, anti-capitalism, opposition to landmines and other instruments of war, charitable giving, AIDS and other health issues and the like. There are flows of information between these networks and co-campaigning, to the point where we are observing the emergence of what Kaldor (2003) calls global civil society with shared values and aims (see also Anheier, Glasius and Kaldor, 2005; Kaldor et al., 2003b; cf. Keane, 2003). The effects of NGOs can be exaggerated, or at least their negative side neglected (on 'bad' civil society, see Chambers and Kopstein, 2001), as we shall see in chapter 3, but the progressive elements of civil society resonate with peace in two ways. These specific issues are often aligned with peace inasmuch as organized violence is seen to provoke them or make them worse; and these global networks can easily be mobilized around peace as a vocation. Paradoxically, organized killings have intensified with globalization to the point where the success of peace processes assumes immense topical importance, justifying sociological engagement with peace. Before making such an engagement, however, we need to spend a little more time thinking about violence.

## Collective or communal violence?

Sociology has long been interested in particular kinds of violence – 'domestic' violence, riots, crowd behaviour, wars, criminal damage, murder, terrorism and so on – and major figures from the sociological pantheon have discussed violence, such as Weber, Elias, Giddens and Foucault. The strong sense of sociological determinism that developed in nineteenth-century European sociology was rooted in part in studies of group violence, for crowds seemed to exemplify the power of the collectivity over individuals. Group violence forms an essential part of sociological theories that seek to deconstruct two Enlightenment meta-narratives, that of social progress – examined in studies of genocide and the Holocaust as examples of social regression in advanced modernity (see Bauman, 1989) – and that of rationality – focusing on how we objectify the 'truth' about mass killings and atrocities (see Cohen, 2001). It also features in sociology's concern with globalization, where communal violence is often linked to local forms of resistance, in which the survival of what Giddens (1996: 15) calls 'little traditions' as a resistance to cultural hegemony can reinforce violent conflicts over such cleavages as 'race', ethnicity and religious fundamentalism.

Violence can simultaneously be against the person and against the group. Group violence comes in many types, such as collective violence, genocide and structural violence. 'Collective violence' is the term in widest currency. The distinction between it and communal violence is thus worth reiterating. Communal violence involves groups, with the violence directed either towards another group as a whole or towards individual members of the group because of their group membership. Where there is intent to destroy the whole group, communal violence merges into genocide. Of course, communal violence is against the person in that an individual Catholic or Tutsi is the victim, but it is their identity as a member of the group that explains their victimhood. It is the group that is being punished or attacked, and the individual only as a proxy for it. Some forms of interpersonal or collective violence may also involve groups, such as gang rape or some forms of riot, but the victim is not selected as a representative of the group, nor punished or attacked as a proxy for others. Or at least, if they are, collective violence veers into communal violence.

It is not the number of participants that makes violence a collective activity. The late Charles Tilly (2003) argued that collective violence only requires three people: two colluding together with the intent to attack the third. What makes violence collective for Tilly is thus the collusion amongst perpetrators and the design between them to attack another. This makes gang rape a form of collective violence, as are brawls on rugby pitches and fights after the pubs and bars close. Tilly's term is thus ambiguous. At one end, collective violence borders interpersonal violence – 'domestic' abuse against children often involves collusion amongst attackers (the parents) against a single victim (the child) or collection of victims (all the siblings). This confusion between collective and interpersonal violence is unhelpful; it is contrary to common sense to think of 'domestic' abuse as a form of collective violence. At the other end, it also borders on communal violence, since people may be involved as participants or victims precisely because of their group membership. 'Collective violence' is thus an unhelpful term concealing different sorts of things.

I want to concentrate on the specific kind of collective violence that I call 'communal violence'. It has three qualities: it involves the mobilization of group identities; its perpetrators and victims act as proxies for group interests; and it is embedded in the social structure in which it takes place. 'Communal violence' is my preferred term because it makes clear that the perpetrators and victims are not random individuals who, through chance circumstance end up in incidents of violence. Accidental circumstance may explain how and why the communal violence broke out there and then, but how and why these perpetrators and victims were involved is not accidental but linked to their identity as group members. This makes the term analytically quite different from 'interpersonal violence' in a way that Tilly's definition of 'collective violence' is not. I prefer this term to 'genocide' because there may be no intent to destroy the whole group and occasionally mass killings are ideological rather than ethnic, such as Khmer Rouge violence in Cambodia. Most acts of communal violence fall below the threshold of the legal definition of genocide operated by the United Nations.

Embedding communal violence in the social structure in which it takes place enables us to focus on the influence of particular kinds of social structure to explain the violence, rather than on the effect of different kinds of political regime or other political explanations. It draws attention to the effect of social processes like 'race', structural inequality, colonialism, ethnicity and religion, and to the impact of globalization in reinforcing violent conflicts over social cleavages. It thus incorporates Galtung's notion of 'structural violence' (1969; for a modern usage see Ho, 2007), where violence is understood as systemic inequality arising deliberately or unintentionally from social structural arrangements (such as apartheid or institutional racism) rather than as direct acts of aggression. The notion of communal violence also touches on the lively debate about whether globalization has created new conflicts or simply transformed long-established ones. Mary Kaldor (1999) and Martin Shaw (2003) are strongly associated with the idea that globalization has created new kinds of war, while Barrington Moore (2000) argues that it has simply allowed older conflicts to appropriate new forms. By tying communal violence to social structural cleavages, we see that some conflicts are ancient in reproducing old divisions.

I am not saying that communal violence only takes place in the country with which it is associated and that it has no international dimension. Structural violence is inevitably restricted to a particular society's set of institutional arrangements, while communal violence stretches social structural conflicts across several societies. Groups are often transnational, describing 'imagined communities' that reflect patterns of extensive migration and diaspora, impacting on social structures stretched across significant spatial distances and territorial boundaries. The point, however, is that these places are seen as extensions of the original group conflict and are proxies for the group identities involved in it. India gets involved in Sri Lanka's communal conflict precisely because of the resonances it has with its own Tamil community in Southern India. India and Pakistan go to war as nation states over Kashmir because both claim communal ties to it. Links exist across social structures to ensure that a nation state's communal conflict is not always confined to one territory: Rwanda's ethnic conflict has infected – and destabilized – Burundi and the Democratic Republic of Congo.

## Plan of the book

Having established the sociological roots to communal violence, I want now to sketch the sociological features of peace processes and explain the format of the book. Whether or not conflict is thought of as new kinds of war wrought by globalization or as older ones appropriating new forms, in the contemporary world there are many societies racked by communal violence. If violence is a mark of late modernity, as Giddens contends (1996: 60–4), or of the clash of advanced civilizations, as Huntington argues (1996), it appears also as a feature of societies at different stages of development, wrenching apart post-colonial societies, former Communist countries, advanced industrial societies and rapidly modernizing countries. There are, however, a number of societies that have progressed from violent communal conflict to a measure of peace, with much-reduced levels of communal violence. These cases form the substance of this book. I develop a sociological category in chapter 1, which I call 'post-violence society', which is applied to those social formations that have undergone transition from communal violence to relative non-violence. A typology is developed of different kinds of post-violence society as they cohere around three axes. Conceptual clarification of the category forms only part of the argument, however. The taxonomy is used to focus on one type of post-violence society, in which peace accords based on consensus have been negotiated as a strategy for managing the fissures that previously provoked communal violence. I focus on this type in order to try to understand better the range of policy issues that need to be faced in negotiated peace agreements.

If sociology can assist in understanding the fragility of peace processes and explain why peace processes are invariably problematic, it fulfils its obligations to discharge a public role. Chapter 2 examines some of the reasons why peace processes are insecure. Part of the explanation is that negotiated peace deals tend to focus on the democratization of politics, the introduction of market economics and human rights reform. There is a wealth of literature within political science, diplomatic and security studies, International Relations and legal studies that champions this approach (for example Arnson, 1999; Atack, 2005; Cejka and Bamat, 2003; Darby and MacGinty, 2000; Hampson, 1996; Maley, 2002; Maley, Sampford and Thakur, 2003; Oberschall, 2007; Stedman, Rothchild and Cousens, 2002). I call it the 'good governance' approach. International Relations theorists know it better as 'liberal internationalism' (Paris, 1997), 'Wilsonianism' (Paris, 2004), 'political realism' or 'Westphalianism' (Atack, 2005). Whether new institutional arrangements are externally imposed by third party intervention – so-called 'market democratization' – or internally devised prior to liberalization from the outside (as recommended by Paris,

2004), new institutional structures and forms of representation and law either solve the violent conflict or institutionalize it in ways that do not threaten the compromise deal. Governance is not unfamiliar to sociology but the discipline's focus has been on the regulation and social control dimensions of governance, particularly in areas like policing, penology and crime. Sociologists have not critiqued governance as it applies to post-violence transitions, yet there are limits to an exclusive focus on good governance.

I contrast this approach with my own in several places in the text, arguing that, as important as good governance is, it does not adequately capture the range of policy issues that negotiated peace settlements need to address if they are to succeed. Stable peace accords require more than good governance, liberal market economies and human rights law – or, at least, good governance in this type of post-violence society has to be understood broadly to cover a range of sociological issues that shape the success of the transition. Chapters 3–6 elaborate on some of these issues, focusing respectively on civil society, gender, emotions, and memory, 'truth' recovery and victimhood. The Conclusion summarizes what a sociological approach adds to our knowledge of peace processes and to the factors that make them stable. The Conclusion takes up again the impact of globalization on new forms of peacemaking and ends with an important distinction between political and social peace processes. I suggest that the relationship between political and social peace processes is recursive and that they facilitate each other: a political deal opens up the room for the social peace process to develop apace, while the social peace process helps to consolidate good governance reforms.

# 1
# *Types of post-violence society*

## Introduction

If war and peace implicate one another, peace processes are obviously affected by the kind of violence that has taken place; and to understand peace, we therefore need first to know more about violence. Violence can be distinguished by its scale, such as interpersonal or collective violence; by the social space in which it occurs, such as violence in the home or in the public sphere; by its motivating force, such as 'domestic', political, racial, terrorist violence and the like; and by its intentionality, which contrasts direct violence with indirect structural violence. A lot of these terms overlap.

The types of violence that occurred offer one way of distinguishing the different kinds of post-conflict society. In this manner there would be post-colonial societies, post-civil war societies and so on. Oberschall (2007) has explored the dynamics of peace building in what he calls 'divided societies', although he restricts the term to those societies divided by ethnicity, focusing on Bosnia, Israel–Palestine and Northern Ireland. Jeffrey Alexander (2004a; see also Alexander et al., 2004) has deployed the term 'post-trauma society' in a similar universalistic manner (used also by the *European Journal of Social Theory*, 2008). Social science interest in trauma reflects the tragic reality of the atrocious events that have marked late modernity, and recovery from trauma has infused social science interest in memory, remembering and 'truth' recovery, amongst other things, and enabled us to see the sociological implications of things like suffering (Wilkinson, 2005). Contemporary genocides have reinvigorated interest in the Holocaust (on which see Alexander, 2004b).

'Cultural trauma' is used by Alexander and colleagues to refer to the scale and effects of the atrocious event and occurs when 'members of a collectivity feel they have been subject to a horrendous event that leaves indelible marks upon their group consciousness, marking their memories forever and changing their future identity in fundamental and irrevocable ways' (Alexander, 2004a: 1). United States' sociologists have 9/11 in mind when they write thus, although it has made them sensitive to earlier cultural traumas in their own history (such as slavery – see, for example, Eyerman, 2004). Cultural traumas can be disconnected from the sort of violence that interests me, since they are often not embedded in the social structure in which they occur; natural disasters can provoke the feelings of cultural trauma Alexander describes. Indeed, Alexander and colleagues draw heavily on Kai Erikson's earlier disaster research in which he made a distinction between individual and collective trauma (1976: 153). Tsunamis, earthquakes, floods and hurricanes can all cause cultural trauma, making the term far removed from our purposes.

Given the inadequacy of existing terms like 'post-divided', 'post-conflict' and 'post-trauma' societies, my purpose in this chapter is to define the category called 'post-violence society' and to develop a typology that distinguishes between three kinds according to how they cohere along three axes. The taxonomy is used to identify one type of post-violence society, that in which peace accords based on consensus have been developed, as the major focus of this book. As we shall see in chapter 2, violence or its threat is rarely eliminated completely with negotiated peace processes, and these societies are characterized by having policy agendas directed to the active maintenance of peace and to the management of the risks surrounding the outbreak of renewed communal violence. The non-violence is thus relative. Peace accords tend universally to be fragile; and there are good sociological reasons why this is so. With this in mind, I want in this chapter to outline the varying ways in which post-violence societies can be distinguished and to assess their potential for stability.

The category 'post-violence society' is applicable to those social formations that have undergone transition from communal violence to relative non-violence, such as Latin America, Rwanda, Sierra Leone, Southern Sudan, South Africa, Sri Lanka, the Philippines and Northern Ireland, to name but a few contemporary examples. Historical examples include Spain after Franco, West Germany after the fall of Hitler, Cuba or Mexico after their revolutions, Poland and other Eastern European countries after the fall of Communism, and so on. These examples offer sociology the opportunity to reflect less on the dynamics of communal violence and more on the transition process that has brought it to an end. There are obvious differences between these societies and it is perhaps important first to celebrate difference before we address commonality.

## A note on the comparative method

The category of 'post-violence society' includes countries that differ in their history of violence, both the scale of conflict and its nature. In some cases it is full-scale war that is being transformed, as in Rwanda; in others sporadic, intermittent acts of communal violence. They also differ in who the victims were. Sometimes the violence was directed at the state, leaving much of the population unscathed, once supporters of the old regime are discounted. In these situations the old regime or toppled dictator can be used to assign away blame. While the abolition of the apartheid regime in South Africa still leaves issues of reconciliation to be dealt with, its dissolution has confined issues of responsibility to the past, enabling the apartheid regime to be a convenient commode into which to pack all the problems that beset contemporary South Africa and explain responsibility away. The fall of Hitler, the ending of the Franco regime in Spain and the toppling of Latin American dictatorships served the same purpose. But in other cases the communal violence was focused on members of other ethnic groups, as in Rwanda, Southern Sudan, Sri Lanka, Northern Ireland and the Philippines; it was neighbour killing neighbour, thus spreading the scale and intensity of victimhood, limiting the capacity to assign responsibility to the past and leaving the policy problem of maintaining non-violence.

The category also includes countries that differ in the lines of social cleavage that structured the communal violence (varying from 'race', ethnicity, religion, national origin and identity to political ideology). Mostly there has been a single line of cleavage, although the cleavage has tended to function as a social marker for much wider inequalities. The capacity of religion in Ireland or 'race' in South Africa to represent broader lines of differentiation is obvious. However, some instances of communal conflict are complicated by the cross-cutting nature of the social cleavages involved. In Sri Lanka, for example, religion (Buddhism, Hinduism, Christianity and Islam are the main religions) does not map easily on to ethnic differences (Sinhalese, Tamil) or variations in wealth, so that addressing the Sinhalese–Tamil ethnic relationship is not a simple solution (see Wijesinghe, 2003). On the other hand, single lines of social cleavage make some peace accords no easier to negotiate, since some cleavages are less easily reconcilable than others, in that they are perceived as inviolable, primordial and absolute and thus lend themselves readily to the worst kind of zero-sum conflicts. Some cleavages can be more readily accommodated by constitutional and institutional rearrangements, while others leave a permanent strain on the accord, increasing the danger of renewed violence.

Attempting a comparative analysis of post-violence societies thus risks over-simplification and perhaps historical distortion. Conversely, sociology's claim to usefulness is that it rises above the particular to focus on the general, continually advancing the grounds on which comparisons between cases are possible, thus increasing its potential for drawing policy lessons and advancing knowledge. It seems particularly apposite with post-violence adjustments that general lessons are drawn from the experiences of individual cases. Nonetheless, taxonomies are heuristic devices intended to illuminate the reality they describe and are only as good as their capacity to do this. They must be sensitive to variations and subtleties. In this vein we can identify three types of post-violence society, distinguished by the basis on which peace was primarily achieved. The distinction between negative and positive peace is important to the categorization.

## Kinds of post-violence society

Post-violence societies come in three forms. For the sake of alliteration they can be called 'conquest', 'cartography' and 'compromise'. They cohere around three axes, which I call:

- relational distance–closeness
- spatial separation–territorial integrity
- cultural capital–cultural annihilation.

Relational distance–closeness refers to the extent to which former belligerents share common values and norms. This might be thought a misnomer for, inasmuch as there is (or was) conflict between them, the belligerents must surely be divided? However, people very close in culture, belief and tradition can be in conflict; if this were not the case, European nations would not have been at war with one another since the Middle Ages and few civil wars would be fought. Or, at least, the lines of cleavage between people and groups who are relationally close can appear greater than they really are and that which divides them is actually smaller than that which unites them. Perceptual cues can be measured and evaluated to exaggerate the cultural distinctions and often rely on finely graded stereotypical flags that are rendered into huge symbolic differences (such as naming practices as an index of identity). Rex (1981: 8) has made the point that conflicts that touch people's sense of ultimate values will move to more and more radical definitions of disagreement. This is the case even where relational closeness otherwise exists, so that groups find the smallest of ways of demarcating their distance from each other, such as the use of colour as emblems in Californian gang culture (see Brown Childs, 2003a, 2003b). The smallness of the degree of asserted difference seems inversely proportional to the degree of relational closeness. For example, as Akenson

(1988) argued, the cultural divisions between Catholics and Protestants in Northern Ireland are quite few, although the respective communities perceive the differences to be larger than they are and to make all the difference. But where relational closeness has some basis in people's experience despite the evident fracture that provokes the conflict, post-conflict adjustments are easier because the line of division can become seen after the event as relatively minor and resolvable. Perceptions of relational closeness can be socially constructed after the conflict where healing becomes associated with the nation-rebuilding project, as happened in post-civil war America and post-war West Germany.

With respect to post-Nazi West Germany, for example, Frei (2002) shows that Adenauer deliberately evaded the USA's insistence on a denazification programme of trials, purges and re-education to transform former Nazis into democrats, and almost immediately set about dismantling the Allies' programme, adopting amnesty laws and employment policies that placed former Nazis back in government and in the professions as teachers, doctors, judges and bureaucrats. The government also took up the cause of war criminals held by the Allies (the United States, after all, employed many pro-Nazi scientists in its own nuclear and armaments industries). As West Germany's importance rose as a base for Allied forces in the Cold War, the Western Alliance gave in to Chancellor Adenauer's demands and by 1958 all war criminals had been pardoned or released, with the exception of the Nuremberg defendants and those held by the Soviets. Geo-politics explains why the Allies coalesced but relational closeness amongst all West Germans gave Adenauer the impetus to want to wipe away the past. Frei (2002: 156) discusses the notion that Adenauer's generosity may have been a ploy to enhance people's allegiance to his government but argues effectively that the amnesty and reintegration policies went much further than were necessary to placate the German right wing. Politicians and church leaders interceded for people convicted of war crimes and the government paid for their legal defence, being excessively keen to absolve ordinary Nazis and Nazi sympathizers of complicity. Frei argues that the West Germans adopted this policy in order to absolve themselves – to attribute blame to the failed Hitler regime rather than allocate responsibility to individuals like themselves; but behind this urge was the principle of relational closeness that sought to avoid the past dividing West Germans any further.

Relational distance on the other hand ensures that the lines of fissure that once provoked the conflict remain and now need to be reproduced in non-violent ways. Relational distance ensures the continued separation of peoples along lines of important social cleavage, fissures that must lose the heat of contention if the post-violence adjustment is to succeed. Some peace accords still leave people divided and proffer ways of dealing politically with the divisions in non-violent ways. This can be achieved moderately successfully where the politics works – such as in the new South Africa or in Francophone-speaking Canada, for example – but the continued social cleavages that feed relational distance can affect groups' perception of the fairness of the politics and destabilize the new arrangements, for example in Sri Lanka, Northern Ireland and the Basque region of Spain. The extent of the new South Africa's achievement is all the more remarkable when one considers the degree of relational distance that the fall of the apartheid regime left untouched and the failure of the African National Congress (ANC) government to deal with social redistribution.

• Spatial separation–territorial integrity describes the degree to which former belligerents continue to share common land and nationhood. Partition is the extreme form of spatial separation. It is not just islands – like Cyprus, Ireland or Indonesia – that have experienced partition as a form of spatial separation to keep erstwhile enemies apart; former mainland states can also be carved up to isolate the belligerents, sometimes with a measure of equanimity, as in the division of the old Czechoslovakia, sometimes with more enmity, as with the former Yugoslavia and the separation of India and Pakistan. But partition is not the only form of spatial separation. Various forms of regional devolution can be implemented within a federal structure to maintain a weakened and limited form of territorial integrity. These federal structures are in themselves different in the way they sustain a sense of spatial separation. The United States seems capable of balancing high levels of commitment to common nationhood, at least in regard to citizens' relationship with outsiders, while permitting local forms of government that furnish strong local state identities. The Basque region of Spain, in contrast, while formally part of the national state and included in a single territorial unit that maintains the integrity of Spain's national borders, is for all intents and purposes culturally and linguistically distinct from the rest of Spain, with the federal structure disguising near total spatial separation.

Spatial separation, in other words, comes in degrees and some forms do not eliminate old enmities, leading to the threat of renewed conflict. This threat is more real where the peace settlement leaves the national boundaries intact. Full territorial integrity ensures the continuance of the national entity within which – and sometimes over which – the former belligerents fought. Government remains centralized and the nation keeps its geographical boundaries and symbolic borders. People and groups share the nation – perhaps now less unequally and with more inclusivity – and groups continue to live as neighbours in a shared if not quite common nationhood. Conflicts that are managed by spatial separation are resolved by keeping the warring groups apart; conflicts that result in the maintenance of territorial integrity require warring groups to find ways of living with each other, side-by-side.

Full territorial integrity is not necessarily a bar to successful conflict management. Europe offers many examples of linguistic groups contentedly sharing territory but not language, as does Canada, but these examples only serve to reinforce the point that peace processes are affected by the kind of violence that has taken place. Accommodation to forms of cultural nationalism is easier to effect if the conflict was restricted to the cultural sphere – in disputes about language, cultural symbols and the like – and was not violent. Retaining full territorial integrity is more problematic when the conflict spread throughout the social structure and led to communal violence as a masquerade for politics. Kaufmann (1996, 1998) has argued persuasively that communal conflicts based on identity that have caused a considerable number of civilian casualties can be pacified only by spatial separation. He notes three caveats to this rule: where such conflicts end with decisive victory by one side that then occupies the entire territory (although this hardly seems to constitute peace); when third parties intervene to end the conflict temporarily (carrying the risk of renewed outbreaks of violence when the third party withdraws); and where each federated region or structure is so small as to be unable to pose an imaginable threat to all the others combined (thus constituting less than full territorial integrity). These arguments rehearse my point about the difficulties faced by post-violence societies that maintain their full territorial integrity in a non-federal system.

𝌆 Cultural capital–cultural annihilation addresses the level of cultural and other resources possessed by former belligerents. I am not distinguishing here, in the contemporary fashion, between types of capital – social, material or economic – but using the term 'cultural' in an old-fashioned imperialistic way to describe all forms of resources, in much the same manner as when the term 'culture' was a synonym for society as a whole. There is the need to make another crucial qualification. Cultural annihilation does not mean total extermination. Genocide rarely wipes out the national, religious, ethnic or racial group entirely, but some groups can be so decimated that their culture does not survive with sufficient vitality to remain a living culture that furnishes people with symbols, oral histories and other material, social and political resources to maintain a separate identity or mount resistance to their defeat. Annihilation is not eradication but rather the stripping away of effective cultural resources for resistance; not the killing of bodies but the spirit. This can be achieved voluntarily by assimilation (although some assimilation policies are imposed from above in a way that is counter-productive to the purpose of assimilation and only assists in keeping the culture alive, such as in modern France with its Muslim immigrants), but annihilation is mostly accomplished by force of conquest or by dint of neglect. People survive but their cultural identity is weakened and reduced to residue, rituals, relics or memory; kept alive, if at all, in an oral or written tradition with a glorious past but little contemporary relevance to their lives. North American Indians, Australian aboriginal peoples, East European Romany culture, and South African Hottentots are examples of annihilated cultures that furnish members with very little material or symbolic capital to resist their original dispossession.

However, some groups can be vanquished in a communal conflict but retain their cultural capital. Colonial appropriation, for example, does not always annihilate the dispossessed, for metropolitan states that depend on the indigenous peoples for their economic labour never destroy the capital of the defeated, for their labour is a form of power. Their culture is kept alive as a resource to be mobilized internationally by diaspora networks that lead to third parties assisting in the maintenance of the legitimacy of the defeated group. The Tamil diaspora throughout the Western world, for example, effectively keeps Sri Lanka's peace process on the international agenda when the country itself lacks the natural resources or strategic location to make it of much interest to Western powers. Maori groups in New Zealand have engaged effectively in forms of cultural struggle via social movement participation; the mobilization of Australian and North American Aboriginal peoples pales in comparison although is not entirely absent since, as noted above, cultural annihilation does not mean extermination. Maori culture also faces a less racist dominant culture than in Australia and North America. That the Israel–Palestine conflict has not culminated in the cultural annihilation of the Palestinians, despite the long pro-Israeli stance of most Western governments, is testimony to the importance of the cultural capital that Palestinians still possess, thus keeping the original dispossession as an international issue. Where the vanquished retain cultural capital, theirs is a living culture and it is not so easily suppressed. Cultural capital remains as a resource to inflame future conflict by providing the stimulus both to readdress the former dispossession and to encourage intervention by third parties. Each axis may become clearer still in the next section when I describe separately the three types of post-violence society that these three axes combine to create.

### Conquest post-violence societies

Conquest is normally associated with conventional wars between nations, but there are historical instances where internal communal violence has been successfully terminated by conquest, such as colonial and civil wars. (I exclude from this analysis UN peacekeeping interventions, which might be construed as a form of military settlement, since the UN's intervention is clearly non-partisan. What I am referring to here is partisan intervention.) Conquest constituted one of the caveats that Kaufmann (1996, 1998) recognized as an exception to his rule that communal conflicts over identity with large numbers of casualties can be pacified only by partition, for one side can achieve a decisive victory through conquest and come to occupy the entire territory.

Conquest results mostly in negative peace – the temporary halting of violence (although this can last for a very long time). More positive notions of peace can occur, however, where the former belligerents are relationally close. Post-violence adjustments after conquest tend to be easier where there is relational closeness between belligerents, such as in the American and Spanish civil wars, since there are few differences other than the allegiance around which the conflict was based, although this should not be disparaged. Post-violence adjustments after conquest are more problematic where relational distance is greater (as with the ethno-cultural and religious differences between settlers and indigenous populations). In these instances, conquest usually succeeds at the cost of the cultural annihilation of the vanquished or their effective subjugation. Many forms of military conquest therefore impose negative peace in the short term only by coercion, which is sustained in the long term by social practices, belief systems and power structures that continually reproduce the subjugation and marginality of the vanquished 'other'. The negative peace disguises the 'structural violence' that the vanquished experience as institutional discrimination.

Where the vanquished retain cultural capital – as a result of their numerical size, labour power and role in the economy, diaspora networks or access to social capital through education and other key resources – cultural annihilation is never complete, and this type of post-violence society becomes susceptible to renewed communal violence in the long term around decolonization or the competing claims of communal groups; the long quiescence of Catholics in Ireland or Africans in South Africa disguised their cultural capital and eventually led to renewed conflict (and a negotiated peace settlement). The examples of colonial conquest where cultural annihilation has been virtually complete, such as with North American indigenous groups and Aboriginal peoples in Australia, often lead to internally directed violence within indigenous communities, drunkenness and dysfunctional family and community bonds rather than externally directed violence to readdress the original dispossession, which is why this form of peace is best understood as 'negative'.

There are some important exceptions to the completeness of this annihilation in Latin America, especially in Mexico, Guatemala, the Andes and Bolivia. Mayan cultural capital has been fairly resistant, despite serious erosion beginning in the sixteenth century. One can see this in everything from the Zapatistas in Chiapas to language revitalization in Guatemala (see Fisher and McKenna, 1996). Indigenous political activism, especially in Bolivia, Peru and Ecuador, also draws on some deep wells of cultural capital still alive despite damaging assaults. The election of the Aymara President Evo Morales in Bolivia, for example, is a dramatic development in the re-assertion of indigenous rights. Morales draws both on the demographic majority of the Andean Aymara and Quechua in Bolivia (plus other lowland indigenous groups) and on the cultural capital of the Andean peoples. For example, the concept of *pachakuti* (meaning the coming around of what once was or the circling of the times) has been employed for centuries to describe a time in which the indigenous will succeed against those who benefited from the Spanish Conquest. Morales had two inaugural ceremonies; the first an indigenous one in the high mountains, the second in the capital La Paz. Simultaneously, Morales speaks to Bolivia being a pluralistic society of many peoples and not just for the indigenous peoples.

This is very much an exception, however, to a general observation that cultural annihilation is difficult to reverse. While conquest can work, by annihilating opposition, it is rarely the organizing principle of post-violence societies in the modern world because it contravenes human rights principles in an international order where human rights constitute the dominant discourse.

### Cartography post-violence societies

Another type of post-violence society is peaceful now only because cartographers have redrawn national borders and new states or devolved regions have developed as a way of dealing with the social cleavages that formerly provoked communal violence. This suggests that post-violence adjustments are sometimes perceived to be easier where former adversaries are separated spatially, which can lead to positive forms of peace. Accordingly, both partition and federal devolution are popular post-violence strategies for separating warring factions. However, the historical evidence for the effectiveness of partition is mixed: sometimes it works, as in Cyprus; on other occasions it merely delays the eruption of communal violence until later, as with the partition of Ireland, or transforms it into conventional wars between nations, as with the India–Pakistan conflict. This suggests their peace was primarily negative. Nonetheless, partition into separate states continues as a popular peace strategy. The new Balkan states are good examples, with new territorial borders attempting to keep apart various ethnic blocs, and partition is proffered as the basis on which the Palestine and Israel conflict can be solved with the 'two states' road map.

As we have already noted, Kaufmann (1996, 1998) has made the strongest case for partition, arguing that conflicts that have been based on communal identity and which resulted in significant civilian casualties require spatial separation of the factions since the scale of the atrocities is said to prevent reconciliation afterwards.

However, the use of cartography is not feasible where the conflict is complex and straddles several social cleavages since it cannot be rendered into simple divisions of territory. Notable examples are the Philippines and Sri Lanka. The conflict in the Philippines, for example, is complex (see Gasper, 2003) and does not map onto regions or geographical areas. It is between the indigenous Moro communities and descendants of Spanish settlers, as well as between Muslim and Catholic, and rural peasant and urban rich, lines of differentiation that do not closely overlap and which certainly have no geography that can lead to one region being excised by the cartographer. Partition is pointless where warring factions live cheek by jowl, or at least can be done only with massive population relocation and the risk of intense violence. Population relocations, however, rarely work. The division of India is a good example. Admittedly the boundaries were drawn in a huge rush – in 1947 the British Indian-born lawyer, Cyril Radcliffe, divided between villages that were to be Muslim or Hindu majorities without much census material in only nine weeks – but the consequent relocations shifted 4 million people as they moved into the relevant state. The massive columns of people moving one way or the other were subject to very violent attacks, many of them against women. Butalia (2000) estimates that three-quarters of a million women were forcibly abducted and numerous others raped and killed, an experience the author likened to the Holocaust. Nor did this pacify the conflict, for in Northern India, where the violence was worst, there has been a legacy of narrow Hindu nationalism that fosters anti-Muslim attacks half a century later.

### Compromise post-violence societies

Many communal conflicts around the world do not involve belligerents with relational closeness, or people who lack cultural capital or who can be separated spatially, so conquest or cartography cannot work. This is why compromise exists alongside conquest and cartography as motifs to define types of post-violence society. This type is one that keeps its territorial integrity and has to find ways of managing internally the social cleavages that formerly caused communal violence through peace accords in which second-best solutions are negotiated as part of a compromise deal. Peace is not imposed by physical force or physical relocation of the population but by a negotiated settlement that forms a compromise deal. It thus involves both negative peace (the cessation of violence) and positive peace (social redistribution, the introduction of equality, fairness, and senses of flourishing and well-being).

Ceasefires – the starting place for negative peace – are an integral part of negotiated peace settlements; positive peace is harder to realize. Where the accord is worked out in the context of continued relational distance, the maintenance of full territorial integrity and with each faction, group or community keeping much or all of its cultural capital, the deal has to achieve a lot within very unpromising circumstances. Second-best solutions are difficult to sell in this kind of setting. Cultural differences of 'race', religion, ethnicity or national allegiance remain despite the peace accord and are open to manipulation by those who seek to retain their local power and patronage or challenge the consensus. The transition process in this kind of post-violence society thus involves implementing peace settlements that eliminate the communal violence while allowing the reproduction of the cultural differences and relational distance that formerly provoked it, having to find ways by which groups can both maintain their differences and, at the same time, develop some sort of sameness.

The effect of relational distance and continued cultural capital is even more problematic when the state is weak, such as Liberia or the Lebanon, since this sustains the patronage power of warlords who use communal violence as an economic or political opportunity. This suggests that this type could be sub-divided according to the viability of the state, for the compromise peace settlement is easier to sustain where the state is more viable institutionally, although strong states that remain partisan despite the accord – or are supported by strong external third parties that are partisan – can also weaken the compromise. Sri Lanka has a strong state but, dominated as it is by the Sinhalese, its partisanship is not conducive to the success of the peace deal (from which the government has withdrawn on several occasions). In 2009 the government seemed bent on the military defeat of Tamil separatists, attacking its geographic strongholds in the north-east of the island. The Northern Sudanese government has balked on its commitments to the Southern Sudanese under several peace accords and uses intermediaries to continue the violence (and in March 2009 the President was arraigned under the International Criminal Court but refused to recognize the court). Post-conflict violence has been at its deadliest in North and West Africa precisely because many of the new states are weak, partisan or manipulated by external third parties.

This type presents sociology with an interesting challenge, for in a context of territorial integrity, relational distance and continued cultural capital, compromise post-violence societies face the most serious task in managing the transition. This kind of post-violence society negotiates peace accords that attempt to enshrine some new consensus and agreement in the midst of the most pressing difficulties. It is hardly surprising therefore that peace processes are often brittle and easily collapse, or go through several iterations before they succeed. This very fragility only reinforces the scale of sociology's task in illuminating the ways in which negotiated peace settlements can be under-girded to deal better with their post-conflict adjustment problems.

## Conclusion

This chapter began by alluding to the commonplace notions that war and peace implicate each other and that, to understand peace, we first need to explore violence. The typology developed in this chapter has attempted to show how communal violence affects the potential for peace in the post-conflict setting by creating three kinds of post-violence society. The typology is structured around three axes that successfully describe the social structural framework within which the communal violence operated, and the intersection between the axes significantly shapes the potential for peace in the three types. They have different mixes of negative and positive peace and combine to create particularly severe problems for post-violence societies based on negotiated compromise peace accords, where positive peace is required. Yet, difficult as these problems are, negotiated peace settlements seem the only solution to contemporary communal conflicts. Some International Relations theorists refer to the 'norm of negotiated settlement' (Walter, 2002), the expectation that conquest or cartography will no longer structure peace processes, but negotiated peace settlements are no easier to manage, irrespective of the norm. This intensifies the need for sociology to begin to offer its special insights. The first of these is recognition of the problems that bedevil peace processes and which bring a high price to peace. This is the topic of chapter 2.

# 2

# *The problem of peace processes*

## Introduction

In an analysis of the violence which accompanies peace accords, Darby (2001: 11) made the telling point that the term 'peace process' has replaced earlier fashionable phrases like 'conflict mediation', 'conflict resolution' or 'conflict management' because the delivery of a peaceful society *is* a process, a long cycle of activities and policy initiatives over a goodly length of time. The process is like walking a series of mountain peaks, a metaphor Darby employed without fully exploiting its force, since there are highs and lows during the process, ups and downs along the way, and perseverance, patience and pluck are needed to get to the final height. Before reaching that point, the journey is very precarious indeed.

It was estimated in 2005 that of the 121 armed conflicts since 1990, covering 81 locations, only one-third were concluded by peace agreements, of which only a minority survived (Harbom, Hogbladh and Wallensteen, 2005: 617). Fragile peace processes are more likely to descend into renewed conflict. Ericksson and Wallensteen (2004) argued that countries that have had wars are up to four times more likely to see conflict break out again. In this chapter I want to explore some of the reasons why compromise post-violence societies are fragile and the negotiated settlements mostly unsuccessful or they bump along from one crisis to another. Peace accords tend to go through several iterations before they are agreed, sometimes with long periods of renewed tension or hiatus before negotiators try again. The Guatemalan peace accord went through nine versions before it was agreed (see INCORE, 2004, for the various iterations of several peace settlements). Many previous Israel–Palestine agreements have been ripped up and discarded as the parties returned to violence. Sudan and

Sri Lanka have witnessed strong governments breach agreed pacts and return to ethnic violence.

Some of the most obvious factors in the failure of peace processes are thus the collapse of the deal as parties abrogate or, despite the best of intentions, cannot deliver, as well as the persistence of underlying grievances and malevolent external interference. Case studies of specific peace processes uncover many localized problems (for example, Paris, 2004). Instead I want to identify some generic issues. Individually they are neither necessary nor sufficient causes of fragility, but together they form a significant sociological backdrop to the problem of peace. While this list is not comprehensive, I want to concentrate on five reasons that help to explain why peace generally is fragile:

- there is often no civil society to provide space and resources for peacemaking and compromise;
- some kinds of post-violence society are inherently insecure;
- the effects of on-going violence are socially and politically destabilizing;
- there are ontological costs to peace;
- most peace processes have a narrow focus on governance reform.

## Peace as a problem

First of all, the communal violence may have been so intense that all searches for compromise have been eroded. Most forms of genocide come close to this. In the Balkan regions in former Yugoslavia, the killings were on such a scale that warring ethnic parties needed to be kept apart by UN peacekeepers and eventual spatial separation by partition. Rwanda proffers another example of genocide but reconciliation since has been facilitated precisely because civil society was not destroyed and traditional forms of justice survived to effect the reintegration of perpetrators and assuage victims, although, as we shall see in chapter 5, commentators have become aware of problems in Rwanda's approach to justice (see especially Cobban, 2006). However, in the initial phases, Rutikanga (2003: 151–3) argues, in a very sympathetic portrayal, that the transitional government of national unity established in the immediate aftermath of the killings was a coalition of eight political parties and was strongly supported by civil society groups that assisted in post-violence adjustment, such as the churches, the National Unity and Reconciliation Commission, the National Human Rights Commission and the National Fund for the Assistance of the Survivors of the Genocide and Massacres. The Ministry of Justice was able to deploy the traditional *gacaca* judicial system to assist in managing the emotional impact of the violence and assuage the demand for revenge, although the *gacaca* courts risk imposing victors' justice, as we discuss later.

With respect to civil society, however, it is not just that the enmity may be stronger where communal violence has been most barbaric: the resources and skills needed for peacemaking may have been decimated in the slaughter. As we shall see in chapter 3, although it has a 'darker' side, civil society is a key agent in peacemaking – civil society being that intermediary set of institutions and organizations that mediate between the state and the grassroots: organizations like NGOs, the churches, trade unions, universities, unions, business, charities and the like. Organizations like these facilitate peacemaking. They harness the enthusiasm there is at the grassroots for peace, and deploy for the benefit of peace the skills, resources and international networks that abound in civil society.

However, rarely is violence so intense that civil society is destroyed completely, yet the peace can sometimes still be fragile. In Northern Ireland and Sri Lanka, for example, countries where carefully negotiated compromise deals were developed, the peace settlements were suspended and the ceasefires collapsed despite civil society structures being in place. One of the reasons for the fragility of peace processes where civil society remains strong has to do with the kind of violence suffered. In a comprehensive analysis of post-conflict elections, Kumar (1998) showed that in some former conflicts, the polarization, fragmentation and division persist after the signing of the accord, and deep cleavages between the parties are not immediately bridged. Commitments to peaceful and democratic means may not readily embed in the new society and former combatants can be reluctant to disarm. As I emphasized in chapter 1, compromise post-violence societies have to contend with territorial integrity, relational distance and the cultural capital retained by the vanquished groups, making huge demands on the second-best compromise deal. Cultural differences of 'race', religion, ethnicity or national allegiance remain despite the peace accord and are open to manipulation by those who seek to retain their local power and patronage or challenge the consensus.

This suggests another reason why peace processes are fragile. The high level of violence that was a catalyst for peace cannot be stopped immediately. Violence often never subsides or at least never subsides quickly enough in the period during (and following) the peace negotiations, as opponents of the peace settlement ratchet up their violence in order to bring the accord to collapse. It is very difficult for peace settlements to be agreed when the negotiations occur amidst on-going violence – which is why most peace accords begin with ceasefires – but those opposed to the agreement can easily break the ceasefire, making negotiations or final settlements difficult to stabilize.

It is worth concentrating on this point for it is perhaps contrary to common sense that violence does not end with peace; after all, many people define peace as a situation of non-violence – the ending of killings. There is a naive assumption that, where violence is a consequence of problematic politics, once a permanent settlement is reached violence irrevocably and swiftly disappears. However, rarely is there a complete cessation of all forms of violence, and the ending of violence in most post-violence societies is only relative. In South Africa's case, for example, there were more deaths *after* the peace settlement than before as conflict between Black parties competing for power under the settlement turned increasingly violent (see J.D. Brewer, 2003a: 85), although it did subside very rapidly once people had voted in the first non-racial election. This is a good example of what Darby (2001: 52–4) calls 'tactical violence' by groups who continue armed conflict for political advantage during the negotiations.

• Tactical violence is only one type of violence provoked by peace. Peace processes have to manage the constant risk of renewed violence from warlords for whom the continuance of conflict maintains their local control and patronage (for an analysis of the economic functions of violence in civil wars, see Keen, 1998). The warlords have developed an economy of war, and profit from the conflict, even perhaps from the aid sent in by the United Nations as they pilfer and corrupt the aid process. Kaldor (1999: 9) refers to the effects on modern warfare of what she calls the new 'globalized war economy'. Fighting groups are now better able to sustain their violence through global processes like remittances from the diaspora, organized corruption of humanitarian assistance, support from neighbouring states, illegal arms trading and involvement in organized crime, particularly illicit trade in drugs, diamonds and oil. Warlords therefore have military and manpower resources – often having well-equipped private armies – to enforce their power; they often have status in a society where otherwise they might have none. And they want to keep themselves in power and use crime, racketeering, corruption and brute force to keep their army loyal. It is not the particular compromise settlement they object to but the very ending of the violence at all.

Weak states in post-conflict settings are often made weak by their inability to assert control over the warlords, as Somalia, Liberia and Afghanistan exemplify, but even viable states can find peace settlements disrupted by the economy of war that privileges some parties and makes the continuance of the conflict a rational means-end. Wijesinghe (2003: 190) has shown that Sri Lanka's war economy is a serious obstacle to peace in that Tamil warlords are reputed to be obtaining undreamt of sums of money from the Tamil diaspora, and the Sri Lankan military benefit through corruption. Ironically, the continued costs of war can cripple states to make them weak and thus susceptible to more cycles of violence from warlords in it for the money. It was estimated that the cost of the war in Sri Lanka reached $US723 million in 1999, 13.2 per cent of the state's budget, a burden not easily borne in non-developed or developing societies (Darby and MacGinty, 2000: 279).

This form of warlord violence is over and above 'spoiler violence' (see Stedman, 1997; Greenhill and Major, 2007) perpetrated by leaders, parties and groups – indeed also by partisan governments that co-opt part of the insurgency – who just do not like the *kind* of agreement that has been negotiated. 'Spoilers' are thus dissidents and corrupt regimes that refuse to go along with the second-best preferences that form the basis of peace settlements and disrupt the process by violence in order to maintain their first-choice preference, either directly or through surrogates. Stedman (1997: 5ff) argues that the damage they cause depends on four factors: position (whether they are inside or outside the peace process), numbers (the size of dissident groups and level of support), type (the kind of goals they have and whether these are limited, total or just plain 'greedy') and locus (their power base and cultural resonance, since even small groups that encapsulate cultural power can be significant beyond their size, such as Loyalist spoilers in Northern Ireland). The anti-Agreement Republican movement in Northern Ireland and groups like the Real and Continuity IRA are examples of spoilers, as are the pan-African groups in South Africa – mobilizing in the first non-racial election in 1994 on 'one settler, one bullet' – or the Afrikaner right-wing, who wanted to kill their way to a White-only homeland. Ironically enough, Stedman identifies physical coercion as one of the policies for dealing with spoilers (along with incentives and inducements and socialization into political norms), which can further destabilize the peace; and imposing democracy at the point of a gun causes people to doubt the quality of the transition.

Spoiler violence can be against the 'traditional' enemy but also against erstwhile colleagues who are now prepared to accept the second-best deal. In Rwanda, moderate Hutus were murdered with as much alacrity as Tutsis. ETA has done the same in the Basque Country. Darby (2001: 55) argues that peace processes in their early years are particularly vulnerable to zealots and the 'family' feuding that is internal to paramilitary organizations. Where this warlord or spoiler violence is kept going, whether for economic or political motives, peacemaking has to operate in a situation where the old enmities continue, where mistrust has not been assuaged and where violence can destabilize elite and grassroots initiatives by closing the space for compromise. The emotions made raw by the past violence are not healed because it continues, albeit in transformed ways and mostly on a much-reduced scale, although some spoilers can be politically co-opted, incentivized and otherwise encouraged to have a change of heart in the way Stedman suggests.

## Vignette: Spoiler violence in Liberia

Following a long period of cyclical violence, leading to its description as a 'warlord state' (Nilsson and Kovacs, 2005: 398), Liberia elected its (and Africa's) first female President in August 2003, which was the culmination of a negotiated settlement between the government and two rebel groups. Its history as a weak state, however, manifested in collapsed state apparatuses and a war economy with lootable material resources exploited by global criminal networks (see P. Johnson, 2008), makes the peace precarious. Nilsson and Kovacs (2005) identify three reasons for this.

First, there is no history of democratic civil culture. This shows itself in inexperience by political and administrative leaders, the failure to socialize combatants into political norms, the fragmentation of Liberia's party system – there are sixteen ethnic groups in Liberia and each has several political parties – and an unwillingness to accept the result of democratic elections (on 'electoral violence' in Africa, see Hoglund, 2008: 86).

Second, there is regional instability in West Africa generally and a legacy of negative external interference. Governments give open support to rebels in neighbouring states, and combatants cross borders to become mercenaries in another's war. The conflict in Liberia contributed to that in Sierra Leone, while fragile peace processes in Sierra Leone, Guinea-Bissau and the Ivory Coast destabilize Liberia further. The failure of Liberia's peace process to reintegrate the combatants economically, in part because of the weak economy, increases the pressure on combatant groups to join global criminal networks wishing access to the country's 'blood diamonds'.

Third, they stress the problem of continued spoiler violence. There is intense violence in Liberia despite the peace accord, which draws Hoglund (2008: 80) to affirm our earlier point that peace agreements do not necessarily stop killings, although the violence has moderated (it is no longer characterized by the eating of human hearts and playing soccer with human skulls, which marked the depravity of earlier violence). Much, if not all, of the remaining violence, however, is from spoilers (for a comparison of spoiler groups in Liberia and Sierra Leone, see P. Johnson, 2008). Many warlord groups survived the democratic transition and fuel violence in both Liberia and neighbouring states. Their continued commitment to violence is in part a reflection of the peace accord's failure to address decommissioning, demobilization and social reintegration, and thus reproduces the weakness of the terms of the negotiated settlement, but also their rejection of compromise itself in the hope of sticking out for their preferred first-choice option. The weakness of the new government's security apparatus compounds these two problems and the United Nations Mission in Liberia, which has deployed police advisors and local peacekeepers, has been largely ineffectual. A war economy continues and spoiler violence is rampant.

However, there is promise in the peace process too. Internecine conflicts between the warlords killed off some gang leaders while others were co-opted. General Butt Naked, for example, found evangelical religion and became a pastor (a familiar Loyalist option in Northern Ireland) and Prince Yormie Johnson found politics (the familiar option of the Provisional IRA in Northern Ireland), winning a senatorial seat after unsuccessfully trying for the presidency. Butt Naked returned to Liberia in January 2008 full of remorse and openly confessing to having killed upwards of 20,000 people, notably dropping his *nom de guerre* to become Joshua Blahyi again. He appeared before Liberia's Truth and Reconciliation Commission urging other killers to do likewise, saying 'I think forgiveness and reconciliation is the best way to go' (quoted in Associated Press, 21 January 2008). The Commission was set up in 2006 and modelled itself on the South African example, although exceeds it in its capacity to recommend that criminal charges be brought for war crimes. The Commission announced in January 2009 that it was setting up a Special Court, similar to Sierra Leone's, which would deal with prosecutions arising from the truth commission's work. Blahyi's candour earned a threat from Mulbah Morlue, head of the Forum for the Establishment of a War Crimes Court in Liberia, which is indicative of the problems surrounding the management of emotions and victimhood that post-conflict Liberia still faces, although Blahyi's response was to say that he was ashamed not proud of his former activities. Spoilers can clearly repent. In February 2009 the President appeared before the Commission begging forgiveness for having formerly supported Sierra Leone's deposed President, Samuel Taylor, although she denied being part of his warlord organization in Liberia after he fled from Sierra Leone. While her testimony was heard in closed session, a recording was made available to radio stations.

The issue of internecine spoiler violence leads naturally to another reason why peace is a problem: peace brings psychological and ontological costs. This is again counter-intuitive and needs further explanation. Peace comes at too high a price for some people. The ontological insecurity caused by violence and which gives the push to the peace process can be insufficiently severe to discourage some people from fully embracing the need to compromise, and the compromises required by the peace process can cause the same severe ontological insecurity and fear as the violence itself. Of course, peace offers the prospect of longer-term ontological security, but in the short term peace may be destabilizing emotionally because it requires change and the overthrow of familiar ideas, routines and behaviours. As we shall see in chapter 6, peace provokes what John Paul Lederach (1997) calls the 'identity dilemma'. People who have defined their identity for so long in terms of the traditional enemy, suddenly in peace processes find they have to reshape their sense of who they and their enemies are.

There is another dimension to this problem. People may not have known anything but the violence, and where the conflict is low-key people tend to be able to learn successfully to routinize and cope with it. Therefore, 'peace' itself is unfamiliar and ontologically strange. These feelings are enhanced for victims and their relatives. The public issues surrounding the search for peace and the reconciliation of ancient conflicts cause psychological grief for the victims and their families. This is reinforced by the habit of peace processes to become almost the sole public issue in the media and in ordinary conversation, enveloping and encapsulating all public events. In the public domain, all they hear is peace, while privately all they feel is grief. Their hurt and bitterness can become defining features of their identity, and peace comes at a cost. The victims and their families are asked to release the bitterness, forgive old enemies and witness them now in parliament, see perpetrators receive amnesty or prisoners released, and generally move forward from their hurt, loss and pain. The testimony of victims at truth and reconciliation commissions bears witness to these costs, and the particular problems around the management of victimhood in peace processes will be addressed in chapter 6; suffice here to say that they bring a particular price to peace.

The continuance of ontological insecurity and anxiety during peace processes is only one kind of cost to peace. In earlier research on grassroots peacemaking in Northern Ireland by J.D. Brewer, Bishop and Higgins (2001), it was discovered that one of the constraints operating on peacemakers was the fear of victimization and intimidation by unreconstructed opponents of peace who wanted to keep the violence going. This leads peacemakers to be accused of 'selling out' their community and makes them vulnerable to harassment and attack from paramilitary organizations on their 'own side'; peacemakers often receive death threats from their former militant colleagues. The 'spoiler violence' referred to above by those still holding out for their first-preference choice is often directed at moderates and peacemakers on their 'own side'. The particular ways in which women experience victimhood in war, a subject discussed in chapter 4, make peace particularly problematic and psychologically costly in gender terms.

There is a final reason why peace processes are fragile, which I will deal with in the rest of the chapter because of its supreme importance.

## The limits of good governance

One of the most important reasons why peace processes and negotiated settlements are so fragile is because the transition process is reduced solely to one of introducing good governance – democratic political institutions, market economies and human rights law. These are good things, but peace processes require much more than governance reform if they are to become institutionally embedded in the longer term. The privileging of good governance tends to leave untouched a whole array of sociological issues that are equally critical to the success of the transition process.

It is necessary to clarify these remarks to avoid any misunderstanding: I endorse the arguments of good governance theorists that institutional reform is needed to permit other aspects of peace building to occur. As I explain in the Conclusion, the relationship between the political and social peace processes is recursive and each facilitates the other. Civil society groups have to conduct their peace work in the context of the rule of law, as well as requiring political reforms that introduce fairer politics and strong economies to pay for reconstruction. Good governance assists in eliminating the sources of conflict, especially when the conflict was about the undemocratic nature of the former regime and the failure of one or more groups to be adequately politically represented as well as being subject to human rights abuses. The stability of peace accords depends in very large part on two things associated with good governance: people's experience of governance and law *after* the violence has stopped; and the way resistance to the accord is managed within the new governance and human rights parameters. Good governance has to work and be *seen* to work. People's experience of the new forms of governance needs to leave them with favourable impressions, for how they experience the reforms will in large part determine their commitment to them. Part of this also involves people's experience of how the new state, government or institutional framework deals with opponents of peace; the on-going spoiler violence may be dealt with so harshly that the new regime's commitment to democratic means and systems of human rights law may be called into question, affecting the way in which the peace process is seen to work.

When governance structures develop legitimacy, much can be achieved. South Africa is an excellent example. South Africa's democratic transition has been remarkable and dramatic. Within a few years, one of the most repressive and unjust systems was negotiated away without a full-scale war. The spoiler violence did not disrupt the negotiations, and four years after the ANC was legalized it took power in South Africa's first non-racial election in 1994 (on the election, see R. W. Johnson and Schlemmer, 1996; Reynolds, 1994). Elections since have resulted in the increasing disempowerment of the White population without any suggestion of a recourse to apartheid. What is remarkable also is that the new ANC government has ignored social redistribution and left untouched the wider issue of equality – partly because of the West's imposition of free market economics on the new government (see, for example, Hart, 2002; Kunnie, 2000). South Africa's peace settlement was based on the dual illusion that, as a result of the settlement, nothing would change for Whites and that everything would for Blacks. In fact, while Black South Africans now control the state, they do not share in the country's economic wealth to any greater degree. The peace thus represents the typical African and Asian post-colonial deal, where the majority group inherit politically, while the privileged minority retain the economy. However, the peace settlement endures precisely because the state's viability is girded by the legitimacy of its governance structures; Black people experience the transition in very positive ways despite the lack of improvement in the material circumstances of most of them because they see the new governance structures as legitimate. This example highlights the risk of renewed violence in weak states and testifies to the importance of good governance in successful peace processes. New systems of governance and law, if legitimate and widely supported, can sustain the continuance of much of the former inequality *without* the threat of renewed violence.

My anxieties with this approach are twofold. First, changes in governance and law alone are no guarantee that communal violence will end, even in viable states. The Basque region of Spain, for example, received devolved government and autonomous elections in 1979 but ETA violence continues sporadically, although on a much-reduced level (see Irvin and Rae, 2001). Brazil (on which, see Pinheiro, 2000) and other Latin American countries continue to experience communal violence even though good governance and the rule of law have been effectively established. In her critique of what she calls 'neo-liberal approaches to peace' in Northern Ireland, Crighton (1998) makes the point that democracy and free markets have co-existed with low-level wars in Spain and Northern Ireland, which suggests that there are limits to 'market and electoral mechanisms in producing peace' (1998: 78). In this regard, good governance does not necessarily protect against fragility in peace processes, even when the state is strong.

Second, good governance becomes limiting if it is proffered as the sole way to peace, justifying the criticism that the approach unduly neglects other concerns. Some International Relations theorists might seem exempt from this criticism because they realize good governance is not the panacea to post-conflict reconstruction. But even the work of Paris (2004), which modernizes Wilsonianism, still places emphasis on political and economic reform. 'Domestic institutions' are needed, he argues (2004: ix), to mediate the market democratization advanced externally by Wilsonianism, yet his depiction of 'institutionalization before liberalization', as he describes his approach (2004: 197ff), shows how wedded to good governance he remains, for he emphasizes electoral reform, conflict-reducing economic reforms and effective state institutions. Only in the emphasis on the promotion of healthy civil society and the control of 'hate speech' is there recognition of the sociological concerns raised here. This reflects the tendency of Western governments, international scholars and research institutes to valorize good governance at the expense of other concerns. Good governance becomes political hegemony when it excludes sociological issues of the kind raised here.

It is worth speculating on the reasons why good governance has this hegemonic quality. It is not just that good governance is believed to epitomize the modern state, or that democratic forms of governance are valued as the best type of governance, it is also that the democratic governments of the West and the World Bank mostly provide the resources to support peace processes and often attach strings to their aid that impose good governance structures on transitional states. In recent interventions, the World Bank, for example, gave $US50 million in May 2008 to support the peace process in Nepal, and districts in Indonesia can get up to 1,000 million rupiah to support local peace initiatives. The World Bank has a special website on peace (https://publicsphere. worldbank.org/usertags/peace-process). It is the West that has the research institutes and training centres that promote good governance as the solution to problematic politics. So, in effect, the West is promoting itself as the model of good governance that newly democratizing societies should follow and providing the philanthropy to reproduce itself (see Vogel, 2006, for a sociological treatment of this).

There are two dimensions that are worth distinguishing here: the way philanthropy is being used to promote peace; and the equation of peaceful transition with good governance. Charity and aid are increasingly becoming mechanisms of democratization and thus the promotion of a Western hegemony. The Carnegie Endowment for International Peace, for example, describes itself as an international donor that has embraced civil society aid as a key tool for democracy promotion and supports thousands of NGOs around the world in the name of civil society development, investing precisely in those organizations that say they promote democratic participation and values and free-market principles (see www.carnegieendowment.org). It funded a 'democracy and rule of law' research programme in Washington, the results of which were collated by two permanent researchers from Carnegie under the revealing title *Funding Virtue: Civil Society Aid and Democracy Promotion* (Carothers and Ottaway, 2000), addressing South Africa, the Philippines, Peru, Egypt and Romania. As Anheier and Daly (2005: 159–62) argue, philanthropic organizations are of several types and those that operate on an international and global stage are not necessarily champions of good governance in such an obvious way as Carnegie. Diaspora organizations support particular religious and ethnic groups quite partisanly, while the international NGOs, such as OXFAM and Save the Children, do not promote liberal market capitalism and democratic governance.

But traditional charities need to be distinguished from what Karl and Katz (1987) call 'modern philanthropy'. New large-scale philanthropic organizations have developed, like Rockefeller, Gates, Ford and MacArthur, which focus on finding long-term solutions to the major public problems of the day. This does not just involve the alleviation of harm and illness but challenges the root causes of the problem; aid is directed to facilitating social and political change. This is done in several ways (see Anheier and Daly, 2005: 162). Some endowed foundations award grants for specified purposes, some develop their own projects and programmes consistent with their aims and remit, while others are linked to multi-national companies and businesses. They function within the developed market economies and established democracies of the West but direct attention to the social problems in the Global South or to transitional societies that have geo-strategic value to the West. Foundations in the United States are more active internationally than European ones (Anheier and Daly, 2005: 163), and the amount of their aid is enormous; the top fifteen US foundations gave over $US19 billion in 2001 (worked out from figures provided in Anheier and Daly, 2005: 164).

Much of this philanthropy specifically targets peace initiatives (the following details are calculated from Anheier and Daly, 2005: 164). Amongst the top fifteen charitable foundations in the United States, for example, the Ford Foundation (which awarded grants of $US6 billion in 2001) 'seeks to strengthen democratic values . . . and promote international co-operation'; the MacArthur Foundation ($US94 million in grants in 2001) 'seeks to promote international peace and security . . . and human rights'; the Hewlett Foundation ($US66 million in 2001) 'supports conflict resolution and US–Latin American relations'; the Starr Foundation ($US53 million in 2001) 'supports international relations'; the Carnegie Foundation ($US44 million in 2001) 'supports international peace and security'; the Mott Foundation ($US31 million in 2001) 'supports the strengthening of civil society globally'; and the Open Society Institute ($US24 million in 2001) 'promotes and opens societies through support for civil society . . . and human rights'. This is not just a feature of US foundations, although the US foundations do dominate modern philanthropy. The Barrow Cadbury Trust in the United Kingdom has a justice and peace programme that has seen monies go to the promotion of civil society in Northern Ireland and the Middle East, and the Hallows Foundation in Australia and the Nippon Foundation in Japan also give generously to 'overseas co-operative assistance'; 353 public benefit corporations in Japan list 'international relations' as the field of their charitable activity (Anheier and Daly, 2005: 165). In their analysis of five trends in global giving, Anheier and Simmons (2004) refer to two that bear upon our point: the tendency for aid to be directed to post-conflict societies and to compensate for 'deficiencies in government or market failures'.

These private foundations work alongside, but sometimes in conjunction with, governments, the UN, the European Union and INGOs as part of a global network of organizations involved in post-conflict scenarios. The US-based Atlantic Philanthropies, for example, has been a significant funder of peace and reconciliation initiatives in Northern Ireland and has complemented the huge amount of resources devoted to the problem by the British and Irish governments and the European Union, the latter's Special Peace and Reconciliation Programme in Northern Ireland being in excess of £1.5 billion by 2001 (see J.D. Brewer, 2003a: 133). This aid not only comes in the form of humanitarian assistance but is also used to police compliance with the terms of the peace agreement. And it is not just governments that threaten to withdraw aid unless structures of good governance are introduced. Leschenko has undertaken a case study of two private foundations that form part of the hegemony pushing the theme of good governance, the Mott Foundation and the Soros Foundation Network (reported in Anheier and Daly, 2005: 170–1), and showed that they tended to fund local NGOs that were involved in good governance, assisted in the training of officials and politicians and policymakers to improve governance, and worked to promote the idea of democracy and open society, monies that were conditional upon the Foundations being satisfied that the recipients served these ends.

It is within this context that good governance sometimes can be simplisticly upheld as the main solution to communal conflict. US-based research institutes and training centres, such as the United States Institute for Peace, the Carnegie Endowment for International Peace and the Woodrow Wilson Center for International Scholars, have training programmes for peace practitioners, give funds to researchers, publish books and invite scholars to visit for the purpose of promoting good governance as the means to effective peace. The conflict prevention programme of the Woodrow Wilson Center for International Scholars is a good case in point. It ran this programme for several years and it was used to invite peacemakers and practitioners to the Center, enabling them to meet US policy makers, and used to fund research projects on how best to prevent conflict or its renewed outbreak after peace accords. The programme worked with the US State Department in assisting US intervention in post-conflict situations. Under these circumstances there can be an easy slippage between peace and US foreign policy interests, with peace becoming part of the liberal hegemony that

associates peace with protecting US foreign policy interests and promoting State Department policies. The Center has since developed new
programmes of research (see www.wilsoncenter.org) which include a
foresight and governance project, international security studies programme and a leadership and state-capacity building project.

The good governance network extends globally. In the Australian
National University in Canberra, for example, there is the Asia-Pacific
College of Diplomacy, headed by Professor William Maley, that engages
with regional conflicts in Australasia to introduce good governance as
the solution, an idea also being advanced by John Braithwaite from
the same university who believes that his famous idea of 'restorative
justice' can be applied to world conflicts, an approach he calls 'restorative peacemaking' (see J. Braithwaite, 2002). Braithwaite's proposals
are addressed in chapter 5, so let me here concentrate on Maley. His
centre offers training in diplomacy for combatants in conflicts, and in
a recent paper (Maley, 2002) he outlined twelve theses for successful
peacemaking and humanitarian intervention. They represent typical
governance rhetoric – things like the importance of getting multi-ethnic
coalitions and keeping them together; political incentives to induce
people responsible for spoiler violence to stop; developing institutions
that deal with the new political actors, making new political demands,
that follow on from the peace accord; and resourcing co-opted elites to
avoid the decline back into violence.

# Conclusion

The coalescence between US foreign policy interests, philanthropic
foundations – mostly based in the USA – and well-funded research
institutes and training centres, ensures that good governance rhetoric
dominates our understanding of the process of transition in post-violence societies. Good governance *is* important to the success of peace
processes. The danger is that good governance brings with it liberal
democratic notions of governance, free-market economic principles
and the hegemony of the West – and particularly of the United States
– in defining what constitutes peace. This makes peace quite partisan.
The risk is that it is the West – and the US government and US-based
philanthropic foundations in particular – who get to define what good
governance is and to control and shape the nature of the institutional
reform that introduces it. This carries with it two problems. First, where
there is significant external intervention by the West, peace processes
can become perceived by protagonists as partisan and thus lose cred-
ibility. For instance, the West is not seen as neutral by, for example,
Sinhalese nationalists in Sri Lanka and Palestinians; nor was it once
by Unionists in Northern Ireland. For those with an innate tendency to

anti-Americanism, the good governance approach can be read as the globalizing of the United States. Second, the focus on good governance neglects a great deal. It concentrates too much on institutional reform in the political peace process, to the neglect of sociological issues within the social peace process.

These twin concerns seem encapsulated by the study with which we began this chapter. Darby's (2001) pioneering analysis of the negative effects of violence on the stability of peace processes was carried out as part of a research programme on conflict resolution at the United States Institute for Peace, an institution that is funded by the United States Congress, although describing itself as independent and non-partisan (www.usip.org). The Institute's mission 'is to help prevent, manage, and resolve international conflicts by empowering others with knowledge, skills, and resources, as well as by our direct involvement in peace building efforts around the world' (www.usip.org). As such, the Institute represents the hegemonic tendency in the West to promote itself as the solution to post-conflict adjustment problems. In funding Darby's research and publishing the book, we see the Institute's commitment to under-girding and supporting fledgling democracies – a worthwhile aim, so long as it does not involve supporting US foreign policy interests: in this case by sponsoring analysis of the destabilizing effects of continued acts of violence in the post-conflict setting. Darby's analysis ended with five propositions (2001: 116–23) that exemplify the strengths and weaknesses of good governance approaches to peace. They are:

- most ceasefires collapse in the few first months, but peace processes that survive are more likely to endure the effects of violence;
- a lasting agreement is impossible unless it actively involves those with the power to bring it down by violence;
- zealot groups can be neutralized only with the active involvement of former militants;
- during peace negotiations the primary function of leaders is to deliver their own people, assisting their opponents in the process is secondary;
- members of the security forces and paramilitary groups must be integrated into normal society if a peace agreement is to stick, without neglecting the needs of the victims of violence.

Their virtue is not in dispute; they simply ignore far too much that is important to stabilizing peace processes. Subsequent chapters address a series of sociological issues that appear to be of equal significance.

# 3

# *Civil society*

## Introduction

We can begin elaboration of my sociological approach to peace processes with discussion of civil society. Using some of the celebrated language of Charles Wright Mills (2000[1959]), civil society is the domain in which people's private troubles become translated into public issues, and the idea of global civil society is heralded as the contemporary antidote to war (Kaldor, 2003). The enthusiasm for the idea of global civil society is not politically restrictive for it has been appropriated by conservatives (Eberly, 2008), while others caution against it being presented as the remedy to war (Keane, 2003). Advocates of civil society – of which I am one – base their arguments on an intellectual tradition that equates it with 'the notion of minimizing violence in social relations, to the public use of reason as a way of managing human affairs in place of submission based on fear and insecurity or ideology and superstition' (Kaldor, 2003: 3). Mills (2000[1959]: 194) articulated similar sentiments when he wrote that sociology's role in making public issues out of private troubles by placing them in the public sphere of civil society is the best way to realize a free society democratically, which defines the purpose of the sociological imagination.

This chapter defines civil society, shows how it impacts on peace processes in good and bad ways, and illustrates these arguments with some examples. I query the claim that it is an antidote to war and highlight the negative contribution of what is called 'bad civil society' (Chambers and Kopstein, 2001), but argue that civil society is nonetheless the primary arena for articulating the sociological strains and policy dilemmas of negotiated settlements in ways that make it, in my view, the cornerstone of a sociological approach to peace processes.

## What is civil society?

Civil society was recently described as an idea whose time had come (Edwards, 2004: vi). What adds weight to these words is that the author is Michael Edwards, the director of the Ford Foundation's Governance and Civil Society programme in New York. The Ford Foundation is one of a plethora of philanthropic foundations, which, in conjunction with business corporations, research institutes and study centres, helps to disseminate the neo-liberal rhetoric about good governance referred to in the last chapter. Whilst appreciating the valuable emphasis on civil society in good governance approaches like this, it is important to rescue the concept from such usage by recognizing its broader connotations. In fact, 'civil society' is a very ancient term, going back to the Roman Stoics, Machiavelli and Adam Ferguson in Scotland – and this brings us only to the eighteenth century – and there are several meanings to the term. Two meanings are in widest currency today (Kaldor, 2003: 1 *passim* gives five): civil society as voluntary association, and civil society as the public sphere. Let us look first at the equation of civil society with voluntary association, which is perhaps the most popular usage in sociology.

This idea resonates with a lot of contemporary sociology. It is implicated in Giddens's notion of the 'third way' (1998, 2000), in Putnam's discussion of social capital (2000) and in sociology's anxieties about 'mass society' (Kornhauser, 1959). The argument goes back to Adam Ferguson in eighteenth-century Scotland (as recognized by: Dahrendorf, 2002; Gellner, 1994, 1996; Keane, 1988; Oz-Salzberger, 1995; Seligman, 2000; Tonkiss, 1998). Modern societies need an array of institutions, organizations and voluntary bodies in which people can participate – trade unions, churches, charities, scouting organizations, parent–teacher associations, NGOs, women's groups, football and sporting groups *ad infinitum*. Various benefits derive from such participation. These benefits affect the quality of the relationships people have, their level of identification with each other, and strengthen what Ferguson called people's 'social bond' (1966[1767]). With a vigorous set of voluntary associations, citizens become actively involved in their society; people do not withdraw into apathy or defeatism, they relate widely to lots of different people; feelings of trust, integration and reciprocity develop between people, so that people's senses of community, or social bonding, are enhanced. Putnam's penetrating analysis of lonely, isolated, modern America (2000) makes the point well: people are happier and society more stable when there is active participation in voluntary associations. While it has been claimed enthusiastically that social capital is the raw material of civil society (Onyx and Bullen, 2000), the equation of civil society with the critique of individualism goes back to earlier notions in US sociology in the 1950s, such as

Donald Riesman's notion of the lonely crowd or the concern of people like Mills and Kornhauser with the emergence of mass society. On the whole the attention within this meaning of civil society is on what sociologists call our sociability: on our patterns of relationship, feelings of belonging and senses of community.

Another meaning of the term extends this argument in the direction of politics. For example, the theory of deliberative democracy (see Dryzek, 2005) places emphasis on the public sphere as a way of under-girding and supporting democracy – public debate in a variety of public settings encourages feelings of shared interests, and a willingness to compromise and work together. In this view, the extent to which this space exists in the public sphere determines the health of the democracy. Civil society is under threat wherever the state centralizes power, reduces the effectiveness of public forums or eliminates the opportunity for free deliberation. Healthy democracies therefore have active civil societies. This means more than the routine consultation exercises that governments and public bodies engage in; it is about citizens using forums to engage politically on any and all issues. It is about the local women's conservative association as much as the Aberdeen branch of the anti-globalization campaign.

There is a moral argument behind this championing of civil society, for both sorts of arguments equate civil society with the good society (a point emphasized by Edwards, 2004). Civil society is seen as mediating between two powerful forces that people need to be protected from – a controlling and centralizing state, and the free reign of people's selfish interests and individualism: civil society is, as it were, a way of mediating between the state and the free market, between the trammelling of political liberties by the powerful and of our sociability by the selfishness promoted by free-market capitalism. These twin qualities give it an inevitable connection with peace processes.

## Civil society and peace processes

In chapter 2 we saw how some peace processes are fragile because the communal violence has been so intense that it has decimated civil society. This gives a clue to my argument: the intermediary sector of institutions, organizations, voluntary associations and groups that comprise civil society is critical to peace processes. Civil society is recognized to have been influential as an agent of social and political change in every kind of transformation – revolutions are rarely peasant-led, but directed by middle-ranking people within civil society; and so it is with peace.

One argument that supports this view is Mary Kaldor's (2003) emphasis on the globalization of civil society as an antidote to war.

'Global civil society' is that range of voluntary associations, INGOs and third-sector groups and social movements that work on a transnational scale, addressing the global dimensions of the local problems that mark their main activities. Civil society, Kaldor argues (2003: 1), is no longer confined to the borders of the territorial state, an idea that specifically confronts the ancient association of civil society with managing the mediation between governments and market within the nation state, to the extent that the existence of global civil society is disputed by those still wedded to this equation (such as Keane, 2003). There are several factors that are beginning to make civil society global. For example, forms of geo-strategic governance have emerged associated with the United Nations, particularly since the then General Secretary, Boutros Boutros-Ghali, in conjunction with the EU, NATO and the Organization for Security and Co-operation in Europe (OSCE), established the notion of international trusteeship for the comprehensive reconstruction of war-torn societies and for the regulation of the conduct of war (on the notion of international trusteeship, see Knudsen and Laustsen, 2006).

As I emphasized in the Introduction, forms of cosmopolitan and humanitarian law that supersede national legal systems have also emerged to impose international accountability for the conduct of war (see Hirsh, 2003). The emergence of global politics has ensured that civil society engagements transcend the nation state (Kaldor, 2003: 78), hence their depiction as INGOs (Kaldor, 2003: 79 *passim*). There are now also networks of exchange and collaboration that are transnational, such as the global women's movement. These global networks place the activities of national groups in a broader framework, moving them literally onto a global stage. Civic networks in the past have linked national civil society groups across different fields of interest (which thus amplified their range of involvement) or within their field of interest (which thus added weight to their campaigning) but these networks are now global, which raises exponentially the scale of their activities. While there is no global state, as it were, to provide a legislative framework for civil society activities, as there is with national NGOs, there are geo-strategic governance structures and rules of law that global civil society groups both work within and help to reinforce. Global civil society is thus both cause and effect of the growth of international organizations and treaties and the emergence of regional blocs of co-operation over security, health, economics and the like (Huddock, 1999).

The emergence of global civil society is important for our purposes because it facilitates peacemaking, if not yet perhaps itself being an antidote to war. Kaldor (2003: 109–41) emphasizes the impact of global civil society on the development of humanitarian law to regulate organized violence, the increase in the international demand for humanitarian interventions in conflicts and the growth of international peacekeeping. Globalization has facilitated peacemaking and brought new kinds of peace work. Global political interconnectedness makes us all vulnerable to conflicts around the world and can heighten our mutual interest in peaceful intervention. The increasing numbers of economic links between states and regional security blocs means that threats to national security are no longer seen just in military terms, so that intervention is more likely to be considered. The development of extensive diaspora networks gives nations cultural links with others far away that may also motivate peacekeeping. The human rights discourse that plays a part in so much of geo-politics is essentially a language of peace as it constitutes a powerful disincentive to violating human rights. It has led to the development of a monitoring regime of INGOs that operate globally, bypassing governments to establish a transnational network of peace monitors. This network allows INGOs to play a global role as peace campaigners, which gives peace an international voice. The impact of this network is boosted by the co-operation between human rights INGOs and the many global networks based around gender, violence against women, the environment, anti-capitalism, opposition to landmines and other weapons, charitable donation, AIDS and other health problems, etc. There are flows of information between these networks, and co-campaigning.

Global civil society resonates with peace in two ways. First, a raft of social, economic, environmental and gender issues are often aligned with peace, inasmuch as organized violence is seen to cause or make them worse and global networks easily get mobilized around peace as a vocation through their engagement with these issues. The globality of civil society is thus a virtue for peace processes in that local conflicts are felt to be everyone's concern and local peace efforts to deal with them are enhanced by their global reach. But civil society groups operate nationally and internationally at the same time, mediating between the local and the global, a process summed up in Roland Robertson's redolent phrase 'glocalization' (1995; for an application see J. D. Brewer, 2000: 176–81). Global activists are – in the famous phrase – urged to think globally and act locally by addressing the local manifestations of problems and issues that often have a global cause. But they also move in the other direction by taking local concerns onto a global stage by means of marshalling global civic networks, in order for such mobilization to impact back on local circumstances. The capacity of civil society groups to negotiate their way between the local and the global allows them to be simultaneously national and international, within and outside a nation state's borders. This 'glocal' quality makes civil society groups an effective go-between on two levels, mediating between the grassroots and the state within a national context and also between national and transnational policy makers. This gives local grassroots people the opportunity for their private troubles to be transformed by civil society into public issues on national and global stages. The protagonists in Northern Ireland's conflict, for example, internationalized the war for the purposes of arms procurement and strategic allies, and then internationalized the peace process, with the US government becoming the guarantor of the process and the EU the financial backer.

This introduces the second virtue of civil society in peace processes. Civil society is the cog in the centre from which all sorts of engagements, involvements, deliberations and dialogue emanates outwards, like spokes in a wheel, towards the state and international regulatory frameworks, transporting local private troubles into public issues in very powerful arenas. Civil society helps to shape the policy agenda in the public sphere by making public issues of the dilemmas that negotiated peace deals provoke as a sociological dynamic. It is in civil society that we meet individuals and groups who are partisanly locked on one horn of a policy dilemma, campaigning for former combatants or victims, who want to commemorate this or that part of the struggle or forget the war entirely, who demand 'truth' recovery on this or that aspect of the past or who call for collective amnesia, who push the demand for justice or the demand for equality. Sociological issues constitute themselves as a dynamic because civil society groups mobilize and articulate, dialogue and deliberate, on one or other policy choice, and engage with policy makers and governments nationally and internationally.

It is because civil society is proactive in peace processes when turning private troubles into public issues that we cannot caricature it in the way some critics do. Keane's dismissal of the idea of global civil society is based in part on the argument that such groups are vulnerable to being misled – 'easily taken for a ride by mercenaries, gangs, wired-up hooligans . . . and psycho killers' (2003: 155) – so eager to trust that they are made fools of by the untrustworthy (2003: 161), and are often mere fly-by-night groups, lacking the social and political embedding necessary for sustained and effective campaigning (2003: 159–60). K. Anderson and Rieff's (2005: 29) scepticism of the concept also concerns its association with a progressive, value-oriented movement that conjures up the image of Swampy, safety pins through nose and ears, a pacifist helplessly fighting the good cause of some soon-to-be-demolished set of trees; or images of well-meaning but naïve ladies making tray-bakes for peace or writing poems about togetherness. This caricature does not fit the reality of well-organized, well-funded, politically astute and sophisticated civil society groups, with great leadership and intellectual skills, resourced sufficiently well to pressure governments and policy makers, moving skilfully between the local, national and international stages; at home in the village hall as much as the halls of Westminster or Washington; attending meetings in the Vatican as well as with the local vicar.

Kaldor, Anheier and Glasius's depiction of forms of global civil society (2003a: 8) illustrates the variety of its manifestations, which make current caricatures quite simplistic. They refer to the following types: *new public management*, in which civil society organizations assist in national government policy making as well as INGO policy making, for example Save the Children and OXFAM; *corporatism*, in which civil society organizations partner transnational corporate businesses and companies, such as Greenpeace and Nike or Starbucks and the World Wildlife Fund; *social capital and self-organization*, which are civil society groups designed to assist community building and develop trust through voluntary association; and *activism*, in which civil society organizations challenge power holders and monitor the actions of the powerful.

When we see below the spaces that civil society groups occupy in peace processes, and the kinds of engagements they have, it will be realized that most civil society groups do not separate themselves from government but use the public sphere to persuade government in ways that impact on the peace process. Long-established civil society groups, notably women's groups and churches, are not fly-by-night, and have campaigned effectively for peace in several post-violence settings. The global peace movement is not some assortment of anti-globalization campaigners, blind to the paradox of rabidly trashing in the name of peace the latest summit, but different sets of civic networks that draw together human rights activists, women's groups, charities, aid foundations, trade unions, peasant groups, new social movements, NGOs and INGOs, churches, para-church organizations, community development and anti-poverty groups and the like; it has participation from popes to peasants, rich and poor, literate and illiterate, secular and sacred, men and women, rough and respectable, and young and old.

However, opponents of peace accords are also global, using international networks in ways inimical to peace, and their contribution should not be ignored when promulgating global civil society as a progressive movement. There can also be differences of strategy, ideology and practice between the groups that constitute global civil society, resulting in them occupying different spaces locally in specific peace processes. The Loyalist paramilitaries in Northern Ireland, for example, thought that the only people who understood them were Afrikaners in South Africa and the Israelis, and both are alleged to have supplied the Loyalists with weapons. The IRA mobilized international networks equally successfully. By playing the anti-colonial card, they obtained most of their weapons from Libya, funded in large part by money supplied by Irish Americans. This tends to be one of the functions of diasporas – the Croat army in the Balkan conflict was largely funded by the Croatian diaspora (H. Smith and Stares, 2007) – and they can sometimes take a harder position on peace settlements than their kinspeople back home. Kaldor and Muro (2003: 151–2) confronted the question of whether religious and nationalist militant groups are part of global civil society without really answering it. In one view global civil society has a normative and progressive content that excludes, for example, Al Qaeda and the Mafia, but both groups are truly global and function as voluntary associations that are active in the public sphere and disseminate social capital and sociability, at least among members. It is worth acknowledging that not all fundamentalists are fanatics, and that some fundamentalists can oppose violence (Kaldor and Muro, 2003: 153), but there are, nonetheless, many forms of extreme militancy that are part of global civic networks, who circulate social capital amongst members and supporters, and are actively engaged glocally in politics for anti-democratic, anti-peaceful purposes. The instance of Al Qaeda should not distort our perspective, for there are many other examples of global networks that do not fit the template of peace-loving global civil society, such as anti-immigration groups in Britain, White supremacist and 'race' hate groups in the USA, far-right populist parties in Western European and the resurgent narrow nationalist parties in Eastern Europe.

There is another important caveat that should prevent us from running away with the idea that civil society is always positive for peace processes. Putzel (1997) referred to the 'dark side' of social capital, meaning the creation of trust, sociability and bonding amongst regressive religious and ethnic groups. This is similar to Chambers and Kopstein's (2001) notion of 'bad civil society', by which they mean organizations and voluntary associations that are malevolent by their resistance to peace – racist groups, xenophobic organizations and spoiler associations are obvious examples. Less obviously 'bad' organizations and associations also exist, in that they are not bad of themselves except that they keep the conflict going or mobilize against the particular second-best compromise that has been negotiated, such as, say, some victim support groups who feel that their experiences of victimhood are being neglected in the peace process or diaspora groups that inadvertently help to fund armaments.

In this regard, the Klu Klux Klan is as much a part of civil society as Northern Ireland's Women for Peace Together, the global anti-abortion movement as much as groups advocating women's rights and choice groups. We should not, therefore, romanticize civil society in a peace process, for some intermediary organizations will oppose the settlement or try to keep the divisions real, deliberately or unintentionally making peace processes fragile; zealots with their 'spoiler violence' (Darby, 2001) rarely work alone but have the aid and assistance of third-sector, civil society organizations behind them. In this respect, H. Smith and Stares (2007) argue that diaspora communities are as much peace-wreckers as peacemakers.

For example, Hindu nationalist groups in India have been responsible for considerable levels of violence against local Muslims and other Hindus who are their political opponents. Three thousand people were killed in riots following the destruction of a mosque in 1992, 2,000 were killed in Gujarat after 58 Hindus were killed on a train, and since 1998 there have been over 500 reported attacks on Christians allegedly by Hindu nationalists. It has been estimated that, lying behind and supporting Barrang Dal, the paramilitary wing of Hindu nationalism, are some 75 organizations for religious education and tribal development (Kaldor and Muro, 2003: 181). Nationalist groups have networks that unite them internally and have a political wing, the Bharatiya Janata Party (BJP), which places them in the public sphere of Indian politics, all of which are linked to diaspora groups to enhance their global connectedness. The BJP has an international political lobbying group known as the Friends of BJP, there are student groups on US campuses, and the Sewa Vibhag, the service or welfare wing of Hindu nationalism, has a Development and Relief Fund (IDRF) in the USA; in the UK, this group is represented by Sewa International UK (SIUK). The UK Charities Commission estimated in 2001 that SIUK raised $US4.3 millions. The US equivalent, the IDRF, dispersed $US1.7 million of its $US3.8 million fund in India in 2001 (Kaldor and Muro, 2003: 181). Renewed conflict is feasible therefore precisely because of global civil society networks and the social capital they generate amongst supporters worldwide.

## Vignette: Civil society in Sri Lanka

Sri Lanka is a good example to illustrate the negative side of civil society in peace processes (this is separate to the claim in International Relations theory that conflict resolution intervention can have negative unintended consequences – on which see Kuperman, 2008). NGO involvement in Sri Lankan society has risen significantly. Between 1981 and 2001, it was estimated that the number of NGOs working in Sri Lanka rose by a factor of three to reach 47,000 (Wild, 2006), in large part because of pressure from the diaspora (Fair, 2005) but also because of the rise of humanitarian concern over its faltering peace process. However, Devotta (2005) shows how many operate on ethnic, religious and linguistic lines, often with separate civil society groups for Sinhalese and Tamils, a divisiveness that is detrimental to the peace process, to the extent that Sri Lankan civil society contains contradictory tensions (Orjuela, 2008: 232). This tends to make Sri Lankan civil society groups locally focused and disconnected from global networks, giving them a limited scope of influence. Some do not challenge the power of exclusivist forms of ethno-nationalism in

Sri Lankan politics, which requires adherents of 'civil society peace-making' to contextualize their advocacy empirically by specifying the groups concerned (Orjuela, 2008: 233).

This makes civil society in Sri Lanka a politically contested space. The Sinhalese-dominated government, for example, tends to dismiss non-Sinhalese NGOs as pro-Tamil, and the Liberation Tigers of Tamil Eelam (LTTE), the main militant group, readily accuses NGOs of favouring the majority Sinhalese (de Silva, 2006). The 'other' group's NGOs are perceived as untrustworthy, thus reproducing the conflicts that civil society normally assists in bridging. Even international NGOs are viewed with great suspicion. For example, the *Island*, a strongly nationalist newspaper, dismisses INGOs as 'self-serving foreign academics' (cited in Devotta, 2005). Thus, Uyangoda (1996), writing in the Sri Lankan magazine *Pravada*, argues that the greatest problem facing civil society in Sri Lanka is a mindset amongst the Sinhalese that NGOs are part of Western imperialism and undermine the Sinhalese right to superiority on the island. That is, civil society is perceived to be part of the problem.

Peace activists thus have to persuade Sri Lankans that civil society is not a Western concept (Huddock, 1999: 3), which perforce tends to keep NGOs locally focused and removed from global networks, and thus outside global civil society. Appeals by Western governments to protect human rights invoke a colonial memory and are represented by Sinhala-Buddhist nationalists as part of a history of imperialist intervention in their affairs. Targeted assassinations are occurring of moderate Sri Lankans involved in civil society peace work. For example, Fr Xavier Karunaratnam was killed by an explosive device under his car just after having presided over Mass on 20 April 2008, the killers suspected of being the Sri Lankan army's Deep Penetration Unit. Karunaratnam was a Tamil Catholic and chair of the North East Secretariat on Human Rights, set up in 2002 after the peace accord, and was responsible for overseeing a great number of cross-community initiatives and human rights monitoring. He was as much an ardent critic of the LTTE as of the government, and liaised with the Tamil Tigers for the return of child soldiers and with the government over its infringement of Tamil human rights (Wijesinghe, 2003: 175 discusses some of the grassroots initiatives he was involved in). A Christian group, Kithusara (meaning 'Core of Christian Message'), continues his work. It holds cross-community meetings, bi-lingual musical programmes, poster campaigns and demonstrations to highlight the commonality of experience for Tamils and Sinhalese. It publishes quarterly journals in both languages. It refuses overseas funding in an attempt to avoid the accusation that it represents Western imperialism.

In a surprising argument, Berger (2005: 12) manoeuvred around these problems by defining civil society as comprising groups who were 'civil' in manners and culture, an adroit but sociologically superficial claim; it is more realistic to hang on to the idea of regressive civil society. However, if civil society is not always progressive, it is also the case that, where they emerge, agents of change come out of civil society; not all civil society is 'good' in the terms of Chambers and Kopstein (2001), but what work there is done in peace processes tends not to come from the grassroots. The grassroots are amorphous, unorganized if not disorganized, and poor. With weak social capital and suffering from social exclusion, the grassroots lack the skills, resources and motivations found in civil society. Civil society is a space where intellectual challenges to the existing order can be first thought, where material inequalities and oppressions are not so immediately pressing as amongst the down-trodden and beaten, so that intellectual envisioning of peace can begin. In civil society lie the educational and communication skills for political articulation, deliberation and mobilization that can motivate people to involvement in peacemaking. Groups within civil society can mobilize international links – through aid agencies, NGOs, the church, diaspora networks or whatever – to get money to underwrite their peace work. Civil society groups can mobilize these resources to such an extent that money can be poured into the peace process simply because they are linked to rich funders overseas. They can draw on these same international links to get trained professional peacemakers, conflict resolution mediators and other peace activists to engage with their particular conflict, none of which can be done by the powerless and globally disconnected grassroots. I am not arguing that the grassroots do not care for peace – the down-trodden and beaten in the grassroots are often the first victims of war and are the people who most suffer its consequences, materially and physically – but it is civil society that has the organizational skill, resource capacity and international network links to mediate grassroots private troubles and bring them to the public sphere where they can be turned into public issues.

We can illustrate this point with an example from the US Civil Rights Movement, focusing, in anticipation of the emphasis below on religion as a microcosm of civil society, on the small rural Black churches in Alabama (I owe what follows to John Brown Childs in a private communication). These churches had been around for a long time with roots in the period of slavery. They were a form of organization that gave African Americans a place in which to perform a marginalized and limited citizenship within their own local communities. They were not the basis for on-going political resistance but were institutions of social and cultural survival for severely marginalized people. They were only in the most marginal ways able to mediate between the African American grassroots and White-dominated civil society, given the oppressively minute way in which segregation impacted the daily lives of people. Thus, even if, as churches, they had the form of civil society, they did not perform its functions. However, when the small rural Black churches in Alabama were approached by the young activists in the Student Non-violent Coordinating Committee (SNCC) – quite independently from Martin Luther King's church-based Southern Christian Leadership Conference – they became transformed. The SNCC activists brought all the aspects of civil society described above, including important connections beyond the 'Cotton Curtain' to the rest of the USA and the world. Although the churches were there to be worked with as already extant organizations, albeit with limited civil society capabilities, it took SNCC to link them with the broader Civil Rights Movement. These churches were grassroots but offered a kind of pre-positioned or proto-civil society that needed better-organized, better-resourced and better-skilled civil society groups to bring their activism to fruition.

## Understanding the roles played by civil society

One way to simplify the multifarious and complex roles civil society plays is to describe the spaces that it occupies in peace processes. There are four:

- *Intellectual spaces*, in which alternative ideas are envisaged and peace envisioned and in which the private troubles of people are reflected upon intellectually as emerging policy questions that are relevant to them as civil society groups. Civil society groups can help to re-think the terms of the conflict so that it becomes easier to contemplate intellectually its transcendence or ending, and through their championing of alternative visions come to identify the range of issues that need to be articulated.
- *Institutional spaces*, in which these alternatives are enacted and practised by the civil society groups themselves, on local and global stages, making the groups role models and drivers of the process of transformation. Civil society thus lives out the vision of peace and transgresses, in its own practice, the borders that usually keep people apart, being institutions that practise, say, non-racialism or non-sectarianism well in advance of the general citizenry.
- *Sociological spaces*, in which cultural, social and material resources are devoted by the civil society groups, drawn from local and global civic networks, to mobilize and articulate these alternatives, rendering them as policy issues in the public sphere, nationally or internationally. With practices that implement, within their own terms of reference and field of interest, this alternative vision

of peace, civil society groups commit resources – labour power, money, educational skills, campaigning and debate – to underwrite their own commitment, to persuade others to share this commitment and to draw society's attention to the policy transformations that peace requires.

• *Political spaces*, in which civil society groups engage with the political process and assist in negotiation of the peace settlement, either directly by taking a seat at the negotiating table or indirectly by articulating the policy dilemmas that the peace negotiators have to try to settle or balance. These political spaces can be domestic and international, inasmuch as civil society groups can focus on facilitating political negotiations internally as well as internationalizing the negotiations, either by using diaspora networks to pressure domestic governments and policy makers to come to the table or by urging involvement of third parties and neutral mediators in the negotiations.

In what remains of this chapter I want to address the single instance of religion as one grouping in civil society to highlight the positive contribution it has made in many peace processes.

*Case study: the role of religion in civil society peacemaking*

Religion is sometimes a source of great conflict and is popularly presented as a negative social force. Established national churches often align with the regime in power, as did the Dutch Reformed Church in South Africa. Churches which are not established but which represent the faith of the dominant class or ethno-national group, and constitute a majority or national church, such as the Presbyterians in Northern Ireland or the Catholic Church in Latin America, can be co-opted by the state into its version of the struggle; even where there is ambivalence about this alignment, the collaboration can be willingly accepted by the church in order to protect itself against the state (for example, the co-option of the Catholic Church under Polish Communism and in revolutionary Mexico, and Russian Orthodoxism in the Soviet Union). A particularly vehement criticism of the Catholic Church in Latin America is that it has tended to side with the descendants of the Spanish and Portuguese settlers – their governments and their armies – against the indigenous Indians (with respect to Peru, for example, see Strong, 1992: 51).

The rise of religious fundamentalism is a barometer of what Putzel (1997) calls the darker side of social capital, and is an example of what is termed 'bad civil society' (Chambers and Kopstein, 2001). Juergensmeyer (2005) highlights the ambivalent and contradictory roles religion plays in global civil society (the ambivalence of religion is a central theme also in Appleby, 2000). Armstrong (2007: 208) argues that Christian fundamentalists are ambivalent about peace – and especially peace in the Middle East – because their interpretation of the Bible is that the end times would be characterized by war, not peace, in the region, and that the antichrist would disguise itself as a peacemaker. This usefully reminds us that concern about religious violence predates, and is broader than, the emergence of militant Islam, since all world faiths have made religion an arena of conflict.

But if religion is, in the language of social movement theory, a 'sentiment pool' (Zald and McCarthy, 1987) that provokes governments, ethno-religious groups and various warlords to believe God is on their side in the war, this sentiment pool can also provoke peaceful intervention in another country's conflict in order to protect co-religionists. The joint Belgian/French paratrooper operation in the Congo in the 1960s began at the point when Congolese rebels besieged Catholic convents; the clamour for intervention in Darfur is motivated in some measure by the desire to protect Christians against the Muslim Janjaweed militia. The Israeli government sent troops into Entebbe airport in Uganda in order to free hostages and airlifted Ethiopian Jews out of the famine. Sentiment pools can run deep when based on shared religious beliefs.

However, religious belief has a role in peace beyond furnishing the motivation for third party intervention, for religion can be an arena of reconciliation (for an analysis of the theological and practical resources for peace within Islam and Buddhism, see Ramsbotham, Woodhouse and Miall, 2005; for Christianity, see Cejka and Bamat, 2003). This is obviously so in cases where the churches and parachurch organizations are outside and above the conflict and can act as a mediator; even more so in cases where religion retains cultural legitimacy against secularization. Sierra Leone is a good example. The *International Religious Freedom Report* of 2005, prepared by the US Department of State Sierra Leone section, revealed that the country is mostly Muslim (around 60 per cent) with a sizeable Christian minority (about 30 per cent) and a small number of practitioners of traditional African religions (about 10 per cent). Amicable relations exist between them, to the extent that interfaith marriage is accepted and blessed by both Christian and Muslim leaders. The Catholic Archbishop for Sierra Leone once remarked that 'tolerance is part of our culture down to the village level. Extended families include members of different faiths' (*Christian Science Monitor*, 13 March 1999). This has been unaffected by the violence in the country. Penfold (2005: 549) summarizes his account of Sierra Leone's conflict: 'tribal differences, greed, corruption and mismanagement all fuelled the conflict but religious differences did not'. Indeed, mosques and churches were key sites for peace work and the Inter-Religious Council of Sierra Leone judged that the war brought the two major religious groups closer together than before (www.c-r.org/accords/s-leone). Established in 1997, the Inter-Religious Council

initiated dialogue between the government and rebels, began mediation with rebel leaders in the bush to release some of the child soldiers,
and played a major role as facilitator in the 1999 peace talks. Not only
did it help broker the peace accord, it monitored conformity to it afterwards. The Council was also instrumental in setting up a Truth and
Reconciliation Commission, headed by Bishop Humper, head of the
United Methodist Church (for details, see Penfold, 2005: 556).

Yet I have in mind something even more powerful, for religion
can become a site of reconciliation even in cases where the conflict is
religious or is experienced as religious (because it is between groups
marked by religious boundaries). How can something that is perceived
to be part of the problem become part of the solution? The answer to this
conundrum is civil society. The application of the term has increased
within the sociology of religion with recognition of the importance of
church – civil society relations to two key debates. The first is secularization. Herbert (2003) has argued that increasing involvement by
the church in civic and public affairs provides evidence to support
Casanova's controversial de-privatization thesis (1994), which accords
continued social importance to religion in opposition to the secularization theorists who claim religion has retreated to the private sphere.
The second debate concerns the rise of conservative evangelicalism
and fundamentalism. This shapes anxiety about the conservative form
in which religion enters the 'public square' (see Audi and Wolterstorff,
1996) and about 'religious terrorism' generally (Juergensmeyer, 2000;
Larsson, 2004). The two debates are not unrelated. The rump of religious believers still left after secularization are people who want their
beliefs to count in the public sphere, using a variety of civil society
groups and associations to place their concerns there, to the resentment
of those with no belief or to the embarrassment of those who prefer to
do their religion in private.

We can first give some general examples of religion as a positive
agent for peace before trying to understand the processes by which it
fills this role. History is littered with cases where the churches rapidly
switched their interpretation of doctrine to challenge inequalities and
to assist the overthrow of unjust regimes, such as slavery, apartheid,
patriarchy and sectarianism. If God thought His word unchanging,
human interpretations can make a rapid volte-face. Sometimes this
engagement with injustice and oppression was official church policy
– as with the Catholic Church's involvement with Solidarity and the collapse of Communism in Poland – and on other occasions it is unofficial,
representing unsanctioned reactions by the local churches and para-
church organizations to localized instances of oppression and violence.
The church hierarchy sometimes withheld its official backing of local
peace initiatives but nonetheless tolerated them; on other occasions
the official church tried to prevent local priests challenging the status

quo. Liberation theology in Latin America was attacked by the same Pope who sought the liberation of his Polish homeland, although local priests in Latin America often disregarded him and were active agents for social change. In Nicaragua, for example, commentators stress that it was 'popular religion', not the official Catholic Church policy, that assisted social change (Lancaster, 1988; Linkogle, 1998). Local churches on the ground in Nicaragua played an important role through which people built a common-sense understanding of the conflict and developed a commitment to social redistribution that supported the policies of the revolutionary parties. Populist Virgin Mary cults were forums for the advancement of social transformation by reinforcing sets of values antithetical to capitalist accumulation (Lancaster, 1988), a positioning that ensured they were opposed by conservative bishops. Popular religion was particularly powerful nonetheless, because it deployed Catholic symbolism that the official church found hard to suppress or limit. For example, Virgin Mary cults did not emphasize Mary's purity and passivity, representing her instead as a powerful decisive figure, able to intervene directly in the lives of poor peasants. In this respect they were institutions in which devotees of Mary could engage in public celebrations of popular religion that were indirectly political and which the conservative church could not disrespect.

In Northern Ireland's case, it was mostly the ecumenical churches that developed ideas about non-sectarianism, inter-faith dialogue, new forms of shared liturgy and the like that challenged the basis of the division between Catholics and Protestants. The ecumenical churches lived out these ideas as a practice in a variety of cross-denominational activities, such as church-to-church contact, joint clergy groups, shared services and joint prayer groups, which they underwrote financially, culturally and symbolically (for the various kinds of peacemaking activity by some of the churches in Northern Ireland, see Appleby, 2000; J. D. Brewer, 2003b; J. D. Brewer, Bishop and Higgins, 2001; Power, 2007). South Africa, on the other hand, represents a state where the churches were highly constrained in the roles they could perform in challenging apartheid. Ironically, however, it was the religious commitment of Afrikaners that ensured the churches some relative protection; Burmese Buddhist monks benefit from this too and can challenge the military regime more daringly than other citizens because of the religious beliefs of the generals (a protection not accorded their co-religionists in Tibet).

In apartheid South Africa, the church was the last set of institutions to be banned, churchmen (there were then no churchwomen) often exploited small areas of wriggle room to use the pulpit to attack the apartheid state, and they set their support firmly behind the anti-apartheid movement, becoming heavily involved in the political peace process (see Prozesky, 1990). The South African Council of Churches

and the South African Catholic Bishops, for example, helped to mobilize the grassroots by giving assistance to communities suffering
oppression in the townships and by trying to effect negotiations with
the government and the ANC to moderate the violence (Knox and
Quirk, 2000: 166). It was no accident, as we shall see in a subsequent
chapter, that the 'truth' recovery process in South Africa was led by the
churches, and Archbishop Tutu in particular, for they had a residue
of legitimacy that came from their strong anti-apartheid credentials.
Wilson's (2001) analysis of the South African Truth and Reconciliation
Commission reveals that, in the Vaal region, religious groups and the
churches were the only local organizations explicitly working with
the Commission towards the goal of reconciliation: 'not businesses, or
health institutions or educational establishments, just churches' (2001:
134). This was also, in a sense, a weakness, since the domination of
the religious redemptive notion of reconciliation, fostered by Tutu,
discouraged the formation of an alliance across civil society groups
to deal with the issue of reconciliation. When the involvement of the
churches puts off engagement by secular civil society groups, or iso-
lates their respective work in hermetic spheres, peace processes are
disadvantaged.

The church has generally involved itself in human rights and 'truth'
recovery processes, in Latin America in particular (see Hayes and
Tombs, 2001; for Bosnia's case, see Herbert, 2003: 229–64). This is in
part because the churches have seen it as their role to help the faithful
forgive, to come to terms with the legacy of violence and to build new,
more democratic, societies. The churches have tended to see themselves as living two Gospel axioms: one from John – that it is the truth
which sets people free (John 8: 32); the other from Matthew – that it is
in forgiving others that people are themselves forgiven (Matthew 6:
14–15). This is true even in those countries where the church did not
officially support the protest against repressive regimes; even conservative churches in Latin America wholeheartedly supported 'truth'
recovery processes. This support furnished the Catholic Church with
two martyrs, Archbishop Romero in El Salvador and Bishop Gerardi
in Guatemala, both assassinated for their part in disclosing past human
rights abuses (for a study of the two, see Hayes and Tombs, 2001:
11–102). In Latin America, however, the official church position often
changed only with the government, being wary of exposing itself to
threat in the way the South African churches did. The official church
often restricted itself to 'safe' peace work – the provision of pastoral
care to the affected communities, criticisms of the violence, calls for
restraint, formulaic statements after each tragedy and the promotion
of national dialogue between the protagonists. The Catholic Church
in Guatemala, for example, urged what it called a National Dialogue
in 1989, which the government and army boycotted, although the

Catholic Church became actively involved in the post-settlement 'truth' recovery process, at great risk (see Levy, 2001: 103–17).

This official church reticence was not evident elsewhere. In Poland, for example, the transition from Communism was strongly supported officially by the church (much of the following is taken from Herbert, 2003: 197ff.). Catholic clubs were formed to envision a new Poland, but they also facilitated the development of an independent movement of intellectuals, utilizing human rights discourse against the government and protesting against the Communist government's own constitutional reforms that delivered much less than ordinary Poles demanded. The church traversed from local parish to diocese, going between national and global networks (and the Catholic Church *is* a truly global church), articulating on many stages its symbolic confrontation with the Communist regime. But the political confrontation was not only symbolic, for the church materially and culturally assisted Solidarity in its active engagement with the political peace process. The Pope provided much of the vocabulary for Solidarity on human rights, although some elements of the underground initially rejected the church's role in politics (Herbert, 2003: 205). Three million Catholics celebrated the Polish Pope's Mass in 1979 and gave witness to the scale of popular resistance beyond the Gdansk-based support of Solidarity. As an urban and industrial movement, Solidarity alone could not have united an essentially rural society without the church. It deployed funds to assist Solidarity with organizational resources and training, it supplied meeting places for Solidarity, gave material support for some of its cultural activities, and funded the provision of alternative social services under the auspices of Solidarity, especially education and public health. Finally, the Catholic Church worked at a political level by mediating between the Gdansk workers in Solidarity and the Communist government, playing the role of third party to broker with a state that might otherwise have ignored Solidarity. When the Catholic Church got its Polish martyr, with the assassination of a Warsaw priest, and with two more visits to Poland by the Polish Pope, the church cast off some of the reservations that had earlier inhibited an overt political role. The government's response was to introduce various freedoms for the church (such as the lifting of restrictions on the religious press and the granting of powers for the church to organize welfare, including hospitals and old people's homes), which only increased the ability of the Catholic Church to act politically. Not surprisingly then, the Catholic Church was at the negotiating table to discuss the transition (Herbert, 2003: 210).

The Polish case, however, illustrates another of the preceding themes, that of the darker side of civil society. Herbert's analysis of the positive role of the Catholic Church in the fall of Polish Communism goes on to discuss some of the negative features of Catholicism post-Solidarity

(2003: 213–28). The equation of Catholicism with Polish nationalism that had once inspired Solidarity in its challenge to Communism ended up in some minds as a xenophobic and exclusive narrow nationalism that is anti-Semitic, anti-gay and supportive of the Polish far right. The Catholic radio station Radio Maryja, while unauthorized by the church, shows how nationalist emotions are not easily turned off and can in some post-violence settings continue to push to *extremis* the freedoms sorely won. But the religious shock jocks of Radio Maryja disguise the extent to which the Catholic Church has officially linked with the new Polish government to implement a conservative Catholic social agenda and is pursuing its own anti-Semitism over the building of a Carmelite convent and crucifixes on the site of Auschwitz concentration camp. Sociability and social capital for purposes of xenophobia – and recall the role that nuns and priests played in the genocide slaughters in Rwanda, to the embarrassment of the Western mother churches – are only some of the problems with civil society.

In the language of Robert Putnam (2000), religion is a form of 'bonding capital', a social network which links group members in solidarity, and, as we have illustrated, the virtues it disseminates amongst them can be desirable or undesirable, producing 'good' or 'bad' civil society. But religion is also, in Putnam's terms, a form of 'bridging capital' that links across diverse groups. Normally, the bonding capital of religion is very high, bridging capital weak. However, one way to understand the role religion plays in peace processes, as a form of bridging capital, is to distinguish the social spaces it occupies in civil society as special locations for religious peace work. These socially strategic spaces give religion weight well beyond that carried by declining numbers in the pews and they bring to higher relief the ways in which the churches operate in peace processes. These spaces duplicate those occupied by civil society itself, identified earlier – intellectual, institutional, sociological and political.

It is clear that in many cases the churches and para-church organizations constituted themselves as intellectual spaces for challenging the terms by which the conflict was understood and for invoking a new society. Some of them think about what for many others (including some other churches) is still unthinkable – non-racialism, non-sectarianism, the ending of repression, political and socio-economic reform, the fall of Communism and the like. Churches are more effective in doing this when they are part of a general coalition of civil society groups that envision the future, much as in South Africa, but they occasionally either lead the opposition, as in Burma, or co-ordinate it, as in Poland. Forms of popular religion, working outside more conservative church hierarchies, are even better at this. Local churches on the ground in Nicaragua, for example, played an important role through which people built a common-sense understanding of the conflict and developed a commitment to social redistribution and transformation. This envisioning of peace not only helps to win the end of violence, it can assist in maintaining the peace settlement afterwards as people suffer the emotional rollercoaster of renewed violence or deal with the after-effects of violence. Churches tend to be able to stake a claim to expertise in dealing with issues like restorative justice, forgiveness and 'truth', which is why the churches have played a role in managing many 'truth' recovery processes.

As a set of institutions and organizations, religion also constitutes an institutional space in which these intellectual challenges are practised, locally, nationally and globally. Liberal Rabbis in Israel–Palestine, such as Rabbis for Human Rights (see www.rhr.israel.net/profile/index.shtml), work in the occupied territories amongst Palestinian groups, confronting the Israeli army in instances of abuse, protecting Palestinian homes and olive groves, and dispersing food and clothing, thereby putting into practice, in a particularly courageous way, their intellectual challenge to Zionism.

When the churches focus less on themselves as institutions – as path-breaking as this may be in some situations of communal violence – in order to work amongst the poor, dispossessed and victims, they occupy sociological spaces in which their resources – financial, cultural and social – get devoted to peace. This is often a two-stage process. From the initial involvement in the 'private troubles' of poor communities and victims often comes the realization that spending resources alone does not solve these ills, recognizing that communal violence makes them worse. From this can follow a wider engagement with the issue of peace and the deployment of resources to help materialize it. The local Catholic churches in Colombia, for example, provided an alternative welfare system to the government's, being a main benefactor of basic services, education and health (as they and other churches have done in many other places too). The Catholic Relief Service (CRS) had been operational inside the country for fifty years, but in 2000 it began a 'solidarity with Colombia' programme, which expanded and strengthened its focus on peace and justice (CRS, 2005). The programme supports civil society efforts to provide emergency and humanitarian assistance and human rights education, as well as promoting conflict transformation. As a global network, the CRS in Colombia was able to draw on international links, and joined with the Catholic Church in the USA to confront the violence.

Through these sorts of global connections, churches are able to encourage co-religionists from outside the country to expend resources that both deal with the private troubles of people affected by violence and transform them into public issues on a global stage. Where religion and ethnicity elide, diaspora networks constitute a further web of co-religionists with potential to deploy resources to enhance the sociological spaces the churches operate in for the purposes of peace. The small-scale actions of Rabbis for Human Rights in Israel–Palestine, for example, are made much more effective when linked to co-religionists in the USA, some of whom are engaged in inter-faith dialogue to further the peace process (Abu-Nimer, 2004: 414). The organization makes effective use of web-based campaigns to highlight its work and to pursue an international campaign for worldwide Jewry to 'return to its moral self'.

When churches and para-church organizations enter the political process and engage in the politics of reconciliation and negotiation, they operate in a political space that is capable of both delivering peace settlements and monitoring conformity to them afterwards. The churches were wholly excluded from the public political process in Northern Ireland that negotiated the Good Friday Agreement, in large part because of anticipated internal disagreements over the settlement, but they were used as back channels of communication prior to the talks, and prominent churchpeople have since been co-opted by the government to lead over-sight of decommissioning and to take forward the question of how the conflict should be remembered. The British government drew up a list of Protestant clergy whom they thought they could recruit to sell the Good Friday Agreement, an idea later abandoned when it was leaked to the press; their principal target was Archbishop Robin Eames, head of the Anglican Church of Ireland. On retirement, Eames led the government initiative to assess how the conflict should be remembered.

In Poland, however, we saw earlier that the Catholic Church was overtly political and was a leading participant at the negotiating table. It is rare in modern times for this to be so overt, since the churches have mostly withdrawn from direct involvement in the political process, but they nonetheless occupy political spaces in peace processes when they mobilize against the effects of violence, criticize governments and rebels, call for peace accords and facilitate the negotiation of second-best compromises. In cases where the churches are open to state repression, such as apartheid South Africa, or are kept at arm's length, as in Northern Ireland, operating in this political space can be difficult for them and their activities take place mostly in secret until the last stages of the conflict. This has been the churches' problem in Northern Ireland, for in this political space it kept well below the parapet for a very long time (as was also the case in Poland). But there are some examples of church involvement in popular uprisings in open defiance and with heads well above the barricades, as with Buddhist monks in Burma and Tibet, Catholics in the Philippines, liberation theology priests in Latin America and anti-apartheid clerics.

There is nothing sequential about these spaces, as if churches and para-church organizations progress linearly from one to the other; nor do they imply a judgement of the quality of the peace work done on each plane. However, it is necessary to emphasize something that by now is obvious. Minority status has a powerful effect on the ability of churches and para-church organizations to occupy particular spaces. Minority status is defined by one or more of three conditions. The most obvious is being one of the smaller denominations or world faiths within the faith of the majority community, with the faith of the majority understood either in the common-sense way as that of the largest number of the population or as that of the dominant group (for example Methodists within Protestantism in Northern Ireland and Christians in Sri Lanka or in Israel–Palestine). Minority status is also conferred on those who comprise a small wing of an otherwise majority denomination, such as liberal Rabbis in Israel–Palestine, ecumenists in Northern Ireland or anti-apartheid members of the Dutch Reformed Church in South Africa. Finally, non-established and non-national churches have minority status compared to those that are state churches.

Minority churches in these senses crop up throughout as leading examples of peace activism, for they have less to lose and most to gain from involvement with peace. Established churches, tied to the state and linked to the majority population's sense of nationalism, find it difficult to mount challenges to the regime or to exclusive forms of ethno-nationalism. Some Protestant ministers in Northern Ireland found it necessary to negotiate carefully even joint carol services with neighbouring Catholic parishes, without risking being hounded out by their congregations. The South African Dutch Reformed Church preached racial separation from the pulpit, and it was left to a few courageous individuals within the Dutch Reformed Church to speak out (such as Beyers Naude), or to minority wings, such as the separate Black Dutch Reformed Churches (notably people like Allan Boesak), or to the non-established churches, like the South African Council of Churches and the South African Catholic Bishops. This is why the Sinhalese Buddhist community in Sri Lanka lags behind the country's small Christian community (representing considerably less than one in ten of the population) in engagement with peace (see Wijesinghe, 2003). Only where a national church identifies itself with opposition to the state, as in Poland, can it distance itself from the state regime sufficiently to engage with the peace process; otherwise, it is left for established or national churches to about-turn only when the failed regime looks as if it is about to collapse.

Minority status, on the other hand, can facilitate an intellectual challenge to the way the conflict is understood and to the envisioning of peace, as well as enhance the churches' critique of existing social relations and thus their commitment to social transformation. Minority status can place one outside the mainstream, leading to feelings of strangeness from the majority and to empathy with other minorities, or of being in a similar position to the victims of communal violence; and it can lead to feelings of marginality and thus to extra efforts to make a difference in the peace process in compensation for what is otherwise a low profile or even relative neglect. The Methodists in Northern Ireland, representing 3 per cent of respondents in the 1998 Life and Times Survey (see J. D. Brewer, 2003c), have been disproportionately involved in the peace process for both sets of reasons; Methodists from Ireland have won the World Methodist Peace Award on three occasions in its thirty-year history. And liberals in one denomination or world faith often find it easier to talk to liberals in another, rather than the hotheads in their own.

Minority status, however, can be associated with limited material and cultural resources, restricted social capital and legitimacy, a low profile in or exclusion from the political sphere, and hostility and oppression from members of the majority church, as is the case for both Christians and the Rabbis for Human Rights group in Israel–Palestine, all of which tends to restrict occupancy to intellectual and institutional spaces. Membership of Rabbis for Human Rights tends to be from Jews with a background in the West, educated in Western universities, and imbued with Western sensitivities towards humanitarian values, which places them in an even greater minority position within contemporary Israel–Palestine. Minority status cuts access to resources fundamental to peace work. This is with the exception of those minority groupings that are linked to dominant faith communities and wealthy co-religionists elsewhere, the global links to which can facilitate them becoming key sociological spaces for the expenditure of resources, facilitating their occupancy of local political space. Some world faiths are global and, although placed in a minority position within particular nation states, they can nonetheless call on international networks and rich resources for local effect. This global interchange certainly helped Catholics back in Belfast. For example, Father Sean McManus established the Irish National Caucus in the USA as a pro-Nationalist lobby that had powerful resonances amongst Catholics in Northern Ireland, although Unionist critics disparaged the Caucus as gun-runners for the IRA.

Religious groups with majority status, conversely, gain easier *entrée* to the political process by dint of their majority status or established church position and have greater resources to dispense in key sociological spaces. They become powerful agents in peace processes whenever this privileged status is exploited to realize a settlement, as mainstream Protestant churches have now done in Northern Ireland and the Catholic Church came to do in Latin America. Majority status, however, seems rarely to be employed in this direction. The Free Presbyterians in Northern Ireland, for example, moved to support the Good Friday Agreement only when their Moderator, Revd Ian Paisley, determined it was in the political interests of his Democratic Unionist

Party (DUP) to do so, and some still rail against him for it. At that point, somehow, divine intervention transformed the DUP's party political interests into the will of God (on Paisley's support for power sharing, see Bruce, 2007).

## Conclusion

I have argued that civil society is the key to a sociological approach to peace processes, for it turns people's private troubles into public issues in ways that mediate between the local, national and global spheres. The corollary of this argument is that post-violence societies with a weak civil society will be short of one of the main pillars that stabilize the peace process, as we have seen to be the case in Sri Lanka. This observation acts as a useful counterweight to the claim that promotion of civil society is the route to democracy in post-violence societies. While this chapter has shown the positive role that civil society plays within a peace process across four spaces, it does not romanticize it. There are some instances where civil society is part of the problem, not part of the solution; some church groups, as we have seen, especially majority-status ones, do not, unsurprisingly, walk on water.

Normally, however, if not quite an antidote to war, global civil society has adopted the process of globalization to develop new forms of peacemaking and to internationalize conflicts by means of global networks. Civil society groups within a country are glocal in the way they traverse local, national and international stages, mediating between the market and the state, between the grassroots and the third sector, and between the local and global. The capacity of civil society to transform private troubles into public issues helps to shape the policy agenda in post-violence societies and assists in managing the policy dilemmas that negotiated peace deals have to contend with. In all these ways, a sociological approach to peace processes has civil society as the font from which everything else flows.

# 4

## Gender

### Introduction

There is a seamless transition from issues of civil society to gender. Women's groups are amongst the most active in civil society and women have played a positive role in peace processes in many ways. If conflict has a great deal to do with masculinity, as we shall shortly discuss, femininity gets stereotypically wrapped up with the peace. This chapter intends to show that women's groups are amongst the longest established and most active civil society groups, and feminist issues around violence against women, amongst other things, have been translated into involvement with peace processes. Women's issues have been internationalized for many decades and evince very well both the impact that global networks have in local settings and the ways in which feminist concerns in local spaces get mediated on a global arena.

The deleterious effect armed conflict has on women has been recognized by the global women's movement as a particularly aggressive form of gendered violence and women's groups have given a high profile to the negative effects of conflict on women. Social science interest has followed. Considerable attention has been devoted to women as victims of rape and other harm in times of conflict (for example Hynes, 2004; Lentin, 1999; Littlewood, 1997), to women as biological and social reproducers of the nation (for example, Yuval-Davis and Anthias, 1989) and to the way women's issues get side-lined in times of struggle for the sake of national or political causes (for example Cockburn, 2001; Carol Coulter, 1998; Enloe, 2000). There is no correspondingly high level of interest in gender and peace. However, the ability of women's groups to move effortlessly between local, national and global civil society when campaigning against gendered violence has been useful in assisting the same mediation for the purposes of peace. Women have played this positive role in two ways:

* by mobilizing on feminist issues, they have broadened the terms of the conflict and prevented its narrow concentration on one zero-sum line of social cleavage, thus offering cross-cutting forms of identity;
* the mobilization of women on feminist issues has had knock-on effects for their mobilization on peace issues, making women amongst the most active peacemakers.

However, I will argue that women peacemakers have to confront cultural values around gender that pressure them into socially stereo-typed peace work. These gendered norms are difficult for women's peace groups to transcend, which tends to distort women's engagement with peace processes. This chapter will address the multiple roles women perform in war and peace and highlight women's contribution in two in-depth case studies: the Sudan and Rwanda. But first let us address the problem of men.

## Masculinity, war and gendered violence

Within sociology, gender is understood as a social construction, with the meanings of femininity and masculinity changing with the social setting over time and space. War is a social setting that impacts greatly on the meaning given to gender, but the attention has mostly been on its impact on women. Masculinity, however, is a feminist issue (for a thoroughgoing analysis of masculinity and heterosexual violence, see Hird, 2002).

It is mostly men who engage in war and violence. Participation can confer status on men as men, allowing them to benefit from all the positive self-images that derive from being 'tough', hard' and 'a man's man'. There is an extensive literature in sociology on how some men in ordinary life respond to the modern 'crisis of masculinity' by 'toughing it out' (Seidler, 1997: 9–10). This 'crisis of masculinity' is the result of the challenge to traditional forms of male power by, amongst other things, feminism, deindustrialization, deskilling, the decline in traditional occupations, and the feminization of labour (see MacInnes, 1998, for further analysis of this crisis). In response to it, some men have taken refuge in aggressive reassertions of the tough-guy image, especially younger males (see McEvoy-Levy, 2001). Indeed Hollywood often exaggerates masculinity for the vicarious pleasure of 'tough' men with the John Wayne, Dirty Harry or Rambo syndromes (for an analysis of masculinity in celluloid, see Gallagher, 1999), with associated portrayals of women as sex objects or coquettish and feminine (for an analysis of the occasional women's 'action' role, such as Demi Moore in the film *GI Jane*, see Williams, 2004; Youngs, 1999). War affords even greater opportunities for 'tough' men to realize themselves as men through aggression (for an analysis of the role of masculinity in the conflict in South Africa's former Natal region, see Campbell, 1992). Indeed, lost wars can be refought in celluloid, allowing Rambo single-handedly to reverse the United States' fortunes in Vietnam; 9/11 was turned by Hollywood into masculine heroism in films like *United 93* or *Twin Towers*.

Away from the fantasy of cinema though, many of the victims of war and communal violence are women and the violence against them often takes a gendered and sexual form. The Soviets regularly gave sexual 'open days' to their troops in the Second World War – the capture of Berlin warranted three; even American allies raped and pillaged in friendly Belgium during its liberation (Hitchcock, 2009). In Bosnia, UN peacekeepers sometimes came across women tied to trees, with their foetuses opened to the ground like entrails. Even in low-level communal violence, the brutalization that takes place amongst male non-combatants leads to increases in the incidence of 'domestic' violence – the powerlessness and emasculation of non-combatant men can sometimes be resolved by doing violence in the home. In colonial struggles, this is compounded by the servile and brutal way non-combatant men are treated in the public sphere, making the domestic sphere the place where the proscribed authoritarian male role is acted out. This is occasionally reinforced by the ready recourse to alcohol as a coping strategy to deal with the strains of the conflict. For example, amidst the large number of deaths in Northern Ireland's 'Troubles', women died regularly as a result of 'domestic' violence. Figures from the Women's Aid Federation reveal that between 1991 and 1994, 24 women were victims of 'domestic' violence related homicide, and, of 1,013 'serious violence cases', 972 victims were women and 52 were men (www. niwaf.org/domesticviolence/factsfigures.htm). In 1998, for example, four years into the uncertain ceasefire and before the signing of the Good Friday Agreement, 9 women died as a direct result of 'domestic' violence and 13,000 women contacted Women's Aid (Bairner, 1999: 126). The easy slippage from communal violence into gendered/sexual violence shows that masculinity is given a particularly brutal and destructive meaning in war.

One of the difficulties faced by male ex-combatants, irrespective of age, is decommissioning, in that giving up their arms is like handing over opportunities for livelihood. Gunmen can also experience emasculation during decommissioning (with respect to Northern Ireland, see Bairner, 1999: 131), and post-conflict 'war stories' can become opportunities for men to relive the 'excitement' of the conflict and the male camaraderie and thus perpetuate unreconstructed notions of masculinity. The acceleration into manhood of the child soldiers in West Africa reminds us that distorted notions of masculinity affect boys as much as men in times of war and play themselves out in specific victimhood experiences for women and girls. Child soldiers whose combat status is mostly reluctant can nonetheless be brutalized by it, although not all are hesitant warriors given the incentives of warlord patronage; Murphy (2003), in particular, resists the notion that child soldiers in Liberia and Sierra Leone lacked responsibility (on the use of child soldiers in Africa more generally, see Honwana, 2006).

Child soldiers have always existed, but contemporary understandings of childhood have come to dominate international discourse and to place special resonance on the phenomenon. The Coalition to Stop the Use of Child Soldiers (see www.childsoldiers.org/), formed in 1980 by leading international human rights and humanitarian organizations, runs a website to highlight both the exploitation of children as combatants and their rehabilitation problems afterwards. Child soldiers have lost their youth as well as their innocence, and with it the chance of education and a more normal entry into adulthood. Human Rights Watch estimated in 2002 that there were 30,000 soldiers under the age of eighteen years, located in thirty-six countries, a third of which were girls (quoted in Murphy, 2003: 73). In Sierra Leone, half of the combatants were children, half of which again are estimated to have been abducted into fighting (Peters and Richards, 1998: 186; also see McKay, 2004; Zack-Williams, 2001). Unwilling child soldiers were kept 'loyal' by means of addiction to brown-brown, a form of raw cocaine, the weaning off from which adds to the difficulties former male child soldiers face in the post-violence setting. Drugs were also used to assist the young boys to overcome their fears of fighting. The experiences of girl child soldiers are somewhat different from those of young males, for most were abducted as 'wives' to male soldiers and as sex slaves (see Itano, 2004), leaving long-term problems around their sexuality and memories of gross sexual violence, although, as we shall shortly see, some were in active combat.

Bereft of a 'normal' transition into adulthood, and lacking skills and resources for entry into the labour market, former child soldiers can be stigmatized, and debates have ensued, motivated particularly by tribal elders whose authority child soldiers undermined, about the degree of culpability of the young fighters (see Peters and Richards, 1998, for the Sierra Leonean case). This adds to the children's difficulties, since they can find themselves ostracized by elders. However, given that combat status was unsought and forced upon some children, as we shall discuss in chapter 6, the Sierra Leone Truth and Reconciliation Commission, organized by UNICEF, agreed that child soldiers should not be forced to give public testimony before the Commission, that they should not be required to seek forgiveness or be publicly shamed and humiliated, and that the local press should not sensationalize their role in the war.

The extent of the difficulty of transforming post-conflict notions of masculinity is shown by the rise in violent ordinary crime that tends to occur in post-violence societies, and by increases in random sexual attacks and 'domestic' violence. Some of this is 'spoiler violence', referred to in chapter 2, deliberately intended to disrupt the negotiations, and violent crime by warlords who want to keep the conflict going to disguise their ordinary crime. In some transitions there is also a collapse of the structures of formal and informal social control that previously inhibited crime. However, some of this increase in violent crime is also the residue of the masculinity to which the conflict gave full vent and which is not capable of being immediately transformed. The analysis of politicized youth in the township of Diepkloof in South Africa by Monique Marks (2001) shows the anomie, powerlessness and emasculation former male combatants felt (for example, see 2001: 89), a point from where, for some, it was a 'slippery slide into the underworld of crime' (2001: 133).

Democratic transitions in other former authoritarian and conflict-ridden societies also witnessed an increase in the crime rate. Publication of the proceedings of an international conference on crime in transitional societies (Mark Shaw, 2001), which reviewed the situation up to the end of the 1990s, highlighted organized crime problems in Russia, Argentina and Nigeria; the rise in general crime levels in Mozambique and Ukraine; relatively high levels of inter-personal violence in South Africa, Northern Ireland and Brazil; and the expansion in power of the drug cartels in Latin America. The growth of organized crime tends to be associated with transitions that also involve changes to the economic system (Mark Shaw, 2002: 15), and with societies where there was already a vibrant informal economy and high levels of crime, with the structural reform of economic relations and the growth of urbanization and consumption providing an opportunity for criminal gangs to cash in. However, crime can extend well beyond Mafia-like groups when the democratic transition is not accompanied by any great economic redistribution or the erosion of economic inequality, and where ordinance from the war remains in ready supply. This fits, notably, the cases of South Africa and Latin American countries. The way crime is handled can put the democratic transition to test, and risks placing in doubt the new commitment to political reform, as the murder of street children by state police in Brazil illustrates (see Neto, 2002).

For all these reasons, it is an important form of peacemaking to work amongst former combatants around issues of masculine identity once the war is over. This is not something that the 'good governance' approach to peace even recognizes as an issue, nor indeed do those feminists who think women's issues are just about women. Even the field of masculinity studies in social science is weak in this area. Vic Seidler, one of the doyens of masculinity studies, when entitling one of his books *Transforming Masculinities* (Seidler, 2006), had in mind the transformation of the theoretical framework of masculinity studies rather than an empirical agenda for assisting aggressive men towards less violent notions of masculinity, although he noted the lack of ways men have for dealing with 'traumatic histories', which includes experiences as combatants (and victims), a problem that can be passed on to generations of their male children. The problem for peace processes is thus plain. Peace processes require the transformation of violent masculinities in two senses: reducing the brutalization of masculinity amongst non-combatant males; and finding alternative non-violent masculinities for former male combatants. But if the problem is known, the solution is not.

Issues around the social reintegration of ex-prisoners and former combatants, including females, will be dealt with in chapter 5 when restorative justice is discussed as a way of managing the emotions aroused by communal conflict. Here I focus on managing masculinity, particularly amongst younger ex-combatants (on young people and conflict transformation, see McEvoy-Levy, 2001). There are, of course, well-developed programmes for assisting men with transcending 'domestic' violence. In the USA, for example, the Men's Resource Center for Change (www.mensresourcecenter.org/about) has since 1982 been offering anger management classes for men, organizing campaigns to highlight 'domestic' violence with a view to raising awareness amongst men, and hosting youth violence prevention programmes. There are numerous examples of similar bodies, such as Men Stopping Violence (see www.menstoppingviolence.org), dedicated to ending men's violence against women 'because they have daughters'. These groups are part of international networks within global civil society that encourage affiliated bodies to, in the words of Men Stopping Violence, 'think globally, act nobly'. Umbrella organizations, such as Men's International Peace Exchange, help local groups mediate between neighbourhood, national and global spaces (www.peaceexchange.org). Anti-war veteran associations also abound (as well as the many veteran associations enthusiastic about war, or at least romantic about it), which are not irrelevant but are not directly involved in transforming violent masculinities after civil conflict. Glocal as they may be, these groups and networks deal with men's violence in the private, domestic sphere and they eschew the problems involved with managing the consequences for men of communal violence in the public sphere.

These glocal networks do, however, dramatize the scarcity of the institutional support for men in need of rehabilitation from violent masculinities after communal violence. There are only a few random examples of this sort of work that can be cited to begin the focus, and many of those merge with initiatives for the social reintegration of ex-prisoners, such as the provision of education and work skills. Initiatives in Sierra Leone with former child soldiers, for instance, assist their recovery through education (and adult education) programmes. Former child combatants interviewed during rehabilitation voiced the need for educational skills and qualifications (see Peters and Richards, 1998) as a way into a more 'normal' adulthood. In South Africa, a minority of former comrades were absorbed into the new defence forces and police. Bairner (1999: 133) refers to the need in Northern Ireland to educate 'boys to become men', but saw no signs of it happening. Elsewhere in Northern Ireland, researchers at the University of Ulster established the Centre for Young Men's Studies in 2004, to assist young men who are coming out of prolonged conflict, especially with respect to their involvement in violence (see Harland, Beattie and McCready, 2005: 3), and have addressed the continuing over-representation of young men as perpetrators and victims of crime in the North of Ireland (McCready, Harland and Beattie, 2006). The Centre has been slow to develop, however, and is primarily concerned with developing a body of knowledge through research that other practitioners can later exploit; by 2007 it was only in the first year of its first research programme.

The Seeds of Peace Organization in the United States of America (see www.seedsofpeace.org) takes youth, including those responsible for perpetrating the violence, from various conflict-torn societies to the state of Maine for an intensive three-week period of familiarization with their former opponents as a way of garnering more peaceful relations. A similar organization, the Creative Peace Network, a Canadian charitable body (see www.creativepeacenetwork.ca), organizes youth peace camps, which it calls Peace It Together, focusing particularly on Israel–Palestine and Sri Lanka, for much the same purposes and in much the same manner. Youngsters are encouraged to break down barriers through contact and communication, with the intention of developing skills and resources that will equip them for leadership roles back home. Part of the problem of similar holiday ventures for Catholic and Protestant youth in Northern Ireland was that relationships were not sustained when participants returned to their segregated communities, but evaluations done of these two youth camp schemes suggest on-going contact is maintained via the Internet (Ungerleider, 2001) and that there are permanent changes in attitudes towards former enemies. Unfortunately, none of this work deals directly with the problem of distorted notions of masculinity in young ex-combatants; it is addressed, if at all, as a by-product of the normalization of relations between young people from conflict zones.

The final examples are more directly useful. The first case involves peace work done amongst former gang members in the USA in an attempt to separate masculine identity from violence. Since gangs tend to cohere around ethnicity as much as neighbourhood it is not irrelevant to communal violence. John Brown Childs (2003a, 2003b) has analysed the 'positive cultures leadership programme' in several cities in the USA affected by gang violence. It works in several ways. It establishes a network of people to work with gang members as positive role models, provides support groups for ex-members, 'safe' spaces where former members can be reintegrated and protected from erstwhile colleagues still involved in the gang, 'love circles' of former addicts who provide mutual respect, caring and solidarity with ex-gang members being weaned off drugs, and a whole programme for intervention to reduce and resolve specific instances of gang violence and introduce life-style change amongst members. On one occasion he described his involvement in six particular projects, spread across California to Connecticut (2003a: 233–47), which were united by a common concern to persuade gang members that the 'enemy' is not members of other gangs but violence itself.

A similar initiative was undertaken in the East Rand of South Africa by a civil society group, the National Peace Accord Trust, with young ex-combatants who had initially turned to crime. This case provides the best evidence of all that intensive work among ex-combatants can be beneficial to peace processes. In an extensive crime reduction programme in three African townships over eight years, the Trust was able to report in 2003 that 80 per cent of former youth activists had now 'turned their backs on crime'. Substance abuse dropped, feelings of trauma were reduced, the number of stable relationships rose by a fifth and the number gainfully employed rose by three-quarters. A few even went into local public service as volunteer police and fire officers. The Trust set up a scheme whereby local businesses in the area could either sponsor one youngster's education or give them employment. The Trust said: '[we] believe that the future stability and prosperity of South Africa can only be built on stable community life. Our [work] shows that, given the right interventions, criminally inclined youths can become positive agents for sustainable development' (see *Mail and Guardian Online*, 27 August 2003).

These sorts of initiatives pale in number compared to the programmes for managing the problems of masculinity in the domestic sphere, which reinforces the scale of the difficulties in transforming violent masculinities in peace processes. The examples suggest that for this to happen there is a need for either an organized economy with a vibrant civil society, furnishing the resources and skills to support and sustain this kind of work, or, in less sustainable economies, active intervention by global civil society from the outside, with international NGOs, foreign governments, charities and philanthropic organizations linking with local civil society groups to achieve the same end. In poorer societies, former male combatants can be left unaided, where they can easily slide into drink, drugs and crime, constituting a ready resource for mobilization by warlords promising patronage, as well as a constant threat to the physical safety of women and children in the home. It is well known that women in war zones tend to have fewer coping strategies available to them than men (see H. Smith, 2007) because of their responsibility for sustaining the domestic sphere – managing the home and bringing up children – but even in peace women can be disadvantaged when the former male combatants form a negative culture that consumes itself in romantic idealizations of the former violence, ongoing 'domestic' violence or a haze of drink and drugs. It is for this reason that Hamber et al. (2006) argued that peace processes were failing women because they left a strong residue of concern over their security – and this based on an analysis of the relatively successful transitions of Northern Ireland and South Africa (but also the more fragile transition in the Lebanon).

Research amongst diaspora communities (H. Smith and Stares, 2007) highlights problems for men even when they migrate to wealthier societies. Displaced Bosnian women in the Netherlands and the UK, for example, found it easier than men to get work because of the feminization of labour, albeit in lower-paid, menial service jobs, assisting their integration in the host society and their active participation in its civil society, at least compared to their menfolk. Displaced men, conversely, experienced a loss of status and identity, and often formed a coterie of disgruntled men locked into the identities – and sometimes also the conflicts – of the past (H. Smith, 2007). Exile can be a more enriching and empowering experience for women, reinforcing, once more, the difficulties in peace processes posed by violent masculinities. Transforming violent masculinities is an important part of peace work and without it communal violence leaves a legacy that can destabilize the peace accord.

## Women and peace processes

My central argument is that women perform a variety of roles in war and peace and, in so doing, face difficulties arising from culturally defined gender roles, the result of which is that men, especially powerful men who are normally in control of peace transitions, either undervalue and ignore women's contribution to peace processes or try to marginalize it to activities that are stereotypically associated with traditional gender roles (for an overview of women and conflict resolution, see Ramsbotham, Woodhouse and Miall, 2005).

According to cultural norms, the private sphere of domestic–family space is women's provenance, and when they enter public space they bring 'feminine' qualities from the home with them. Traditional gender stereotypes of women as carers, nurturers, healers and reconcilers form powerful imagery and are applied liberally in discussions of women's roles in peace processes, even amongst those who should know better. The United Nations Development Fund for Women in 2000 (UNIFEM, 2000: 33) described women peacemakers in traditional terms, motivated by the practical day-to-day concerns of wives and mothers – lofty humanitarian and ideological concerns presumably require the intelligence of men – and motivated by improving relationships, the 'normal' nurturing role for women. Their concerns over war and violence are the concerns of wives and mothers (their loss and bereavement as their sons and husbands do the fighting, the anxiety of mothers caring for traumatized children) and of women dealing with the problems of domesticity (keeping hearth and home together and children alive), while men deal with political and military strategy. In a later report (http://unifem.org/attachments/products/securing_the_peace.pdf), the body repeated its view that women have special qualities as peacemakers because they are women, including that they are better at building ties and at fostering reconciliation, and are consistently more highly motivated to peace (UNIFEM, 2005: 2–3).

In a study of seven peace processes, Cejka (2003: 28–9) found, however, that male and female peacemakers showed no difference in their motivations and concerns. In contrast, public surveys of people's perceptions of male and female participation in peace activities, reported by Tessler, Nachtwey and Grant (1999), found that in Western countries people tended to *feel* that women were more peace-oriented than men, reflecting widespread cultural notions of female nurturing. This should be no surprise, for social surveys tap into social stereotypes and reproduce socially constructed gender roles. This social stereotypical view of women's peacemaking qualities was confirmed in an experimental research design amongst three groups of Israeli–Palestinian respondents (see d'Estree and Babbitt, 1998) and it has been repeated in an analysis of the role of women in Northern Ireland's peace process (Potter, 2008: 142–6).

I argue that the position is more complex, for women play four roles in war and peace, discussion of which will focus the remainder of this chapter. The roles are:

- Combatants
  Some women do the fighting. Women combatants, however, struggle not only against the state, regime or ethno-national group to which they object, but also against the unreconstructed gender roles perpetuated both by some of their co-combatants and by society at large, resulting in highly gendered forms of combat.
- Victims/survivors
  Everyone suffers in war but women experience particularly gendered forms of victimhood. Violence against women in ethnic conflicts is

more than merely sexual violence driven by male biological drives and socially constructed notions of masculinity; it is gendered violence driven by the symbolic association of women with the nation: the bearers of the nation's children, the progenitors of the generations to come. Their victim experiences can be especially traumatic in consequence.

- Healers/reconcilers
  In this role, women enter the public sphere as peacemakers but bring qualities and skills that are supposedly displayed ordinarily in the private sphere, qualities and skills operative within the family and domestic life, such as repairing relationships, healing divisions, bringing people together, caring and nurturing others, and the like. Here, too, women confront traditional stereotypical views of what their peace work should be.

- Social transformers
  In some settings, women break out from traditional gender roles and become genuine social transformers, gender being the base from which women develop a wider engagement with peace issues. Women may initially mobilize themselves as women, restricting their focus in the first instance to women, but their campaigns and ambitions develop, seeking to realize peace by the transformation of the social relations that provoke the conflict.

### Women as combatants

Traditional stereotypical evocations of femininity are incompatible with the idea that women are equally as capable as men of being violent. There are two separate claims involved here, however. One is that ordinary women have an 'essential' nature that is denied by participation in violence. Longley (1994), for example, writes that women who support terrorism are in thrall of a death cult and abuse themselves by so doing. The other claim challenges the conventional allegiances of feminism towards politically Left and liberal causes (this is couched broadly because I am aware there are differences within feminism between radical and liberal feminists), disputing any 'natural' connection between feminism and political radicalism.

Evidence shows, however, that women can be as violent as men in communal conflicts. Itano (2004) has complained at the tendency to treat women only as victims. It was estimated that one-third of the women who were involved with rebel and government forces in Sierra Leone were in active combat roles (Mazurana and Carlson, 2004), and that just over 16 per cent of the rebel Revolutionary United Front were women (McKay and Maurana, 2004: 92; on the reintegration problems faced by young girl ex-soldiers, see McKay, 2004). Itano (2004) claims women have been combatants in fifty-four conflicts since 1945. Hutu women were amongst the worst killers in Rwanda's genocide and, in crowd violence their victims were often Tutsi men, although women represented less than 3 per cent of those jailed (www.womensnews.org/article.cfm/dyn/aid/1602/context/cover). Gibiro (2004) estimated that one in ten people suspected of genocide in Rwanda were women, perhaps the most notorious being Pauline Nyiramasuhuko, ironically the former Hutu government minister for women and gender, who has been charged with several counts of genocide and war crimes, including allegedly presiding over the rape of Tutsi women.

Examples abound of women's militancy and could be reiterated to saturation with very little added to the point. What is interesting sociologically about women's combat role is that it occurs even in countries where women are normally accorded low status and subject to strict social control, and that its form there is highly constrained by the kinds of social relations that patriarchy entails. In these settings, women combatants are required to observe dominant gender conventions. Kashmiri women, for example, wearing *burqas* in compliance with strict Islamic law, participated extensively in the protests calling for Kashmir to be absorbed into Pakistan (see Manchanda, 2001), many being members of the Muslim Daughters of the Faith organization and inspired by Islamic political activism. It is noteworthy, according to Anjum Habib, the General Secretary of the Kashmir Council for Muslim Women, that their combat roles were mostly in service to the men: 'We did training in the use of guns but we never used them' (quoted in Manchanda, 2001: 52). They visited jailed militants in prison, smuggling in contraband, acted as guards in combat missions and decoys, transported armaments in their large flowing *burqas*, and readily came out on the streets to fill the crowds. Their activism, in other words, was rooted in large part in their cultural roles as women (Manchanda, 2001: 51).

There is a parallel here with women's combatant role in Palestine, the Lebanon (on which see Shehadeh, 1999) and other Middle Eastern conflicts, where women combatants have been prominent, for the patriarchal society in which they fight allows them full participation in the national struggle but gives no space for campaigning for women's liberation at home or for the overthrow of patriarchy itself. Of course, feminism faces severe problems in Third World and post-colonial societies because it can be easily derided as a form of Western imperialism, used to promote the culture of the colonizers and undermine indigenous values. This is not to suggest that women there have been passive or docile, in the way that Western gender stereotypes would imply they should, for women have been active in many colonial struggles for independence – just over a fifth of the people arrested in Gandhi's salt marches for Indian independence were women (Jayawardena, 1986: 100), for example – but that their incorporation in the national struggle co-existed with conservative attitudes towards the position of women culturally. Lacking Western gender stereotypes, no incompatibility is perceived in colonial struggles between anti-feminism and full partici-pation by women in combat.

Cultural norms governing traditional gender roles have another impact on combatant women. Inasmuch as they offend the stereotype of women as carers, reconcilers and nurturers, those who uphold these norms criticize combatant women for their militancy because they are supposedly denying their essential femininity. There are at least two sides to this problem. On the one hand, male combatants can resist the participation of women in the fighting; conversely, strong cultural forces are levied against women combatants when they infringe social mores by engaging in militancy. South Africa's young comrades who battled against apartheid in the 1980s tended to exclude women from their groups because of masculine senses of social solidarity and a brotherhood of comrades (see Cock, 1991: 225) – a weakness that meant that women were not involved in the post-conflict leadership of the youth movement (see Marks, 2001: 49) – or restricted them to gendered roles as spectators, cleaners and cooks. Male comrades spoke of women in stereotypical terms as weak, in need of protection, not suitable to be involved in violence (see Marks, 2001: 105). In Northern Ireland's case, women combatants were subject to considerable vilification by the British media, especially when assassinated (such as Marie Drumm) or killed on active service (such as Mairead Farrell), for offending the cul-tural assumptions about women. An extension of this sort of gendered criticism is found in the negative portrayals of women combatants in films and popular culture (see Edge, 1995, 1998). Women combatants, therefore, struggle not only against the state or regime to which they object, but also at times against unreconstructed gender roles that undervalue their militancy.

## Woman as victims/survivors

Large numbers of civilians are affected by war at random – bullets from helicopter-mounted machine guns or blast bombs dropped from planes hit men, women and children without discrimination. In particular, internal and civil conflicts lack a determinate space for the conduct of war; everywhere is a battle site. This tends to increase the indiscrimi-nate targeting of civilians, which explains why nine out of ten deaths during wars in the 1990s were civilian (Garfield and Neugut, 2000). But some civilian victims are specially selected for particular kinds of treat-ment, and their experiences are far from random. While there may be a tendency to undervalue the relatively small number of women who act as combatants, it remains the case that women's experience of conflict is mostly as victims.

Northern Ireland's case is interesting, since one of the many paradoxes of 'the Troubles' is that women were not special targets of communal violence and only very few fatalities were female (McWilliams, 1995: 16); the Cost of the Troubles Study, undertaken by the University of Ulster, put the figure at 9 per cent (Fay, Morrissey and Smyth, 1999: 161). These fatalities were overwhelmingly coincidental to the gender of the female victims, and, when women were involved (with the exception of female combatants), cultural norms ensured public outrage and revulsion towards the perpetrators. It is all too easy, however, to explain this as the result of traditional gender roles, which gave them protection against communal violence because of the 'sacred moral code' surrounding women (for example Colin Coulter, 1999: 133–4). It is traditional gender roles, after all, that forced many women to suffer the indirect effects of communal violence in the form of 'domestic' violence, disproportionately higher levels of mental illness and emotional strain, and material deprivation in the home. It is estimated that at the height of the Hunger Strikes in 1981, 35 million tranquillizers were prescribed in Northern Ireland, two-thirds of which were swallowed by women (M. Ward and McGivern, 1982; for children's narratives of 'the Troubles', see Holliday, 1997).

What mediates the impact of gender roles on women's victimhood is not the lack of provision of distinct spaces as battlefields for the fighting that move it away from the home (as argued by Renner, 1999), but the extent of relational distance or closeness that exists between the warring sides. This axis has been referred to before in chapter 1 as one of the principal variables determining the severity of the post-conflict problems confronting the various types of post-violence society. Where relational closeness survives between the groups in conflict, such that they share much in common culturally, familially and economically, save for the issue(s) provoking the violence – although small differences can make *all* the difference – cultural norms persist through the violence, which regulate its severity, limit its brutality and restrict its direct targeting to only certain sorts of victims. Traditional gender roles are part of the cultural norms that relational closeness allowed to continue in Northern Ireland, ensuring that women were not special targets.

Relational distance, however, can have the opposite effect, encouraging warring parties to victimize certain targets specially in order to resist the imposition of their culture, or as a way of rejecting it. Relational distance occurs in societies where social cleavages around ethnicity, nationality, religion and 'race' reproduce marked social divisions, and in instances of relational distance, traditional gender roles, far from protecting women, can make women special targets of violence from male combatants. This is only in part because there is no common cultural code between warring groups. Women's experience of victimhood in societies with relational distance is highly sexualized and gendered – that is, their victimhood is a direct consequence of their status as women, of the manner in which men use women's bodies, and of the way femininity and masculinity are socially constructed and understood in the context of the contestation over nation, culture and identity. It is the experiences of women as victims in instances of relational distance with which we are concerned hereafter.

It is necessary to distinguish sexual and gendered violence in order to understand the different kinds of experiences women have as victims in societies with relational distance and thus the sort of private troubles women face in post-violence settings that peace processes have to try to turn into public issues. Sexual violence is a significant component of the non-random treatment women experience as victims and, simply put, involves the use of women's bodies by combatants for sexual gratification against their will. This desire for sexual gratification derives in part from male biological drives but mostly from socially constructed notions of masculinity, which associates the sexual act with social control of women and reproduction of women's vulnerability. Women caught up in communal conflict may occasionally initiate sex as a means to obtain food or protection, but this is still sexual violence because it hardly represents consent. Sexual violence is an attack on women's bodies as objects of sexual lust and social control, irrespective of whether women were forced into sex at gunpoint or through fear and hunger. However, gendered violence is done for different reasons from sex, and involves attacks on women because of what is culturally associated with femininity and women's bodies in contexts of relational distance, especially the connection between nationhood and womanhood. This results in their bodies being attacked for reasons of sociology not biology, as supposed carriers of the nation, the bearers of the nation's children. It is worth drawing out this distinction further.

Sexual violence is – and always has been – commonplace in conflicts where relational distance is involved. Rehn and Johnson-Sirleaf (2002) prepared a report on behalf of UNIFEM in October 2002 that charted the experiences of women in their own words, during and after communal violence, covering fourteen countries, to harrowing effect. Rape, torture, deliberate impregnation, premeditated infection with HIV/ AIDS, foetuses ripped from wombs, sexual enslavement, forced prostitution and trafficking bespeak, as Hynes (2004: 438) says, of the sexual aggression unleashed in men by war. In Sierra Leone, nine out of ten households surveyed reported sexual assault of one kind or another, 59 per cent in a similar study in Cambodia and 75 per cent of Khmer women. Doctors treating rape victims in the Congo reported that victims' vaginas had been punctured and destroyed with weapons and tree branches in systematic gang rapes of girls, some as young as five years old, other women as old as eighty (taken from Hynes, 2004: 438). The Clinic of Hope in Rwanda, an INGO providing medical services to victims of the genocide, estimated that half a million women had been raped in less than 100 days (McGreal, 2001), such that the country now has one of the world's highest rates of HIV, with around 50,000 dying each year of AIDS (see Human Rights Watch, 1996). This sort of targeted victimhood led Littlewood (1997) to coin the phrase 'military rape'; it has persuaded the United Nations to host a special web portal Women, Peace and War as a hub for data on the impact of war on women and girls (see www.womenwarpeace.org).

When sexual attacks have to be witnessed by victims' husbands and male children, as is often the case in genocide and ethno-national conflicts, the acts are designed to control the men as much as subjugate the women. And fear of rape makes it difficult for women to exist independent of their menfolk, who are seen as sources of protection, reinforcing traditional gender roles (Meyers, 1997: 9), furthering their sexual exploitation. But it also reinforces women's reliance on their men carrying arms, which ironically only increases the likelihood of women being targeted as a way of imposing social control on armed men by opposing groups. Even when women look to UN or African Union peacekeepers for protection by entering refugee camps, they can sometimes not escape male sexual aggression, for sexual violence against women is even engaged in by military peacekeepers. The UN set up a commission of enquiry in 2007 to investigate allegations that African Union peacekeepers sexually attacked women in Darfur. The United Nations High Commissioner for Refugees and Save the Children published a joint report in February 2002 substantiating the allegations that girls in refugee camps in Guinea, Liberia and Sierra Leone were being sexually exploited by male aid workers and UN peacekeepers (Hynes, 2004: 438). Sex was being extorted for food aid. On the other hand, of course, many aid workers work courageously in war zones and in the refugee camps. Amidst the tragic statistics from Darfur, where, in four years, 2,500 civilians have been killed and 2.5 million displaced, 7 aid workers have been killed. Western aid workers are special targets for kidnap and ransom.

Gendered violence, however, has other motivations than the purely sexual, although quite clearly it is still sexual. A medical student working in North Darfur told Human Rights Watch in February 2004 that fifty women had been raped in one village by Janjaweed militia and Sudanese government soldiers, reporting one victim being told, as a knife was inserted in her vagina, 'you get this because you are black' (Human Rights Watch, 2004a). As the perpetrator displayed, sex is still involved in this kind of act but it is secondary. Ronit Lentin (1999) emphasizes how violence against women in ethnic conflicts – a good instance of relational distance – is more than sexual violence driven by socially constructed notions of masculinity; it is gendered violence driven by the symbolic association of women with the nation, the bearers of the nation's children, the progenitors of the generations to come (for similar argument, see Yuval-Davis, 1997; Yuval-Davis and Anthias, 1989). Nations are symbolized in feminine terms – the nation as beloved motherland – and mothers are symbolized as bearers of the nation. To invade the bodies of the enemy's women is to take their territory; to oppose the nation is thus to attack women. Rape is thus an instrument of ethnic and nationalist conflict. This kind of violence is gendered *as well as* sexual and tends to feminize the phenomenon of genocide.

Gender gives women other victim/survivor experiences that carry into the peace, such as widowhood and the death of children (more children died in armed conflicts in the 1990s than soldiers, an estimated 2 million, see UNICEF, 2001). These issues will be addressed in chapter 6. The point here is to acknowledge the trauma faced by women who have been subjected to sexual and gendered violence that peace processes need to address. Women can spend decades as refugees in camps or foreign lands; at the beginning of the new millennium, 80 per cent of the world's refugees and internally displaced people were women and children (Ashford and Huet-Vaughn, 2000). Often, however, this trauma is taken back into the private domestic sphere and, through internalization by the female victim, is rendered into guilt, shame and ostracism, reproduced in 'domestic' violence and further psychological or cultural trauma. Sometimes memories of the experience can be banished from the women's consciousness, in a form of amnesia, or banished by the community in a form of repressed memory. This not only creates a 'memory gap', as Lentin (1999) describes it, for the women themselves, it hides their experiences from history. In some societies with strict honour codes, the women are never quite allowed to forget. The dishonour felt by the women victims can become a family dishonour that in the private sphere is used as a form of social control by husbands and male relatives. The 'memory gap' tends to be filled eventually, sometimes only after lengthy delays (with respect to Afrikaans-speaking women in the Boer War, see Stanley, 2006). The experiences of Indian women raped and abducted in the disruption caused by the massive population relocation at the time of partition in 1947 came to light only years later when, ironically, intellectual developments in Western feminism inspired local feminists to collect the personal narratives of the women (see Butalia, 1997). Significant anniversaries or commemorations often encourage the revisiting of the past. Japanese treatment of Chinese and Korean women during the Second World War became a media issue on the sixtieth anniversary of the War's ending (see Soh, 2009).

The experiences of some women victims can enter the public sphere in another way, in the form of medical aid to deal with the crises left by HIV/AIDS, unwanted children born after rape, medically shattered bodies and emotionally scarred memories. Medical charities assume even greater public significance for welfare delivery when the new or reformed state remains weak, as in Liberia, the Congo or Sierra Leone, but there are instances of them assisting in stronger states when the scale of the medical problem faced by women victims is immense, such as in Rwanda. Global civil society has a role here. Women's groups in Bosnia, for example, were mobilized as victim groups (such as the Zagreb Centre for Women War Victims) and as self-help support groups working in conjunction with global civil society NGOs like Medicare, to enable rape victims to tell their stories, in order to avoid psychological or cultural amnesia, and as a strategy for social and personal rehabilitation (Lentin, 1999: 4.7). UNICEF (1997: 110) reported over 100 self-help groups amongst women in Rwanda in 1997 dealing with support to survivors, widows and returning refugees, many with links to global civil society. In many post-conflict societies, women have organized themselves into co-operative associations, development groups and feminist groups as they attempt to address specific post-violence problems experienced by women.

*Women as healers/reconcilers*

In moving to the two roles that more directly relate to women's engagement with peace processes, it is necessary to distinguish two features – women's contribution to the negotiation process, and their work in assisting with post-conflict reconstruction. Both are kinds of peace work in which women and women's groups have been prominent, and the distinction will form part of the following discussion. What continues to structure the argument, however, is the gendered nature in which women make these contributions, for it is only when women engage in social transformation – whether in the negotiation process or in managing post-conflict adjustment problems – that they transcend the constraints and limitations of cultural notions of femininity.

In the role of 'natural' healers and reconcilers, women enter the public sphere as peacemakers but bring qualities and skills that are supposedly displayed ordinarily in the private sphere, such as those of repairing relationships, healing divisions and bringing people together. They are often brought into this public role by forms of communal violence that violate the private space of the family and prevent the performance of their traditional roles as women, wives and mothers. The home is not a 'protected' space in most civil conflicts, and violence prevents women from carrying out their stereotypical duties in providing care, food, nurturing love and stability. These sorts of domestic concerns are thought of as a crucial motivation for women to get the violence to stop, as well as providing an array of women-related issues that they bring into the public sphere as part of post-violence reconstruction.

Paradoxically, women peace activists assist in the reproduction of these stereotypical roles in the public sphere when they mobilize other women for peace work by evoking the traditional concerns of women as wives and mothers. Women's groups in Sri Lanka, for example, tend to be local and in desperate need of skills, resources and personnel, and are often attached to the Catholic Church and organized by nuns, embedding them in patriarchal structures which limits their capacity for wider engagement. Some women peacemakers focus their activities on the effects of communal violence on families, children, food, welfare, health, education and the home, aspects tied to women's lives in the domestic, private sphere. Their peace work is not about challenging these gender stereotypes but complaint that the violence prevents the better performance of their domestic roles. Sometimes they may work alongside men in peace groups and organizations that mobilize on these issues, but mostly they form groups aimed specifically at women to help women and children cope with the effects of communal violence in order to perform better women's traditional roles in the private sphere. It is worth giving some examples to illustrate these points empirically.

Good exemplars of 'feminine' healing and reconciliation peace work – feminine because it draws on women's cultural association with the private sphere of domestic life – in the context of post-conflict reconstruction are wives and mothers coming together to form groups championing claims for 'the disappeared', the husbands, sons and brothers kidnapped and killed without trace in the fighting. Recognized as a strong feature of Latin American conflicts, groups of wives and mothers of the disappeared also exist in Kashmir, Mindanao, Bosnia and Northern Ireland. Women's groups have been slow to get involved in Kashmir (Butalia, 2002: xx), for example, but the Parents of the Disappeared group is largely dominated by women and they have taken their private acts of suffering and grief as wives and mothers into the public sphere (Butalia, 2002: xxi). They eschew involvement in wider politics and mobilize on a single-issue agenda, justice for the disappeared, for which they are resoundingly criticized by those who demand a more aggressive political position, a complaint which tends to neglect the heavy cultural and religious pressure on women in Kashmir and to ignore the way renewed violence has masculinized the conflict and squeezed the public space for women's activism (on this last point, see Manchanda, 2001: 96).

Another example, in this case in the lead-up to peace negotiations, is peace work done to raise awareness of the costs of violence for women civilians. The Mindanao Commission on Women, for example, formed in 2000, promotes the cause of multiculturalism in the Philippines, since intolerance between its ethno-national groups contributes significantly to the communal violence between indigenous American Indian communities, descendants of Spanish settlers, Islamic militant groups and various politically Left and Marxist movements (for a study of the conflict in the Philippines, see Gasper, 2003). The Commission sponsored the Mothers for Peace Campaign, a national movement of women to draw attention to the effects of violence in Mindanao and nationally in the Philippines, which has engaged in public awareness campaigns, such as the Mindanao Women's Peace Caravan Campaign, which involved brightly painted caravans motoring around the region, emblazoned on their sides with peace slogans. It publishes an annual record cataloguing the damages of the war (see Mindanao Commission on Women, 2004). The Sierra Leone Women's Movement for Peace was very active in urging the country's warring parties to come to peace talks, although it was excluded from the eventual talks between the government and rebels (see Jesu-Sheriff, 2000) and concentrated its public activities on ensuring the voices of women victims/survivors were heard above the noise of war.

Feminist writers note the impact of 'the Troubles' on the profile of women's groups in Northern Irish civil society (see Connolly, 1999: 148; Morgan, 2003: 250). It has been estimated that, of the 1,500 women's organizations active in 2000, over two-thirds were 'traditional' organizations in which the primary focus was on women's issues within the family and domestic sphere, the remainder being described as 'activist' groups, mobilizing as women but on broad issues of violence, conflict and transformation (Morgan, 2003: 250–1). The large number of women's groups illustrates the way in which violence can increase the scale of women's involvement in civil society, and points to the important space women's groups occupy. The North of Ireland is not exceptional in this respect. Communal violence has spurred women in other conflict societies to action on women's issues and equality generally; the Report by the United Nations Development Fund for Women on women peacemaking (UNIFEM, 2005) encouraged participation by women as one way to raise the profile of gender, for peace processes 'create a space for negotiation of deeper-rooted societal and political issues' that gender inequality can become part of (2005: 1). The communal violence in Sierra Leone, for example, brought to fruition over 50 women's groups, which in 1993 organized themselves under the umbrella of the Sierra Leone Women's Forum and then Women Organized for a Morally Enlightened Nation, with the apt acronym WOMEN (see Barnes and Polzer, 2000).

It is possible to criticize this kind of work for failing politically to address what Bairner (1999) terms 'hegemonic masculinity', and for assisting in the reproduction of the very cultural notions of gender that women peacemakers experience as a constraint. However, we should not be too disparaging of traditional women's groups, partly because women have particularly gendered experiences of communal violence that explain their narrow focus on women's issues rather than politics more generally, but also because these traditional groups can transform into broader peace organizations. Women in traditional groups learn leadership skills, develop networks of relationships – often with international groups – learn finance, the arts of communication and deliberation and develop confidence in handling the press and so on, which are good in their own right as forms of empowerment for women but also advantageous when these groups become active in a wider peace agenda. And traditional women's groups often come to realize that their concerns as women with conflict and its after-effects have a wider context that requires them to act more broadly. In promoting the place of women in peace negotiations, UNIFEM's 2005 Report listed amongst the chief purposes the mainstreaming of a gender perspective that would allow women to overcome their exclusion from public decision-making (2005: 1; for a review of practice, see Porter, 2003).

One of the best examples in Northern Ireland of this frame extension, as social movement theory would describe it, is the Women's Coalition, formed in 1996 as an amalgam of several women's groups that wanted to make the transition to a broader political agenda, led by sociology professor Monica McWilliams (who went on, rather conventionally, to head the Equality Commission). It did not succeed electorally: it gained two seats in the power-sharing Assembly but soon lost them. This suggests that women did not vote for it in large numbers, or, at least, there were not enough women in any one constituency imbibed with commitment to vote for women representatives (women get elected but as representatives of traditional political parties); but it fleetingly displayed the potential of women to be agents of change. Fearon (1999), its principal biographer, tellingly entitled the Coalition's story *Women's Work*, for, as Zalewski (2006) makes clear, its status as a gender-specific women's party was significant for its inability to transcend gendered constraints and to become genuinely transformative. They were still, in Zalewski's terms, a feminized movement – choosing as their colours the emblem of the old suffragettes (green for hope, purple for dignity and white for purity) – by insisting on calling on the 'feminine' qualities of women's supposedly 'different' form of rationality to knock sense into Northern Ireland's male-dominated politics. A few individual women were empowered (temporarily) but patriarchal relations were left unblemished by the Women's Coalition.

It is too simplistic, however, to blame women for some supposed lack of will, ambition or foresight. The transient career of the Women's Coalition in the North of Ireland (discussed, from contrasting gender perspectives, by Fearon, 1999; Murtagh, 2008; Roulston, 1999) reflects the wider problems faced by politicized women, since they pose a threat to normal male-dominated politics. The paradox of women peacemakers is that they are more acceptable when conforming to traditional gender roles as healers and reconcilers, but, when this role politicizes women, they tend to be excluded from formal politics. The reaction to the Women's Coalition by Peter Robinson, First Minister in the Northern Ireland Assembly, was noteworthy only for its public expression: 'the Ulster woman in the past has seen herself very much as being in support of her man. You women should be at the kitchen table not the talks table. "Go and make the tea"' (quoted in R. Ward, 2004: 499). Helms (2003) discusses the same problem with respect to Bosnia-Herzegovina. Assumed to be the best at ethnic reconciliation as a result of stereotypical gender roles, women peacemakers in Bosnia-Herzegovina were effectively marginalized from formal political power. The traditional gender roles of women, placing them outside and marginal to the public sphere, affected both the way male politicians treated women peacemakers and how women voters perceived them electorally. This is not just because of the orthodox cultural evocation of women as wives/mothers; the underlying stereotype is that men occupy public space, making politics men's work. Interviews amongst women peace activists tend to catch this frustration. Those conducted with women peacemakers in Northern Ireland, the Lebanon and South Africa by Hamber and colleagues (2006), for example, identified their feelings of marginalization from the institutions of peacemaking and peace building (2006: 497). Mary Ann Arnado, from the Mindanao People's Caucus, spoke for many when she said:

> We seem to have the distorted notion that men are for public concerns and women for private life – hard issues for men, soft issues for women. Thus the Mindanao peace process should be left to men while women do their usual mediation within the family and at the community level, the latter an extension of the women's kitchen. This is where we miss the point. What is important is that we start to bring our sisters into this negotiation process. Then perhaps we can start to rebuild peace in Mindanao for ourselves, for our children and for the generations to come. (www.peacewomen.org/wps/philippines.html)

This captures the conundrum admirably: most women peacemakers tend to be kept boxed in as 'feminine', valued for their womanly ways as healers and reconcilers but steered clear of politics by men (but on occasions also by traditionalist women voters). According to Meintjes, Pillay and Turshen (2001), in their study of women in post-conflict transformation, the desire for profound social change is strong amongst women, and they resist the mere reconstruction of pre-conflict social relations. While this is a very broad generalization, which arguments here would dispute as accurate for all women, many women show 'great eagerness to take on roles as transformative agents' (Hamber et al., 2006: 495). Traditional gender roles often defeat them, but some women try nonetheless.

*Women as social transformers*

Despite the gendering of their work by men, some women peacemakers are committed to political engagement and are empowered by their peace work to commit to a broad agenda of socio-political and economic transformation; on occasions with real success. They mobilize women, mostly restrict their focus to women – remaining therefore, women's groups – but their ambition is to realize peace by the social transformation of the social relations that provoked the conflict, including hegemonic masculinity. Not all women's groups possess sufficient social or economic capital to overcome their social exclusion, but there are examples of women who have campaigned for peace in such a way as to try to transcend gender relations by advocating wider social change. Thus, in Northern Ireland, one might compare the Women Together for Peace group with feminist and politicized women's groups like the Socialist Women's Group, Belfast Women's Collective or the Women into Politics project.

Sometimes their efforts realize little, except, perhaps, for the women participants themselves. For example, in a study of Israeli women peacemakers, Lentin (2004; see also Lentin, 1997) emphasizes the challenge they made to what she calls the Israeli racial and masculinist state. They tried to be social transformers by dodging the draft and by dialoguing with Palestinian women across the divide. They challenged the traditional roles of Israeli women as mothers and homemakers and took political positions on the conflict. However, the Israeli state's response to them was to invoke conventional conservative images of women, trying thus to reduce their potential political threat by rendering it into the 'natural' concern of women for their husbands and children rather than as a challenge to the very foundations of the state. If they were listened to at all by the state, it was as mothers of soldiers not as political agents in their own right; when they acted politically, then, they were either ignored or imprisoned. On occasions, however, women's groups can achieve much more; but hardly ever in isolation from wider global civil society. As remarked in the Introduction, globalization has brought new forms of peace work, allowing local peace groups to mediate between local, national and international arenas in glocal ways, and this is nowhere better exemplified than in the case of women as social transformers. I will first give examples of the glocalization of women's peacemaking, then outline some of the international networks that local women peace groups connect with.

Women were an active part of the civil society groups that participated in an Inter-Congolese Dialogue to try to effect peace in the Democratic Republic of Congo (the following details are taken from UNIFEM, 2005: 6). UNIFEM persuaded the facilitator of the talks, Sir Ketumile Masire, former President of Botswana, to allow a separate women's meeting in preparation for the main event and in order to get gender issues on the official agenda. A delegation of African women led by Ruth Perry, the former Liberian head of state, travelled to the Congo to help establish a branch of the Women as Partners for Peace in Africa group, a body sponsored and funded by the African Union, UNESCO and UNIFEM, amongst others. Billed as a peace and solidarity mission, the delegation added weight to the local women's call for the inclusion of women in the Dialogue and for the agenda to address wider social transformation. A further preliminary meeting of 60 women took part in a women's caucus in Nairobi in February 2002, in order to negotiate amongst themselves a platform for peace, producing the Nairobi Declaration and Action Plan, which demanded the mainstreaming of gender issues throughout the Inter-Congolese Dialogue as well as international assistance to underwrite any social reforms that it might produce. Amongst the 300 delegates to the Dialogue in 2003 were 36 women, and Article 51 of the transitional constitution guarantees women full participation in decision-making during post-conflict reconstruction.

With women comprising the bulk of the survivors of the war in Guatemala, they have been more active than men in forming civil society voluntary associations, such as the Mutual Support Group and the National Coordinating Committee of Guatemalan Widows. Kaur (2003: 63) found women there more likely than men to be involved in peace groups and to engage in confrontational forms of peacemaking; and, notably for a Catholic country, to have non-religious motivations for their involvement, compared to men. The negotiations to end the war were mediated by the UN, and encouraged the establishment of a Civil Society Assembly to represent the diverse views of Guatemalan society, such as indigenous organizations, women's groups, business, the universities and others. The Assembly was used as a forum to discuss the range of substantive issues raised by the war and its ending, and as a review body for the final draft peace accord. UNIFEM (2005: 8) argues that the Assembly assisted local women's groups in uniting behind a common agenda within civil society, and they were successful in getting a women's representative at the formal peace talks. The accord gave specific commitments on gender equality, especially for rural and indigenous women, one result of which was the establishment of the Indigenous Women's Defence Office, which has subsequently transformed socio-economic relations and the position of rural and indigenous women in the country by winning land ownership rights and equal access to credit, education, housing, health care and political participation.

Women in Burundi, to take but one example, have been less fortunate. Burundi is a little-known state in East Africa bordered by Rwanda and Tanzania. It is arguably the poorest country in the world based on nominal per capita GDP, at $90, making it 182nd in the international rankings. Gaining independence from Belgium in 1963, it has experienced military dictatorships and ethnic violence between Tutsi and Hutu ever since, with several ceasefires but no lasting agreement. In 2000, Nelson Mandela acted as mediator at the Arusha peace talks, sponsored by UNIFEM, the Mwalima Nyerere Foundation, the UN Departments for Political Affairs and Public Information, and the Swedish International Development Agency (what follows is taken from UNIFEM, 2005: 13). An accord was signed on 28 August 2000. Several women leaders were given rights as permanent observers at the negotiations but barred from the formal deliberations. After pressure from international bodies, women were guaranteed direct involvement in the implementation of the agreement and an All-Party Burundi Women's Conference was established as a means to operationalize the guarantee and monitor women's post-agreement advancements. Among the clauses were agreements to ensure returning women refugees have a legal right to their former lands and properties. Unfortunately the agreement stalled, two subsequent ceasefires were broken and women's rights were not enforced. This is all too typical of the fragility of women's gains in post-violence societies, and highlights that glocal connections do not necessarily permit local women's groups to deploy international networks to advantage.

There is, however, an impressive array of such networks; and they are not just a product of the flourishing of the women's liberation movement in recent history. Jane Addams, a minor sociologist from the USA, winner of the 1931 Nobel Peace Prize (see Deegan, 1988) and Chair of the American Commission on Conditions in Ireland that produced a report in 1921 condemning Britain's policies in Ireland (see Conway, 2006: 11–12), was foundational in establishing in 1915 the Women's Peace Party that very quickly became the Women's International League of Peace and Freedom. The League is the oldest women's peace movement and took a gendered approach to the ending of the First World War, offering itself as a mediator (for details, see Alonso, 1993; Foster, 1989). This has been amplified since into a worldwide campaign for peace and encouragement to women to participate in peace processes. Its headquarters today are in Geneva and it keeps an office in the UN in New York, where it has observer status; it has branches in thirty-seven countries and focuses on global justice for women, disarmament and sustainable economic development (see its website, www.wilpf.int.ch). It has a dedicated Peace Women Project (www.peacewomen.org). As commentators note (for example Alonso, 1993), this example shows that not only has peace been seen as a women's issue for a very long time, but women peace activists have always recognized the need to internationalize their work. Although it was not part of the League of Nations, the forerunner to the United Nations, the Women's League has always seen strength lying in international links between women themselves and with other international bodies, notably the UN itself; it works with the UN in monitoring the Security Council's Resolution 1325 on women, peace and security.

The United Nations Development Fund for Women (about which, see www.unifem.org/) is active in both gendering peace work and internationalizing it. As the UN's women's fund it provides financial and technical assistance to programmes and strategies that promote women's rights and economic security, political participation by women and an ending to violence against women. It works in partnership with other UN organizations, governments and INGOs to enhance gender equality and women's empowerment. Issues of war and peace are thus not its direct concern but it has been very active in mobilizing against war, because of its negative impact on women, and supporting women's involvement in peace processes as part of their general empowerment. It forms another of the women's organizations that help to monitor the UN's international instruments that seek to guarantee commitments to women's equality and security. These instruments include the General Assembly and Economic and Social Council resolutions calling for equal participation of women in decision-making processes; the Security Council's Resolution 1325 on women, peace and security, part of which commits UN member states to supporting local women's peace initiatives and to involving women in peace agreements – a commitment supported also by the European Commission, the Organization of American States and the African Union; and the UN's Women 2000 document (for a review of the operation of some of these declarations, see Porter, 2003). The latter commits the UN member states to: 'Ensure and support the full participation of women at all levels of decision-making and implementation in development activities and peace processes, including conflict prevention and resolution, post-conflict reconstruction, peacemaking, peacekeeping and peace-building, and, in this regard, support the involvement of women's organizations, community-based organizations and non-governmental organizations' (cited in UNIFEM, 2005: 21).

Beyond the UN's own networks lie an enormous number of other networks of women's groups. The following list is not comprehensive: Coalition for Women and Peace (an Israeli–Palestinian umbrella organization), Femmes Africa Solidarité (Swiss-based group that focuses on African women), Follow the Women (concentrates on solidarity with Arab women), Gender and Peace Building Working Group (Canadian), Mano River Women's Peace Network (addresses women in West Africa and publishes its own online journal *Voices of Peace*), NOW Working for Peace (the US-based National Organization of Women's peace body), West African Network for Peace Building (regional umbrella group in West Africa), Women Building Peace (an umbrella organization of 200 women's peace groups launched in 1999 by International Alert), Women for Peace (a Swiss group interested in Israel–Palestine), Women's Action for New Directions (a political empowerment programme for women), Women's Commission for Refugee Women and Children (focusing on the experiences of particular women victims/survivors) and the Initiative for Inclusive Security, formerly known as Women Waging Peace (an initiative of the Women and Public Policy programme at Harvard's Kennedy School of Government and the Hunt Alternatives Fund, which addresses women's role in conflict prevention, peace negotiations and post-conflict reconstruction).

There is merit in using the last example as a case study of the glocalization of women's contribution to social transformation through peace work. The Initiative for Inclusive Security, Women Waging Peace (http://womenwagingpeace.net) is part of an extensive network of programmes for women's empowerment funded by the private US foundation known as the Hunt Alternatives Fund, named after Swanee Hunt (see Hunt, 2006; also www.swaneehunt. com), whose fortune derives from Texan oil. She heads the Hunt Alternatives Fund, money from which was used to establish the Women and Public Policy programme at Harvard, which she directs, and to set up the Initiative for Inclusive Security, which she chairs. Hunt was a former US Ambassador in Austria (1993–7) and is a member of the US Council on Foreign Relations and sits on the board of Amnesty International. From a conservative, Republican and Southern Baptist background (she has a Ph.D. in theology), she developed a commitment to expanding women's roles in social change and political life and became part of the network of friends and advisers around Bill and Hilary Clinton. The Initiative for Inclusive Security describes itself as primarily concerned with promoting women's participation in peace processes in order to make peace sustainable and citizen-led (www.womenwagingpeace.net/content/aboutus. asp). It is based around 400 or so women peace activists (whose biographies are included in the website), who act as role models and galvanizers for over 3,000 women and women's groups that are part of the Initiative. The core group of 400 women includes elected and appointed government officials, members of NGOs, lawyers, academics, businesswomen, journalists and religious leaders. It has its own research unit, the Inclusive Security Policy Commission, created in 2001, to permit research and analysis to underpin women's policy advocacy. The Commission has produced a series of case studies of women's involvement in peace processes, as well as a directory of women experts on peace issues, all of which it disseminates on the website. The expertise ranges over Africa, the Americas, Asia, Europe and the Middle East, and concentrates around the themes of conflict prevention, peace negotiations and post-conflict reconstruction.

It is noteworthy that the Initiative does not feminize women's contribution to peace processes by invoking some special feminine virtues that make women 'natural' peacemakers. Equally noteworthy, it does not advocate the 'good governance' approach to peace, which, as we saw in chapter 2, reduces peace processes to institutional reform. It is thus perhaps remarkable amongst US private foundations for not advocating the reproduction of Western notions of politics and economics. Its structure and organization help to explain this. It works through women's groups in the local arenas of conflict, offering labour power, financial aid, administrative skills and other practical support, as well as constituting a global network by which local groups can mediate their concerns internationally and mobilize Hunt's extensive personal networks and influence. The individual women and local women's groups that form the Women Waging Peace network represent a diversity of perspectives and come from very different sorts of conflicts and regions. To be as encompassing as possible in its advocacy of women's contribution to peace, it eschews taking a political stance and is willing to have represented within it public and private bodies with widely contrasting political positions, united only by two views: that women-led peace processes will make peace more sustainable since it is citizen-led; and that women's participation in peace processes is beneficial to women's general empowerment. It cut its teeth in the conflict in Bosnia (for her views on Bosnia, see Hunt, 2005), which is hardly coincidental given Hunt's connections to Clinton, but has involved itself in all the obvious conflicts, such as Rwanda (for Hunt's views on the role of women in the *gacaca* courts, see Hunt, 2003), Sudan, Sri Lanka, Iraq, Afghanistan, Colombia and East Timor; perhaps only Northern Ireland is missing from the litany of names that mark the globalization of organized violence in late modernity.

## Case studies: women in the Sudan and Rwanda

The case studies have been selected to illuminate the contrast I made earlier between women's roles in pressurizing for peace negotiations and in dealing with post-conflict reconstruction. We will deal first with the lead-up to peace talks and thus the Sudanese case.

The contemporary concern over the genocide in Darfur since 2003 (on which, see de Waal, 2007) disguises the fact that conflict in Sudan has been on-going between the Arab, Islamic North and the African, Christian South since 1957, one year after independence from Britain, although the discovery of mineral and oil deposits in the South in the 1980s intensified both its demand for independence and the North's refusal, leading to a more extreme period of civil war. The South's war of independence intensified the Northern government's Islamification of Sudan, and the imposition of Sharia law served to enrage further the Southern rebels. After the warring parties agreed to a memorandum of understanding in 2002 (the Machakos Protocol), a 'comprehensive' peace accord was signed in January 2005, but it proved short-lived and did not stop organized violence in Darfur (the UN's Integrated Regional Information Network has details of all the agreements, see www.irinnews.org/webspecial/sudan/). Several rounds of negotiations have not delivered a peace deal. There has also been considerable internecine conflict between various rebel groups in Darfur and the South generally, keeping it weak and prey to Arab paramilitary groups like the Janjaweed, which the Northern-based government uses to sub-contract most of its military violence since the signing of the 2005 accord, leading the International Criminal Court in March 2009 to issue a warrant against the President. The South, however, remains a battlefield in two wars at the same time: one between North and South for control of the South's mineral reserves, the other amongst Southern factions over control of the war. One family in three in the South has had at least one member die in one conflict or the other (Duany, 2003: 214).

According to Duany (2003: 214), Southern women have experienced the violence in several (highly gendered) ways: the death of loved ones; displacement of families and communities; survivor medical injuries, especially disablement through the use of landmines; sexual and gendered violence; starvation; and the withdrawal of centralized welfare, particularly medical, health care and educational provision. The continuing violence makes it difficult for aid agencies to operate, especially in the rural areas. There are many refugee camps but they tend to be surrounded by Janjaweed forces, making them dangerous places for INGOs to work. The absence of facilities to care for victims of violent rape has been noted by INGOs; Amnesty International USA reports one girl victim as saying that 'a child born of rape is considered an "Arab child", we still look after them but they do not enter our hearts' (see Amnesty International, 2005). Living in a conservative and patriarchal society, tribal women who were interviewed about the war saw themselves as having special experiences rooted in their status as women, as well as particular insights into peace: 'childbirth teaches women the value of life'; 'we women, having given life, always know what life costs, men just go out and kill, it is easier for them to destroy life'; 'I hate these guns around here, men just take and shoot anything around them' (taken from Duany, 2003: 214). A Darfurian woman acknowledged that 'men are still the lead decision-makers' (quoted in Amnesty International, 2004). Women suffer, therefore, from the effects of masculinity as it is expressed both through the war and in subordinate gender roles within a patriarchal society. These are normally conducive to feelings of powerlessness.

However, drawing on the example of women's worldwide activism, and with the support of international networks of women's groups, the Hunt Alternatives Fund, local NGOs and the Southern Sudanese diaspora in the USA and Kenya, several women's groups and networks were established in Southern Sudan with a peace vocation (see Itto, 2006). These include the Sudanese Women's Voice for Peace, the New Sudan Women's Federation, New Sudan Women's Association, the Darfur Women's Solidarity Society, and the Sudanese Women's Empowerment for Peace; several women activists from these groups feature in the directory of experts on the Women Waging Peace website (see, as an example, Amna Adam, who is a social worker and human rights activist working with women and children in Darfur, at: www. huntalternatives.org/pages/209_amna_adam.cfm). UNIFEM has also been involved in assisting the mobilization of local women for peace. Working in conjunction with UNIFEM, who assigned two 'gender experts' to help, the UN and World Bank led a Joint Assessment Mission to Sudan in 2003 in order to evaluate the potential for implementing Security Council Resolution 1325, widening women's participation in peace negotiations, and mainstreaming gender issues in any agreement (UNIFEM, 2005: 15). Consultation took place with local women's groups in Sudan when the Norwegian government hosted a conference of donors to the Sudan in April 2005, and fifty Sudanese women travelled to Oslo to attend. Separate from its main donor event, the conference held a dedicated gender symposium that called for a gender-responsive approach to donor aid, affirmative action for women in any post-war reconstruction, and assistance with the rehabilitation of displaced women.

Two of the women's groups who utilize this global space are the Sudanese Women's Voice for Peace and the South Sudanese Women's Association (on which, see Duany, 2003: 216). Both bodies are based in Kenya, which has a large South Sudanese diaspora community, in order to prevent suppression by the Northern government (there is a separate Sudanese Women's Association of Nairobi, which works amongst displaced women in Kenya). The level of violence prevents them from being highly visible in the public sphere, such as by holding peace demonstrations, so they focus on local empowerment strategies for women in the form of organizing training in peace building, supporting small-scale development projects for women farmers and growers, and establishing women's centres in the villages that assist in their education towards peace work and women's rights, and they collect information on the effects of the war on women for outside agencies. This is about capacity building amongst women, forging a community of women leaders in the villages capable of conflict resolution and peace building. They work with local churches, aid agencies and INGOs and are keen to emphasize connections with the wider women's movement, locating women's plight in Sudan and Darfur as part of a generalized experience for women. As Amna Adam writes on the Women Waging Peace website: 'it's not just a Darfur problem or Sudanese problem. It's the whole world's problem and we feel the solidarity of women around the world.'

The Sudanese conflict, however, is a mix of religion, ethnicity and gender, and because women experience the conflict in part as a religious one, women's groups also work with the local churches and mobilize international Christian church networks, charities like Christian Aid and Christian INGOs. The best example of a Christian INGO that works in the area is the South Sudanese Friends International, based in Bloomington in the USA (see www.southsudanfriends.org). It is not affiliated to any particular denomination but it is avowedly Christian. It describes its mission as to 'share the love of Jesus Christ with the people of Southern Sudan in a way that leads them toward peaceful and self-reliant living'. It was originally conceived by two Sudanese exiles to the USA working at Indiana University, Wal and Julia Duany, but has since developed significantly in size and scale. Julia Duany, who is Presbyterian, co-joins religious and feminist concerns, and works upfront in the diaspora in an advocacy role and behind the scenes on the ground in Southern Sudan as a facilitator. She is involved in many grassroots campaigns to bring sustainable economic development to the region's women farmers and has drawn in a number of North American Presbyterian churches to support her work.

In moving to the case study of Rwanda, we make a transition from pre- to post-agreement peace work by women; for this reason there is less need to dwell on the genocide (for a variety of perspectives on the conflict, see Adelman and Suhrke, 1999; Melvern, 2004; Taylor, 2001). Relational closeness historically was high, since cultural, linguistic and residential differences were minimal, although the policy of the colonial administration and the Catholic Church, the main religion in Rwanda, was to favour the Tutsis, widening the socio-economic and political gulf between the groups. This included unequal access to education (which the Catholic Church controlled) and employment. The Tutsis constituted a co-opted elite during the latter part of the colonial period but, unusually, on independence, power was transferred to Hutus, leading to their political domination. Control of education and the economy remained with Tutsis – the complete reversal of most post-colonial deals, where the dominant minority (who are usually White) cedes control of politics to keep mastery of the economy.

Hutu resentment was unabated and riots in 1959 resulted in 20,000 Tutsi deaths and massive population relocation by Tutsi to neighbouring states. The desire of Tutsi refugees to return coupled with the Hutu government's refusal to permit them to do so, led to the formation of the Rwandan Patriotic Front as a guerrilla movement that sought the overthrow of Hutu political rule. Tutsis within the country were accused of supporting the Patriotic Front. Outbreaks of conflict inside Rwanda oscillated with temporary ceasefires, and ethnic hostility was never far below the surface, which is why the revelation (see Adelman and Suhrke, 1999: 97–100) that Rwandan 'hate radio' broadcasters were fanning the flames describes nothing unusual. The conflagration started in April 1994 when it was believed that the Patriotic Front shot down the Hutu President's plane, killing all on board, including the President of Burundi, provoking wholesale slaughter, of both Tutsis and moderate Hutus (considered as traitors in an imagined historical rivalry). UN peacekeepers withdrew after the killing of ten soldiers – a legacy of which has been to hasten intervention in many later conflicts, with the exception of Darfur – and murderous venom was unleashed, although it was reported that some ordinary Hutus had to be forced into participating and were given food and money by the military as incentives. Many other Hutus needed no encouragement. Counter-violence by the Patriotic Front led to 2 million Hutus fleeing to Zaire (now the Democratic Republic of Congo).

Strangely, the peace process required no great push. The Patriotic Front quickly declared a ceasefire, by July UN troops had returned, and a new multi-ethnic government of national unity was popularly acclaimed. If peace was won easily, the war's legacy continues to cause difficult problems of reconstruction (on which, see Eltringham, 2004). There is the question of what to do with the perpetrators – although 500 or so were sentenced to death, 100,000 remain in prison while victims' relatives await restorative justice via the *gacaca* courts (this is expanded in chapter 5). While women experienced exceptionally aggressive sexual and gendered violence, with attendant problems of rejection by a culture that normally stigmatizes rape, high levels of HIV/AIDS, unwanted children born through rape, medically damaged bodies and psychological trauma, women survived the genocide in greater numbers than men, leaving issues of its own. Seven out of ten people in Rwanda are female, six out of ten women are widows (World Bank, 1998: 6); women now head 35 per cent of households and there are large numbers of orphans (Powley, 2003: 13). Many women victims/survivors find insufficient time and health to cultivate the land, resulting in high levels of malnutrition. Post-war reconstruction is occurring amidst high levels of poverty; GDP has not returned to pre-war levels and 70 per cent of households were below the poverty line in 1997 (World Bank, 1998).

Women's groups have tried to turn this situation into an opportunity and have taken a leading role in reconstruction (for a general discussion of women's role in reconstruction, see Ciabattari, 2000; Elbert, 2005; Powley, 2003, Wallace, Haerpfer and Abbott, 2009). Gender relations have been redefined with the older male family members who survived, with a change in patterns of authority; inheritance laws which prevented women from owning land have been retracted, and women have assumed greater prominence in the public sphere – women make up the majority of the adult working population; half the seats in the legislature are held by women, the largest number of women parliamentarians in the world (Wallace, Haerpfer and Abbott, 2009); one-third of judges in the *gacaca* courts are women and the head of this community-based judicial system is female (Human Rights Watch, 2004b); women now dominate the teaching profession (Kirk, 2003); women hold key public offices in the 'truth' recovery process (the National Unity and Reconciliation Commission); there is a government ministry of gender and women, headed by a woman, which has an obligation to ensure all policies are gender-sensitive; programmes exist to encourage the entry of girls into science subjects at school and university; and local women's groups and self-help groups have come to fill the void left by the collapse of welfare and social services. Ngengahayo (1997) reports that reconstruction in the Butar region is done almost exclusively by women.

Civil society in Rwanda is vibrant, ironically enough partly because of the scale of the violence, in that it has caused heavy involvement by the international community in reconstruction and persuaded the new government of national unity to adopt a decentralized state, with local autonomy and innovative structures. However, in its commitment to forging a single national identity around Rwandans rather than Tutsis, Hutus and Twa, the government has threatened INGOs (and some local groups) when they allegedly promulgate what it terms 'genocide ideology' or are critical of the country's form of transitional justice, leading human rights groups within global civil society to feel civil society is at risk (this is taken up again in chapter 5). The global women's movement, on the other hand, enthusiastically applauds the political inclusion of women and the empowerment of Rwanda's women's movement, illustrating that global civil society contains within it groups that occupy different spaces locally (a theme we return to in this volume's Conclusion).

Pro-Femmes, an umbrella organization, has forty women NGOs affiliated to it, and there is also the Rwandan Women's Network. The May 2003 Constitution (formulated by a Commission of twelve, three of whom were women) stipulates that 30 per cent of all decision-making posts should be filled by women (less than their proportion of the population but larger than is normally the case), and twenty-four seats of the eighty in the Chamber of Deputies – although thirty-nine women have been elected, sufficient in number to organize themselves into a Forum of Women Parliamentarians. In order to address women's political exclusion in the past, there is a system of women's councils and women-only elections (there are reserved ballots for women and youth alongside a general ballot). Martin Shaw (2003: 197) notes that it is a common feature of genocide for women to transform traditional patriarchal relations if they survive in sufficient strength, and to make radical alterations to their lives. He must have had Rwanda in mind.

## Conclusion

Women suffer violence of different types. Biology partly explains this victimhood, but sociology sees it as the result of socially constructed notions of masculinity and the particular positions women occupy in society. Women have social locations that are unusually vulnerable because they are the ones with the children and they are invariably always socially, economically and politically 'less' than men. Rape is sexual violence by another name; but it can in certain social settings also be gendered and sexual at the same time because of the cultural association of women with the nation. Sex, gender and violence are thus inextricably intertwined in the experiences of women caught up in communal conflict.

This linkage also impacts on women's roles in peacemaking. This chapter has attempted to show the complex ways in which sex, gender and peace intersect. Traditional gender roles give women special victim/survivor experiences and particular roles to perform in peacemaking. These traditional gender roles tend to undervalue women's role as combatants and to undermine their political role as agents of social transformation. Communal violence, however, *is* gendered and women have been unusually vociferous in the cause of peace. In some instances they have pushed for wholesale social transformation.

To explain their peacemaking as due to their femininity, to women's 'natural' interests and skills in reconciliation, relationship-building and nurturing, is to reduce their public roles to an extension of their private ones, carrying into the public sphere skills honed in the domestic sphere of family and home life. Not only is this disparaging, it is exclusionary. It assists in the political marginalization of women by encouraging the retort that women would be better to return to their 'natural' domain (the home) and leave the business of developing peace to men. This chapter has shown the immense contribution women have made in times of war and peace – in one or more of four roles – which, it is true to say, finds no parallel elsewhere in global civil society groups.

There are several ways to explain women's position at the vanguard of peace processes without having to reproduce gendered stereotypes of women's 'natural' peacemaking virtues. Women are, prosaically, half the population and their exclusion from peace processes thus negatively affects a very sizeable slice of the population. In some post-conflict societies, women can represent a much larger proportion of the surviving population, reinforcing the scale of any exclusion of women. The silence of this number of voices is actually deafening; it is raised in volume further by the universal acceptance of women's equality in international discourse. Women also have special experiences in war that rebound into very high levels of engagement with the peace. These experiences are gendered and the gendered nature of women's mobilization during peace processes simply reflects the reality of war and peace as lived experiences. The long-standing mobilization of women in opposition to 'domestic' violence has also benefited women's engagement with other forms of violence, acting as a role model of organizational structure, resource management and mobilization strategies. The glocal nature of women's campaigns against 'domestic' violence has carried over into peace processes, demonstrating the advantages of internationalizing their peace work. A huge number of global networks of women's peace groups facilitate women peacemakers in moving effortlessly between local, national and global stages, allowing grassroots women's groups to exploit well-funded, well-organized and well-connected international networks that are driving the peace agenda. Finally, women's issues in times of war and post-conflict reconstruction fit into a universal moral code of late modernity that emphasizes equality in all its respects, which sees equality as indivisible, allowing it to extend its reach into an ever growing number of areas, including, now, peace processes.

# 5

# *Emotions*

## Introduction

The emotions aroused in communal violence can be very intense and generously widespread, since communal violence causes an emotional response in everyone touched by it. These emotional responses are not assuaged on the signing of a peace accord, and peace processes carry the effects of the emotional baggage of war well into the post-conflict period. Emotions, therefore, are highly relevant to our purposes in demarcating a sociological approach to peace processes. In this chapter I wish to introduce specialists in peace processes to the sociology of emotions as a way into discussing the problems posed by post-conflict emotions. After focusing on some of the negative emotions that are aroused in post-violence societies, I seek to establish the potential spaces for progressive sociologies of hope and forgiveness within peace processes.

## The sociology of emotions

Before considering some of the problems posed by emotions in peace processes, a prior set of analytical questions arises. There is confusion in the way emotions are understood when applied to peace processes, which reflects a general uncertainty over whether emotions are the dependent or independent variable. At one and the same time, emotions get used to explain different behaviours and outcomes in peace processes and the outcomes get used to explain varying emotional responses to the settlement. This is an irresolvable tension in the sociology of emotions.

However, if we think pre-analytically for the moment, combatants, victims and bystanders do not experience this as a contradiction, since ordinary people do not interrogate their emotional responses by logic; emotions are *felt* and involve the suspension of reason. Emotions, after all, are known to induce senses of urgency and impatience that short-circuit people's usual prudence (see Elster, 2004: 218–19). There is a deeper analytical paradox here, however. As Elster noted (2004: 219), the remarkable feature of emotions is their short shelf life, yet people who are subject to them lack any anticipation that these feelings will decay: we expect to continue to feel what our emotions tell us at the moment of their experiencing. Emotions have an intensity of the moment, as it were, that those experiencing them believe transcends that moment, making them seem permanent. Emotions can be kept alive whenever the stimulus that provokes them remains (or, at least, remains at the same level of impact, since the law of diminishing returns normally reduces its bearing over time). There is also a range of personal and cultural practices for keeping emotions alive to delay their decay. In this respect, people's emotions transcend their momentariness and can be kept vivid. In this maelstrom of feeling, whether the emotion or the behaviour takes analytical precedence is not an issue for the person or group subject to them. For sociologists interested in peace processes, these analytical concerns draw us to the necessity of rendering momentary all those negative emotions (anger, rage, hate, revenge, shame, guilt) that the war and peace seem to make permanent, while trying to make permanent all the momentary positive emotions (hope, forgiveness, empathy, charitableness) that can be so easily undercut by the destructive legacy of war and the travails of peace.

There is another analytical problem with emotions. We need to separate feeling and behaviour. Emotion is a feeling (what used in classical antiquity to be called a 'passion' or 'appetite'; it is not an action. Emotionally induced urgency, impatience and intensity can inflame feelings within us that result in action that is thought of as unavoidable, yet these feelings need not be enacted; the behaviour is entirely avoidable. We may choose (or not be able) to act out the emotions we feel at the moment of their experiencing, for while all emotions have behaviours related to them, these action tendencies can be overruled by prudence and time (by proverbially 'counting to ten'); by reason, such as fear of the consequences of enacting them (by what theologians call 'conscience' and sociologists term 'the social self'), in that we may dislike being seen as someone governed by passions and under the control of our emotions; or by culture, which attaches opprobrium to particular emotionally induced action tendencies, which in some cases it reinforces by legal sanction. Behaviour that is avoidable is preventable. This holds out potential that policy making in peace processes can eliminate the acting out of negative emotions while encouraging positive emotions to be enacted.

This analytical discussion can be taken a stage further. When emotions become behaviours, they transform. The action tendencies associated with particular emotional feelings are performative behaviours – actions that are performed, behaviourally and linguistically, according to the socially learned scripts by which emotion work is conventionally done and talked about (for an elaboration of this view, see Katz, 1999).(Thus, when emotions become behaviour, they are transformed into the standardized actions, forms of language and interaction rituals that are culturally recognized by people with the same social learning as the appropriate ways for acting and talking emotionally.)In this sense, emotions are socially constructed through the ritualized behaviours by which they are performed and talked about. This does not deny that the emotional *feeling* is 'real' (or felt to be real) or raw; it means that when acting what are (or what we believe are) raw emotions, we use standardized performances that distance our behaviour from the emotional feeling. The debate within the sociology of emotions about whether emotions are corporeal or discursive is thus irrelevant, for, either way, emotions are performative.

Emotions are artful in one of two senses, therefore, in that the feelings are constructed in their performance and this performance can be uncoupled from what is being felt. The latter may occur because either we may lack any of the feelings associated with the ritualized behaviour we are enacting and talking (we are pretending an emotion) or we are performing behaviours and talking entirely contrary to how we feel (we are disguising an emotion). The social practices we experience as constraints preventing us from acting out our feelings of the moment can be used to persuade us to act and talk in ways opposite to our momentary emotional response, whether for individual reasons, like conscience or personal gain, or because of social and cultural pressure and legal sanction.

Hochschild's famous distinction between 'deep' and 'surface' emotions (1983) touches on this, showing how in organizational settings employees who interact with the public are taught how to display appropriate emotions, whose superficiality is disguised as part of their skilled public performance. This is reminiscent of Goffman's (1959) contrast between 'front-' and 'back-'stage selves, where our emotion work is performed differently depending on whether it takes place in public or in private. With respect to post-violence societies, just as individuals who feel aggression towards others need not act upon it, societies can be at peace even though masses of people still feel at war, either because the violent emotions within them are not performed in public front-stages or because we display appropriate 'superficial' emotions in public, leaving our 'deep' emotions for back-stage.

Peace processes, therefore, do not require people to stop feeling negative emotions; consensus needs to emerge around agreement to perform the ritualized behaviours and talk that enact the positive emotions that people may not personally feel but which are recognized as socially productive for the future. And while Hochschild had the like of air hostesses in mind, 'emotional labour', as she calls it, applies no less to forgiveness or reconciliation. Our ability to separate feelings and behaviour explains the common-sense remark that people sometimes seem to be 'feeling' (that is, acting out) different emotions at the same time, for not only can people be observed to be performing contradictory scripts, but also, when people act in ways they do not feel, the performance may lack authenticity if they are not skilled in emotional labour.

One final sociological digression needs to be made. As Elster (2004: 217) makes clear in his discussion of transitional justice, emotions are triggered by beliefs and modulated by social relations. It therefore matters a great deal for the stability of peace processes what beliefs are held about the communal conflict and about the people involved in it and their behaviour and character. What people *did* during the communal violence is thus part of the problem of managing the emotional dynamics of post-violence societies. These beliefs, however, are mediated by the quality of the social relations that once existed between the erstwhile enemies or which survived despite the conflict. Relational closeness or distance (on which, see chapter 1) is important to this. But even in instances of relational closeness, it matters greatly for on-going social relations in the peace process whether one group faces another as wrongdoer, victim or both simultaneously, and what senses groups have of the fairness and justice of the peace settlement. What people *do* in the peace is thus also part of the problem of managing the emotional dynamics of post-violence societies.

Some of the issues around emotion are taken up in chapter 6, since, in terms of the question of what people did during the violence, emotions implicate discussion of 'truth' recovery procedures and social processes of remembering, while in relation to what people do during the peace, the issues raised by emotions revolve around the nature of victimhood experiences and the moral and political mobilization of victims, amongst other things. In this chapter, I intend to deal with the more immediate concern in peace processes of managing the emotional legacy of the violence. Inasmuch as emotions can be worked out in action (although they need not be), this also involves consideration of the action tendencies that are threatened by these emotions if they are left unmanaged, which can cause renewed outbreaks of violence, social withdrawal, ostracism and even suicide.

This chapter will also broaden the discussion away from negative emotions. Human emotions exhibit great variety. The discussion of emotions in post-conflict settings invariably focuses on managing problematic emotions (for the latest example, see *European Journal of Social Theory*, 2008) – anger, rage, shame and guilt – although some note the positive functions of shame (Katz, 1999: 147; Scheff, 2002: 363) and anger (Muldoon, 2008). This ignores the range of positive emotions that are critical to peace processes, such as hope/anticipation, love/ charity, forgiveness/redemption and pity/consolation. The concentration on negative emotions is a consequence of the popularity of the restorative justice paradigm as a way of managing emotions during peace processes. I will argue that the application of restorative justice to post-violence societies, while valuable, has limitations because of the exclusive attention to shame–guilt–reintegration.

## Emotions and communal violence

The starting place for any assessment of the usefulness of restorative justice to post-violence societies is with the comparison between communal violence and ordinary crime. Communal violence is connected with very strong emotions and particularly high senses of urgency and impatience, which quickly release actors from normal prudent constraints – people can find it hard to make second thoughts their first. What is more, instances of communal violence can be very large-scale in the number of protagonists involved and thus in the panoply of emotions let reign. The memory of the scale of the killings provokes very strong feelings of hatred and revenge amongst survivors (Scheff, 1994), as well as a sense of obligation to keep faith with the dead, to honour their memory and justify their sacrifice, all of which can hamper reconciliation (on this 'cult of the dead', see Ignatieff, 1998: 188). And where there are vanquished victims, there is the emotional legacy of feelings of 'defeat', 'surrender' and 'humiliation', if not also of the cultural annihilation of the group.

Perhaps with the exception of 'hate crimes', the ordinary crimes processed by restorative justice systems rarely reach the range or intensity of emotions aroused in communal violence. Hate crimes are structured by group membership, and their unusualness in this regard has had the effect of generating public comment that only reinforces their difference from ordinary crimes. While the emotions provoked by the majority of criminal law offences are public and disseminated collectively to the generalized other, perpetrators and victims rarely have a sense of 'groupness' (a term borrowed from Brubaker, 2002). Victims of ordinary crime are not singled out because of their group identity, and perpetrators are not homogenized as if acting on behalf of a group. Ordinary crime is experienced as an individual attack, and while we may put ourselves in the victim's place and share their emotion, the attack is not taken as one that threatens people's group identities. Where personhood is absorbed in the group, however, an attack on one group member is felt by all, and people suffer the thousands of cuts themselves every time an injury to a group member is experienced as personal.

The public's reaction to criminal law offences might well render us into 'highly emotional "moral spectators" in the spectacles of distant suffering of victims', as Karstedt richly put it (2002: 303), but the empathy is at a distance and is not perceived to affect the bystander's very ontological self. When self-identity is absorbed into the group, however, members are not diffuse individual spectators, for the emotional experience becomes a collective one. This is not to suggest that identity is inflexible and unchanging, but in rigid social structures where patterns of cleavage coalesce around a major fault line, people participate in fewer groups, and group membership subsumes and envelops more of an individual's total identity. This has the effect of broadening communal violence, for group interest defines the position taken on all other issues and ensures that every issue is reduced to a simple matter of whether or not group interests are served by it. This makes for no bystanders to communal violence. Ordinary crime rarely generates this level of emotion, giving restorative justice approaches to peacemaking a challenging starting point.

## Restorative peacemaking

The shame–guilt–reintegration paradigm has been proffered as an effective way of dealing with emotions after communal violence and as a viable form of peacemaking. The potential of restorative peacemaking is huge. There are at least four possible usages, all of which in different ways privilege shame–guilt as the key emotion. We can consider them briefly in turn, followed by two case studies of restorative peacemaking in practice. The usages are:

- restorative justice in reintegrating belligerents;
- restorative conferences in healing divisions between people;
- 'truth' commissions as a way of handling the past;
- the use of shame apologies for assigning culpability.

The strongest (and most successful) application has been to use restorative justice in the reintegration of perpetrators and ex-combatants as an alternative to the criminal justice system (for example J. Braithwaite, 2002; Ciabattari, 2000; Dinnen, Jowitt and Newton-Cain, 2002; Justice Network, n.d.; McEvoy, 2003; Roche, 2002; Wilmerding, 2002). This kind of usage is nearest to its original application in ordinary crime. Victims and their relatives chiefly desire retributive justice, if not revenge, but most peace accords involve amnesty for combatants, which is often deeply troubling to victims/survivors and bystanders alike. Demands for retribution intensify when, as Elster explains (2004: 220–1), the crimes have been thought of as heinous, there is a short time-span between the deeds and the peace settlement, culpability is specific to a few known individuals, knowledge about the abuse is widespread and perpetrators have an absolute and relative prosperity compared to victims. Blanket amnesties are even more troublesome emotionally (see Cobban, 2006, for discussion of three cases). John Braithwaite (2002: 202–3) stresses that, for them to work, amnesties need to be perceived as contributing to the ending of the war, the agreement to offer amnesties should be made part of the peace negotiations and all stakeholders should be party to it, and those benefiting from them must show public remorse and commit to service or reparation to the new nation.

Restorative peacemaking also emphasizes the importance of 'truth' recovery procedures as a way of dealing with the emotional impact of communal violence. 'Truth' commissions, or other 'truth' recovery projects, have strong restorative justice elements (as argued in South Africa's case by Leman-Langlois and Shearing, 2003, and Gobodo-Madikizela, 2008) which are intended to achieve much the same purpose as individual restorative case conferences by means of dealing with the emotions around memory of past violence (for a discussion of memory as a problem in peace processes, see chapter 6, as well as J. D. Brewer, 2006). Archbishop Tutu explicitly made the traditional African idea of *ubuntu* central to South Africa's Truth and Reconciliation Commission (what follows is taken from Wilson, 2001: 9–10). It is a term used to describe traditional African ideals of community, based upon reciprocity, respect for each other's human dignity, and strong feelings of solidarity, and it contains a notion of justice that is restorative rather than retributive, seeking to restore harmony rather than obtain revenge. 'Truth' is thus thought to dissipate emotions rather than reproduce or inflame them. It is for this reason that 'truth' commissions proliferate (for a review of earlier examples, see Hayner, 1994; for later comparisons, see Chapman and Ball, 2001) or take different forms as judicial enquiries, recovered memory projects (in Guatemala's case, see Recovery of Historical Memory Project, 1999; in Northern Ireland's, see Smyth, 2003) or commemoration projects through the collation of people's narratives that bear witness to their life stories (for example, see Lundy and McGovern, 2001, 2005). The popularity of 'truth' recovery projects in post-violence societies suggests that the restorative peacemaking paradigm touches on a universal concern when prioritizing 'truth' recovery as a way of managing emotions.

The connection within restorative peacemaking between 'truth', emotion and recovery is made through elaboration of the sentiment of shame–guilt. Communal violence is thought to involve 'shame displacement' and 'narcissistic pride'. The former deals with questions of responsibility; the latter, justification. Both questions bear with great force on the emotions of perpetrators (assuming them not to be anti-social psychopaths incapable of feeling), for combatants have to live with themselves in the quiet moments after battle. Shame displacement involves projection of the blame for the violence onto the victims themselves because of their group membership. Shame displacement often occurs by claiming the victims brought it upon themselves by some historical offence or recent wrong, real or imagined, which the violence corrects (see Ray, 1999, for how imagined wrongs in the Balkans worked to displace blame for the violence). Narcissistic pride justifies the violence in terms of the other groups' inferiority, a standard capable of being judged in terms of racial purity and heredity, moral values and civilization, religious righteousness or ethnic and national supremacy. Restorative peacemaking in post-violence societies seeks to transform shame displacement into shame acknowledgement, and narcissistic pride into humbler notions of the position of one's group, and in the process to readdress group power relations. 'Truth' recovery projects are starting points for dealing with shame acknowledgement for groups (victim–offender mediation does the equivalent for individuals), while memory work addresses the latter. 'Truth' is thus a way of managing shame.

What matters, however, is how the 'truth' is received. Events may be denied and shame unacknowledged or hidden. Historical memories in this case are open to being revisited in order to discern unacknowledged/hidden truths as a way of shaming parties into a subsequent apology. Algerian soldiers who fought on the French side in the 1954–62 Algerian war of independence have periodically expressed their sense of betrayal, and in 1997 a group went on hunger strike in the hope of shaming the French government into an apology for neglecting them. History is littered with similar examples of seeking to shame others through sacrificial acts. The sociology of emotions helps us to understand how this works. The inducement of shame for unacknowledged or hidden historical events not only requires them to be disclosed via 'truth' recovery processes, there needs to be embarrassment upon their revelation. This is rarely achieved by directing violence towards those it is intended to shame, for this confuses the emotional dynamics by extending them sympathy; the violence is mostly inwardly directed and usually takes on sacrificial and martyred forms. It comes as hunger strikes, setting oneself alight to make a human torch, and various forms of dramatic public suicide. The purpose is to make oneself a victim, to retake some of the moral high ground by self-sacrifice, so that opponents are morally challenged sufficiently to feel intense embarrassment and thence to make shame apologies. This is to be distinguished from suicide bombing, of course, because in its case the martyrdom is intended to cause physical harm to others.

Even where shame is acknowledged and 'shame apologies' voluntarily made, these have to be heard as genuinely meant. Both Scheff (1997a: 8) and John Braithwaite (2002: 203) see the genuineness of the shame apology as critical to the effectiveness of restorative justice and 'truth' recovery processes in managing post-violence emotions, making authenticity central to the possibility of restorative peacemaking. Shame apologies (when genuine) help with victims' feelings of moral indignation and soften the emotional reactions to amnesties. Drawing on the examples of the twentieth century's two world wars, Lu (2008) has argued that shame apologies can inspire communities to social transformation and to take responsibility for past crimes.

However, shame apologies are a highly problematic form of discourse (on the sociology of apology generally, see Tavuchis, 1991). The failure of Ulster Protestants, for a very long time, to hear what they considered should be an apology from Sinn Fein was used by anti-Agreement Unionists as one of the grounds for suspending the Belfast Agreement, bearing witness to the importance of shame apologies in dealing with emotions in post-violence settings when formulated using just the right wording, and their ineffectiveness when not. The discursive difficulties of shame apologies arise because they involve a two-party dialogue, requiring a willingness in one party to use just the right form of words and a readiness in the other to accept them as sufficient. The post-violence civic responsibility to apologize can, however, be undermined by tragic victimhood experiences, continued loyalties to the cause of violence and so on. Shame apologies require careful orchestration to ensure both parts of the two-part exchange follow (or are anticipated to follow, since the offer of the second part may be some time later). This is feasible in individual restorative case conferences managed by a skilful facilitator, where victim and offender are brought together and can offer both parts of the exchange almost simultaneously. However, as we have emphasized, communal violence invokes group membership, and in some forms of shame apology afterwards there is ambiguity about who the parties to the exchange are and for whom individuals speak. We might thus contrast what can be called 'literal' and 'figurative' shame apologies.

In one sense all shame apologies are symbolic, for they are representational of emotions after the fact, once the deed is done and has been reflected on (normally only after one party has been caught or exposed). Literal ones, however, at least occur in the presence of the parties irrespective of the time lapse. Figurative ones are symbolic in another sense, for the parties as much as the emotions are representational. Most shame apologies after communal conflict are made, if at all, in a figurative form, normally a long time later, and do not involve the specific parties to the conflict but representatives speaking on their behalf without explicit consent to do so. In figurative shame apologies there is a less clear-cut exchange, and neither part of the two-part dialogue is offered with sufficient clarity to assuage individuals' specific emotions. They can even be counter-productive. The public apology for the treatment of Aboriginal people made by the newly elected Labour Prime Minister in Australia in February 2008 resulted in mixed reactions from the intended recipients. One Aboriginal leader remarked that the 'blackfellas get the words, the whitefellas keep the money'; without reparation, words can count for little (see T. Smith, 2008). Figurative shame apologies that appear grudging can thus backfire and insult parties to the exchange – some group members obligated to the first part may feel they have little enough personal responsibility to merit apologizing for anything, and some group members obligated to the second part may consider the first part too ambiguously worded and indirect to do its proper work in earning redemption. Figurative shame apologies therefore have a different function in restorative peacemaking from literal ones, and are normally part of a wider orchestration that *begins* a process of peace negotiation that may or may not involve more literal shame apologies (or more robustly worded figurative ones) later. Either way, shame apologies in one form or other are a necessary element of restorative peacemaking, helping to repair relations and mediate the transference of power between parties.

*Case studies of successful restorative peacemaking: Rwanda and Bougainville*

Rwanda has become world-known now as much for the process by which justice is being implemented as for the genocide itself, giving us a new word, *gacaca*, for the very old practice of shaming. Rwanda's *gacaca* courts are being universalized as the country teaches the rest of the world how to manage the problems of transitional justice – there is hardly an international conference today on conflict resolution, transitional democracy or human rights/justice in transition that does not applaud *gacaca* courts. However, Rwanda came to this solution chiefly by accident and not before some resistance from the new government of national unity, and *gacaca* justice is imperfect.

Since responsibility for acts of violence was dispersed throughout Rwandan society, the number of perpetrators was huge; the prospects for the peace process were not thought to be good (Clapham, 1998). Three-quarters of a million people were suspected of having some involvement in the killings and, at one time, 120,000 Hutus were in jail awaiting trial, a backlog made worse by the scarcity of lawyers – many of whom were Tutsis now lying dead – as well as a shortage of police, some of whom had fled the country as a result of their participation in the violence (see Destexhe, 1995). In 2003, Rwanda still had only fifty trained lawyers (Ciabattari, 2000: 1). The new government of national unity's first approach was to apply orthodox retributive justice through the criminal courts, rejecting amnesty and restorative principles.

After an international conference in Kigali, the country's capital, more imaginative solutions were adopted. The new 'Organic Law' was decreed in 1995, on the advice of Canadian lawyers. Article 2 of the Organic Law established four categories of offender to try to manage the scale of the problem: organizers and planners of the massacres, due the death penalty if guilty (interestingly, this category also included 'persons who committed acts of sexual torture'); individual participants in the killing, due life imprisonment if guilty; persons responsible for serious assault, due up to five years' imprisonment if guilty; and persons responsible for attacks on property, punished with civil damages if guilty. This proved not imaginative enough for between 1996 and 2000, only 2,500 cases were tried in the state courts, and in 1999 120,000 alleged offenders remained in over-crowded prisons, some still not knowing the charges laid against them. Other agencies responsible for retributive justice fared no better. The International Criminal Tribunal for Rwanda was established in 1994 under the auspices of the UN, concentrating on bringing to justice the ringleaders. The Rwandan government opposed it for its refusal to impose the death penalty, but it handed down only seven convictions in the first five years.

The Justice Network Report on Rwanda (Justice Network, n.d.; see also Sarkin, 2001) claimed that retributive justice models like these were Western and not suited to dealing with the complexity of Rwandan society, although retribution was the national unity government's preferred option, including access to the ultimate sanction of capital punishment. It was not preference for the principles of restorative justice that moved the Rwandan government; it was logistics that defeated the attempts to impose retributive punishment, for murder on this scale had not been channelled through a criminal justice system before, nor were there sufficient prison places to cope. (Their enduring commitment to retribution resulted in the *gacaca* courts retaining the capacity to return people to prison, as we shall see shortly.) At first a variety of more innovative strategies were adopted to process this number of alleged offenders, rather than restorative justice, including a return to amnesty policies. Prisoners on remand or awaiting sentence who confessed to their crimes were summarily released once they had completed half the sentence, with the remainder of the time spent doing community service, such as work in agriculture and forestry, building and construction, and support for victim groups and vulnerable communities. In 2002 (see www.restorativejustice.org), the number of offenders who confessed jumped from 5,000 to 32,000. In 2003 a presidential decree was passed that people who were teenagers at the time of their alleged offence would be released from prison irrespective of the length of time spent there. Over 40,000 were released and made to undergo 're-education', including learning the history of the genocide, AIDS/HIV awareness, and counselling. The imminent release of thousands of genocide prisoners, angry over years of imprisonment without trial, into communities still themselves angry and bitter over the violence, was perceived as a risk by various civil society groups, who responded in ways typical of this key sector of society.

Several Prison Fellowship groups were set up, notably the Christian outreach group called Prison Fellowship Rwanda that worked amongst the genocide killers in prison (and encouraged those who had not yet done so to confess to their crimes), helping to prepare them for release and assisting them in practical ways on the outside. It trained eighty facilitators to work with the prisoners inside jail. Some women prisoners, upon release, have established various self-help associations specifically for female ex-combatants. One example is the Ndabaga Association, named after the legendary mythological figure Ndabaga, who became a warrior after disguising herself as a boy. Their idea is to try to bring together female ex-combatants from both sides, to foster development, unity and reconciliation, and to work together to overcome poverty and unemployment. (The Association has offered itself as a regional peace broker elsewhere in Africa.) While there is no formal 'truth' commission (Rwanda and Cambodia are unique amongst countries that have experienced genocide in not setting up 'truth' commissions), there is a National Reconciliation Commission, and in 1999 it was this body that suggested utilizing traditional *gacaca* courts, bringing restorative peacemaking to the centre of the twentieth century's most intense and rapid case of genocide.

*Gacaca* describes a field of grass or open space, which symbolizes the gathering of tribal leaders and elders who dealt with offences under traditional authority and arbitrated disputes within the community (for details of how *gacaca* courts work, see Corey and Joireman, 2004; Hodgkin and Montefiore, 2004). In the past, *gacaca* courts did not deal with serious crimes and were designed for low-level offences that could be appropriately handled by village elders. They have their parallel in the 'sentencing circles' found in Canadian indigenous peoples, in South Africa's adoption of *ubuntu* as the approach to 'truth' recovery (Wilson, 2001: 9–10), in transcommunal mediation practices in Native American peoples (see Brown Childs, 2003a, 2003b) and in the *mato oput* ('blood atonement') ceremonies in Northern Uganda (on which see S. Bloomfield, 2006; Justice Reconciliation Project, 2007). *Mato oput* involves ceremonial cleansing of the soul, and many returning child soldiers in Uganda are undergoing them to be exorcized of their guilt and as a way of re-entering normal society. The Ugandan Commission of Human Rights endorses their use in cases of communal violence. Perpetrators confess to tribal elders, who then approach the elders of the clans of the people whose murder is being confessed to, and during a *mato oput* ceremony a public shame apology is made, reparation paid (normally goats or cattle) and forgiveness offered and received. Advocates describe the process as 'cooling of the heart' (Justice Reconciliation Project, 2007).

*Mato oput* ceremonies are separate from Uganda's formal legal system and this is what makes *gacaca* courts unique, for they have been co-opted into the criminal justice system to provide a restorative justice approach to assist the over-burdened and logistically inadequate retributive punishment system. They were formally adopted in this role in January 2001, some years after the genocide and only when the formal courts proved not up to the task; they did not become nationwide until 2006 (Caesar, 2009: 36). In 2004, there were 11,000 *gacaca* courts (www.inkiko-gacaca.rw) compared to 12 courts set up under the International Criminal Tribunal for Rwanda (which operates from Tanzania). *Gacaca* courts do not deal with category 1 offenders as defined under the country's Organic Law (organizers and planners), who remain in the formal court system and subject to the death penalty, focusing instead on individual perpetrators responsible for deaths and serious assaults; category 4 offences – civil damages for attacks on property – are not thought to require further intervention. These traditional courts do not operate separately from formal criminal courts, for the cases they hear are those of the early-release prisoners, for whom appearing before tribal elders is a condition of their release, and *gacaca* courts can return people to prison, for short sentences or to complete the original term. People can be returned to prison for not showing sufficient remorse; requesting forgiveness invariably results in a community service sentence. They thus combine both restorative and retributive elements, seeking to heal as well as punish. This ambivalence led Cobban (2006) to compare transitional justice practices in Rwanda unfavourably with those in Mozambique and South Africa. The restorative element aims to bring offender and victim/survivor together face-to-face to hear each other's stories, with the elders determining the sentence with an eye on reconciliation and repair for both the individuals and the community.

Because women can be judges, *gacaca* courts are heralded amongst the international networks of women's groups, championed for their gender equality (see, for example, Ciabattari, 2000: 3) and supported by Western women's activists, such as Swanee Hunt of the Hunt Alternatives' Initiative for Inclusive Security (www.womenwaging-peace.net/content/articles/0118a.html). Wallace, Haerpfer and Abbott (2009) saw them as boosting significantly the empowerment of Rwandan women. Human rights groups are less sanguine. Amnesty International reports of confessions being forced under torture and in January 2007 Human Rights Watch published a report on killings in Eastern Rwanda, complaining at the way *gacaca* courts abrogated the most basic of Western legal norms, such as provision of counsel for the defence, properly trained and impartial judges, and protection of witnesses (www.hrw.org/backgrounder/africa/rwanda0107/0107web.pdf).

Allegations have been made (see Le Mon, 2007: 16–17; McVeigh, 2006: 1) that witnesses are subject to intimidation and harassment by offenders; some witnesses have been murdered. Entire communities have refused to testify against some perpetrators out of fear. To try to deal with this problem, the government set up an office for witness protection in 2006 that received twenty-six complaints within the year, but Caesar (2009: 37) provides qualitative evidence of intimidation well beyond that date; one witness had his tongue cut out for giving testimony. Ibuka, the umbrella organization for survivors in Rwanda, estimated that, in the first eight months of 2008, seventeen witnesses were murdered (cited in Caesar, 2009: 37). Judges can be afraid of dispensing justice: in November 2006 a female *gacaca* judge was murdered on her way to work. On the other hand, suspicions have been voiced in local media about corruption amongst *gacaca* judges; at least one has been discovered to be in receipt of bribes (the judges are unpaid). Chakravarty (2006) complains of conflicts of interest, as community members adjudicate on trials of people responsible for killing their own family members. Justice in Rwanda has been politicized. To disagree openly with *gacaca* court decisions puts people at risk of being charged with 'divisionism', a new crime established in 2007. Human rights groups – and other civil society organizations – have been accused of disseminating 'genocide ideology' for criticizing the courts (Cobban, 2006: 98), and they apply very selective notions of justice by excluding revenge attacks committed by the Tutsi-dominated Rwandan Patriotic Front, which now forms the government. This suggests the courts represent victors' justice (a term used by Cobban, 2006, and Corey and Joireman, 2004). The courts have tended to operate on the basis of dividing Rwandan society simplistically into two camps, the guilty Hutus and the Tutsi victims, making it difficult for them to deal with more complex issues of culpability amongst Tutsis.

Some of these weaknesses are procedural to the way restorative justice is applied by the *gacaca* courts, but others reflect the inevitable difficulties experienced by people coming out of genocide. Others represent Western legal sensitivities towards the primacy of the rule of law that the traditional authority underpinning *gacaca* courts could not be expected to satisfy (for example, see Sarkin, 2001). The sociologist Max Weber's long-established distinction between what he called 'traditional' and 'rational-legal' authority (Weber, 1947: 324–406) highlights the disjuncture between 'rationalized' Western legal norms and traditional forms of authority that concentrates differences in the *gacaca* courts, reflecting essentially cultural differences towards legitimate authority. On the other hand, restorative peacemaking has been put to a sterner test than the euphoria over *gacaca* courts implies. The process has been used to settle old scores and to pursue the same old vendettas as before the war. There is a lack of trust that the outcomes are fair and a feeling that they have been designed to marginalize one group. The courts have not found a way of dealing with a critical dimension of shame–guilt, which Elster calls 'bystander guilt' (2004: 243–4) or the 'guilty knowledge' of people who did nothing to prevent the killings but now sit in judgment in *gacaca* courts on those they were unwilling to stop. The quality of mercy in this situation is inevitably strained.

The second case study of restorative peacemaking in practice is far less well known and has virtue for that very reason. The Autonomous Region of Bougainville, as it is called, also known as the North Solomon Islands, is now, after successful peace talks, an autonomous region of Papua New Guinea. The largest island is called Bougainville (named after the French explorer who was author of the famous calculus book). The island is rich in minerals. The civil war in Bougainville was over the secession of the island from Papua New Guinea. The Bougainville Revolutionary Army unsuccessfully declared the independence of Bougainville in 1975 and again in 1990. On the latter occasion, the factional violence between secessionists became very intense, and was overlaid with violence between the rebels and the state; the assassination of Paul Bobby, leader of the Bougainville Revolutionary Army in Buin District in South Bougainville; and deep memories of division going back to the collaboration of some islanders with the Japanese in the Second World War (for details of the case, see J. Braithwaite, 2002: 176–80). In 1997 a ceasefire was negotiated as the starting point for a wider peace process. Australian and New Zealand military peacekeepers restored calm and the New Zealand Overseas Development Agency's PEACE Foundation Melanesia (also partly funded by the Princess Diana Fund), in combination with local civil society groups, began a process of restorative justice to deal with the emotional dynamics left by the conflict. A Peace Monitoring group was established to orchestrate the peacemaking. Some 10,000 Islanders were trained in restorative justice, 500 as facilitators and another 70 as trainers, equipping nearly 800 active-village mediation schemes. Some of the mediators are traditional chiefs, and Bougainvillians are implementing traditional Melanesian restorative justice principles known as *wan bel* ('one belly') as a form of reconciliation and communal healing.

Advocates of restorative peacemaking promote the case (J. Braithwaite, 2002: 179; Howley, 2002, 2003; Reddy, 2008) and the Peace Foundation considers it a huge success (PEACE Foundation, 1999). Perpetrators were persuaded to desist from killing, warring groups came together in joint meetings, locals were able to define their own ordering of priorities in dealing with the issues that drove the war, peacemakers were sufficiently supported to win local elections and the criminal justice system on the island was reformed along restorative justice principles. Former combatants in the Bougainville Revolutionary Army were absorbed into the new police force. The broader peace negotiations were highly productive. The peace agreement finalized in 2000 provided for the establishment of an autonomous Bougainville government, and for a referendum in the future on whether the island should become politically independent. Elections for the first autonomous government were held in May and June 2005, when a new President was elected. Within a month, the main rebel leader, Francis Ona, died after a short illness. A former surveyor with Bougainville Copper Limited, Ona was a key figure in the secessionist conflict and had refused formally to join the island's peace process. His death proved timely for the ending of further resistance; the Bougainville Freedom Movement was abolished and absorbed into the broader Solidarity South Pacific network, which unites several groups in opposition to the state of Papua New Guinea. Reviewing the case years later, Reddy's (2008) interviews with locals showed that the peace was being kept.

By all measures the Bougainville peace process is a success. It is noteworthy, however, that, as in Rwanda, the conflict did not destroy traditional forms of authority, which were readily adapted to deal with post-violence adjustment problems, and these traditional structures already contained deep respect for restorative justice principles that were easily reoriented to the new setting. Local senses of place remained strong in Bougainville, in part because of the strong identity fostered amongst small island peoples, which allowed local value systems to be drawn on in indigenous orderings of priorities after the violence. The war did not destroy relational closeness amongst the islanders, and the quality of social relations amongst islanders after the war modulated the beliefs they held about some people's conduct during it (and in other conflicts as far back as the Second World War), assisting in assuaging their emotional impact afterwards. Civil society remained intact and mediated these concerns in the public sphere ensuring that public space was dominated by the discourse of restoration, forgiveness and healing. The military peacekeepers played a positive role in relationship building: they were unarmed and the local commander placed emphasis on soldiers developing good relationships with villagers through sport, music and shared meals. John Braithwaite (2002: 179) saw their presence as complementing the restorative approach to peacemaking of the Peace Monitoring group. There was significant involvement by regional powers both on the ground and financially. By 2007, the Australian government had given $AU200 million (see www.ausaid.gov.au/country/png/bougainville.cfm) to consolidate the peace and assist in service delivery, a staggering sum in the context of a population count at the 2000 census of only 175,160 people. There was no population relocation amongst the islanders, no returnees from refugee camps, nor any wide-scale targeting of specific victims for particularly horrendous abuse.

Many instances of post-violence reconstruction, however, are not so accommodating to restorative justice principles because they occur in the midst of relational distance. In some conflicts, traditional authority either is destroyed in the atrocity or has not survived modernization, and restorative justice is an alien idea. Involvement by regional powers and peacekeepers can be non-existent or negative and some conflicts involve multiple localities and value systems that lead to no agreement even on whom the indigenous are, let alone what priorities they have. Bougainville – unlike Rwanda – offers a good illustration of restorative justice working in post-violence societies, but it has a social structure unusual enough to permit little wider generalization.

## The limitations of restorative peacemaking

Restorative peacemaking is, admittedly, a new venture for the shame–guilt–reintegration paradigm, and the arguments advanced in its favour are not fully formulated. Even at this early stage, however, it is possible to identify two weaknesses which we can consider in turn: naivety over what post-violence means, and the privileging of shame–guilt as post-violence emotions.

As we saw in chapter 2, violence very rarely ends with peace processes, not even in the medium term. Restorative peacemaking has to operate, in other words, in a situation where the old enmities continue, where mistrust has not been assuaged and where violence can destabilize elite and grassroots initiatives by closing the space for compromise. This in itself would not be problematic except that restorative justice conferences, to be successful, tend to assume the communal violence to be at an end and that the emotions are not continually being inflamed and reproduced by events surrounding them. Restoration conferences in criminal justice offences may not prove to be successful – the offender may be recidivist and the victim's fear undiminished – but offender and victim bring into restoration conferences an event that is over and done with, the emotional reaction to which requires management but is not reinforced during the conference as a result of repeated victimization. The paradigm assumes willingness to compromise, even the desire to *want* to participate in restoration conferences, which cannot be guaranteed after communal violence or may only exist for a very short 'honeymoon' period before renewed conflict and killing destroy them. The suggestion by Scheff (1997b: 11) that 'forums of conciliation' be established prior to community restoration conferences as a foundation setting presupposes there is enough willingness to search for common ground; and the experience of many peace processes shows that rarely do spokespeople talk in the way Scheff says is required: 'exquisite courtesy, avoiding any kind of language or action that might occasion insult' (1997b: 11).

Another example of naivety will suffice. Facilitators for large restoration conferences that deal with post-violence emotions need 'to have considerable skill and cunning in order to manage the intense emotions . . . be trusted by both sides prior to the meeting . . . and need the skill to detect unacknowledged emotions' (Scheff 1997a: 3–4). These people may exist, and they may exist in sufficient number to deal with the thousands of such conferences that will have to take place in every town, neighbourhood and locality if every incident of communal vio-lence is to be dealt with separately, as Scheff suggests is the case (1997a: 3), but the on-going violence may undermine facilitators' efforts, lose them trust and never put an end to the emotions they need to manage. The trustworthiness of the facilitator is the key to successful mediation and this is the first thing to go when people from both sides complain of one-sidedness and, despite protestations of neutrality, attribute a stance on the conflict to the facilitator. With on-going violence, facilitators themselves are likely to become targets exposing them to high levels of risk. The error Scheff makes is to transpose too literally the restoration conference techniques in criminal justice cases to communal violence.

However, the restorative elements of 'truth' recovery processes offer nationwide mechanisms to achieve much the same purpose without exposing individual facilitators to any risk. John Braithwaite notably omits mention of individual restorative case conferences in restorative peacemaking, preferring to emphasize 'truth' commissions as a way of ensuring grassroots consent, particularly mentioning South Africa's commission as 'touching the hearts' of its people (2002: 170). As we shall explore further in chapter 6, more critical assessments of the Truth and Reconciliation Commission exist (Jeffrey, 1999; Wilson, 2001). In most settings where 'truth' commissions are being counselled, peacemaking has to take place alongside sporadic violence and where the political agreement remains unsettled or insecure. Sometimes governments and other parties to the conflict design 'truth' recovery procedures in order to disguise their own culpability or expose partisanly that of their opponents. In addition, 'truth' may merely be a bludgeon with which to beat the other side, to criticize their position as elected representatives or dispute their place in parliament, and disclosures and revelations used to continue the war, not end it, inflaming not assuaging emotions. 'Truth' in these settings may lead to revenge killings rather than emo-tional recovery. As we shall see in the next chapter, 'truth' commissions work best, if at all, as part of a settlement that has already stopped the killing, not as a mechanism to end the violence.

Misconceptions about the nature of violence impact negatively also on the paradigm's focus on shame–guilt as the primary emotion through which restoration and reintegration are delivered. There are two dimensions here – the paradigm's failure to address the counter-productive effects of shame–guilt and its neglect of the posi-tive emotions that are important to the envisioning of peace. Positive emotions are particularly crucial in instances where the peace process does not stop the violence, for hope for the future can quickly degenerate into despair at more of the same, undercutting people's support for the negotiated settlement. It is necessary to take some time to explore both omissions further.

*The limitations of privileging shame–guilt as post-violence emotions*

The restorative peacemaking paradigm under-estimates the array of negative emotions in post-violence societies by its concentration on shame–guilt. This is in part because it overlooks the negative emotions aroused by the peace process itself. Peace, as much as violence, provokes emotions that need to be managed. As we saw in chapter 2, peace threatens feelings of ontological security because it requires the overthrow of familiar ideas and ways of understanding the world. People who have defined their group identity, tradition and loyalties for so long in terms of 'the enemy' suddenly find they have to reshape their sense of who they are and what groups they feel loyalty towards. These feelings are only exacerbated for victims and their relatives. People can find an emotional anchor in the continuance of the old routines, behaviour, language and moral codes, rather than in change, encouraging a resistance to peace, opposition to peacemakers, whom they accuse of being 'sell-outs', and a fear of compromise. Emotions lose their vividness over time as memories of how we felt emotionally in the past fade, but peace processes tend to keep negative emotions alive for longer for those people for whom the peace comes at a cost. Shame–guilt does not describe the emotions that fear of peace generates in these people. Their emotions need management too, which limits the utility of shame–guilt in effecting restoration.

The most serious objection to the paradigm's characterization of emotions after communal violence is that shame–guilt can be problematic, even counter-productive, in peace processes (see Lu, 2008: 373–5). There are three difficulties with shame–guilt in post-violence societies – problems around its elicitation, appropriateness and desirability. Dealing first with its elicitation, what unlocks reintegration once emotions are elicited is the perception that they are genuine. The sociology of emotions teaches us that emotions involve performative behaviour, so their display can be artful. Shame–guilt in particular is socially constructed by institutionalized practices and expressions that are socially learned and performed. Communal violence can in some cases destroy the social bond, abolishing the moral system in which shame–guilt could operate, or cause the collapse of the institutionalized practices and codes through which it is expressed. Even if this is not the case, large communal restoration conferences are not conducive to picking up the subtle cues that display genuineness. It is likely to be community representatives making figurative shame apologies in public on behalf of the group whose genuineness is put to the test, and since most of these will be political representatives they will be under considerable constraint in their use of wording. And where violence continues, even sporadically, expressions of shame–guilt are difficult to hear as 'true', so the whole group will be perceived as duplicitous. The failure of Sinn Fein to say the precise words Ulster Unionists wanted to hear, despite Sinn Fein's genuine commitment to the Belfast Agreement, shows the political constraints peacemakers are under when offering shame apologies, and the temptation of opponents to impose a specific set of institutionalized practices and expressions in order to obstruct the process.

One other key to reintegration is that the elicitation of shame–guilt has to operate under what Karstedt (2002: 309) calls a 'fairness rule', in which the emotion is genuinely felt by the perpetrator but the victim's anger is channelled or controlled in ways that preserve some self-esteem for the offender. When political philosophers write of the 'moral legitimacy of anger' (for example Muldoon, 2008) amongst those who suffered through conflict, or portray anger as 'an indispensible political virtue' in the politics of reconciliation after trauma (such as Ure, 2008: 288), they always see the emotion held under control by 'norms of reasonableness'. With respect to ordinary crime, judicial procedures themselves prevent the arousal of additional emotions because offenders can 'tell "their stories", are not humiliated before their own peer group and their self-esteem is not stripped from them' (Karstedt, 2002: 309). Shame–guilt works in criminal justice settings on the basis of benign assumptions about the willingness of both parties to listen and learn within this shared sense of what is fair. However, after communal violence, it is often harder to be non-judgemental, to hear the other's narratives reflexively in order to learn something about your group from it, and to avoid the temptation to rub it in. The level of atrocity may have intensified judgementalism. Restorative mediation after communal violence may thus continue the vendettas of the past and provide an opportunity to settle old scores, as we saw in the case of Rwanda. Ure (2008: 288) thought that where 'norms of reasonableness' were not already constituted, they might become so by public debate about the conditions under which anger can be legitimately expressed. In the absence of a peace agreement, though, such deliberation is likely to become a proxy for the continuance of conflict.

When notions of fairness have been destroyed or made one-sided by the level of atrocity, restorative mediation can degenerate into what the sociologist Harold Garfinkel once termed 'degradation ceremonies' (an observation I have taken from Maruna, 2001: 158, who uses it with respect to the way some ex-prisoners experience restorative mediation after ordinary crime; see also Garfinkel, 1956). In an ordinary crime setting, degradation ceremonies involve the lowering of the actor's esteem in public attacks on their social identity, whereas reintegration ceremonies involve disapproval of the act while sustaining the identity of the actor as a good person (on the application of this distinction to juvenile delinquency, see J. Braithwaite and Mugford, 1994). The restorative mediation of ordinary crime must eliminate all sense of degradation so that the status as a criminal does not overwhelm the offender's identity. The problem for some forms of restorative mediation after communal violence, however, is that identity concerns may need to be addressed and people's sense of group identity impugned. Degradation ceremonies, therefore, may be just what is appropriate to reduce the 'groupness' that gets wrapped up in communal violence or to correct people's distorted notions of the 'superiority' of their group. Conversely, the 'fairness rule' is sometimes deliberately abandoned for the purposes of humiliation, resulting in simplistic notions of victimhood in restorative mediation, as we saw in Rwanda, where the notion of 'good Tutsis' and 'bad Hutus' was employed as a cognitive map to distort the complexity of issues of shame–guilt after the genocide. The problem with humiliation like this is that it may be resisted and not lead to shame–guilt, encouraging the arousal of further emotions.

In coming now to the second of the objections about shame–guilt that make it counter-productive as an emotion, the appropriateness of humiliation and shame–guilt depends entirely upon the nature of the communal violence. In some cases the violence may have been one-sided, victimhood thus being unambiguous, and an outright winner to the conflict has emerged able to look down from the moral high ground with world opinion on their side, with the vanquished – the corrupt regime, toppled dictator – having no cultural capital or moral claims. There are instances that approximate to this, such as the collapse of Nazi Germany, the ending of apartheid and the overthrow of Latin American dictatorships. In most cases of communal violence, however, victimhood is widespread across the social structure and most, if not all, groups are victims and perpetrators at the same time. Victimhood is every group's experience; every group a perpetrator. Thus, people need to enter restoration conferences as both victim and offender at the same time if they are to be successful.

Multiple victimhood might appear to make it easier to develop 'norms of reasonableness' after conflict; however, others' victimhood is likely to be unacknowledged, for victimhood tends to become politicized. One's own group's culpability may be denied or a hierarchy of victims imposed, based either on partisan preferences for victims from one's own group or on a hierarchy of crimes in which the other groups' actions were more heinous. A violent struggle is rarely if ever equal – morally, politically and militarily – but senses of proportionality are more quickly lost when the conflict involves multiple victimhood, for the others' actions are more likely to be perceived as dispropor-tional. Restorative mediation has to try to reduce this partisanship; the problem is that it can also perpetuate it. Self-righteous indignation and moral superiority distort victimhood (noted by Scheff, 1997a: 12) so that victimhood has the effect of perpetuating rather than healing the conflict. Shame–guilt in these circumstances seems not to fit the emo-tions required for peacemaking.

It does not fit for another reason: shame-guilt is an emotion that some do not feel. Who it is that does the disapproval is important to the degree of shame felt and thus the level of repair and reintegration achieved. Ahmed et al. (2001) found that, if the person who is doing the shaming is not respected, it may lead to defiance. The flip side is that the person being shamed may not feel the emotion. When disapproval is from the erstwhile 'enemy' in the opposing ethno-national group, as occurs often in cases where relational distance continues during the peace process, feelings of shame can be lessened because disapproval is anticipated (which gives additional impact to any expressions of dis-approval from members of the offenders' own ethno-national group). Anticipations of disapproval can also increase rather than diminish offenders' tendencies to justify their conduct. Shame–guilt is not only unacknowledged, there is an ardent refusal to countenance it. In con-ventional restoration conferences, offenders may well use techniques of neutralization to explain to victims their recourse to ordinary crime, but these are not moral claims. Perpetrators of communal violence, however, can under certain circumstances genuinely feel themselves morally justified. They may use restorative mediation to 'explain' why they took recourse in violence rather than express shame, which does little for the victims/survivors and offers no entry into repair or reinte-gration. Unlike ordinary crime, communal violence mostly comes with its own morality through 'just war' claims, making shame–guilt inap-propriate. Since 'just war' claims are open to challenge, shame–guilt becomes morally contestable; of all the post-violence emotions, it is the one most likely to be politicized. Shame–guilt thus risks perpetuating the conflict.

If shame–guilt is inappropriate because people feel they have nothing to be ashamed about, another problem of privileging shame–guilt is that post-violence societies can sometimes have too much of it. Elster (2004: 241) writes of his impression that, in the immediate aftermath of transition, many wrongdoers are overwhelmed by such a strong sense of guilt that they find it almost impossible to bear. One reaction to this cognitive dissonance is to engage in neutralization, as we have empha-sized. Where this is not feasible or permissible, it inevitably impugns wrongdoers' views of themselves as likeable people, from which can follow shame–guilt as an identity. This shame–guilt, like their accusers' sense of bitterness, can become a master status that both locks them in the past and makes them equally incapable of moving on. Too much guilt is problematic (as problematic as too little); it is as socially destructive as too much bitterness.

In addition to protagonists overloading themselves with too much shame–guilt, the ritualized performative behaviours and forms of talk associated with it spread to other categories of people not directly responsible for acts of violence, so that a culture of guilt–shame takes hold, contaminating too many undeserving people. Irena Sendlerova, for example, was a Polish social worker in Warsaw during the Second World War and used her access to the ghetto to rescue over 2,500 children and babies before she was caught by the Gestapo (she was eventually rescued by the partisans). Yet still this courageous woman could say, at the age of ninety-seven: 'the term "hero" irritates me greatly. The opposite is true. I continue to have pangs of conscience that I did so little' (quoted in Humphrys, 2007: 268). Think, too, of Oscar Schindler saying he could have done more. Bystanders in the 'grey zone' between combat and collaboration, neutrals not partaking in resistance or regime support, can come to feel shame–guilt simply for having done nothing (see Elster, 2004: 241). 'Standing by' can mean different things, of course, from not intervening to stop acts of violence directly witnessed to withdrawal from active involvement in peacemaking through apathy or fear. It goes from being unwilling to do something to being unable to do it. For some bystanders, therefore, their shame–guilt can be overdone – a bit like the 'irrational' survivor guilt experienced by those who did not die in plane crashes or, indeed, in the Holocaust (on survivor guilt amongst American Jews, see Novick, 1999).

This shame–guilt profligacy is problematic for society generally, for, as Elster (2004: 242) notes, bystander shame–guilt can encourage sufferers to resolve these emotional feelings by intransigence in the demand for retribution and by unforgivingness towards combatants. Aggression towards wrongdoers disguises their own sense of shame–guilt by projecting it onto people more directly responsible for acts of violence. Bystander guilt thus reduces the space for compromise and restorative mediation. To counteract the tendency for a culture of shame–guilt to permeate post-violence societies, therefore, transitions require that positive emotions be performed too. Two in particular command emphasis, hope and forgiveness.

*From the sociology of shame–guilt to the sociologies of hope and forgiveness*

Although the Greeks saw hope as dangerous – it was one of the evils contained in Pandora's Box – social scientists understand it as one of the most important emotions (for example Elster, 1989; Harvey, 2000). However, part of the problem in addressing emotions like hope and forgiveness is that they appear the domain of Christian theologians and to be virtues that arise primarily out of religious faith; the Catholic Church considers hope one of three 'theological virtues' (along with faith and charity). Jurgen Moltmann (1967) once developed a theology of hope and even Desroche's intriguingly entitled study *The Sociology of Hope* (1979) restricted itself to religious themes and consideration of divine manifestations of hope, mostly Messianism. While there is a philosophical tradition of utopian thinking that is separate from theology, culminating most recently in Rorty's *Philosophy and Social Hope* (1999), which focuses on alternative political societies, hope and forgiveness as everyday emotions appear to exist within the framework of pious forward-looking to the eternal world hereafter, or to consist of inspirational dreams of a different world on earth, in which, as Christian scripture writes, nation speaks peace unto nation and we beat our swords into pruning hooks. The political philosopher Michael Ure (2008: 286–90) has identified Christianity as one of two pillars for locating the discussion of forgiveness and love as emotions in post-traumatic societies. To the vast majority of ordinary people, this makes them useless emotions.

Of course, hope and forgiveness are widely acclaimed as wonderful things by virtually everyone until people have something or someone to forgive or are caught in a situation of despair and seemingly endless despondency. Hope and forgiveness in those situations are challenges that even the most devout religious believer finds it difficult enough to muster the faith to perform, let alone non-believers. The emptying pews tell a story: that many people today experience religion as distant and detached from their lives (G. Smyth, 2004: 127) and society needs a secular eschatology to replace religious notions of hope. The paradox, however, is that in societies where religion is a source of conflict or where the conflict is between groups socially marked by religion, a religious discourse of forgiveness and hope is likely to be rejected, making a secular eschatology of greater relevance.

Unlike other emotions, it is at the moment of their provocation, when feelings are most intense and urgent, that hope and forgiveness seem the most irrelevant: when hope and forgiveness are needed most, they seem the hardest of feelings to contemplate and enact. The young African mother gang-raped and now dying of AIDS, with no one to care for her several children, will tell you that, as can the child whose family was killed in a burned-out Rwandan church, the widower grieving his only child lying dead after Bloody Sunday, or the Sierra Leonean child soldiers whose thoughts are consumed by the atrocities they have committed, the screams of their victims invading their nights. The key is for peace processes to establish reasonable grounds for hope and forgiveness, to create spaces of hoping and forgiving, to develop public policies that enact hope and forgiveness, to effect social changes to create the social conditions that sustain hope and forgiveness; and to do so outside the framework of religious faith (although religion can assist believers in all these things, as we saw in chapter 3). Let us look first at hope.

As Bar-Tal (2001; see also Jarymowicz and Bar-Tal, 2006) noted with respect to Israel–Palestine, collective fear can dominate people's emotional repertoire in situations of intractable conflict and prevent the development of hope. For this reason, peace processes require an envisioning of the future as much as an emotional packaging of the past. Politicians and lay people alike may lack a peace vocation, being concerned only for the killings to stop rather than enacting an agreed future. People can also be dominated by short-term expectations – wanting change now and quickly – rather than being prepared for the long haul. The likelihood of travails during the long haul requires there be a vision to sustain them. Hope, in other words, is as critical to peacemaking as shame–guilt. This point is made with respect to prisoners of ordinary crime by Burnett and Maruna (2004: 395; see also Maruna, 2001), who show hope's positive role in preventing recidivism. Over a ten-year study, they found that hope for the future, prior to release, made former inmates better able to cope with the problems they experienced after leaving prison, although the impact of hope shrank as the number of problems rose, leaving even the most hopeful ex-inmate overwhelmed by reality (Burnett and Maruna, 2004: 398–9).

The value of this research is that it illustrates that hope is not enough on its own without the conditions to sustain it. Herein lies the potential for a sociological approach to hope. A sociology of hope, in summary, explores the impact social arrangements have on structuring hope and in creating the conditions for its realization, analyses the social practices by which hope is socially constructed, explores the use of hope to help construct and achieve societal goals, and the way in which hope is used to manipulate and manage people's private and personal loyalties. Psychologists define hope in personal terms as the ability to formulate achievable goals (see Snyder et al., 1991: 570; see also Bandura, 1989; Stotland, 1969), which makes it more than just wishing or optimism, recognizing that hope will be reducible to wishful thinking unless the means are perceived by which the goals can be attained (for example Burnett and Maruna, 2004: 395). Even so, the emphasis is upon perception – people envisioning means and ends – making hope a cognitive process (for example Bar-Tal, 2001). It can easily become a circular argument when couched in these terms: those people who succeed in achieving their goals are the ones with the cognitive processing skills called hope, those who fail lacked them. However, a thoroughgoing sociology of hope explores the impact social conditions have on structuring these means–ends. The means–ends also need to be seen as collective rather than personal ones, focusing on societal rather than individual ambitions. Furthermore, hope within sociology should be understood as something more than means–ends, a calculation reducible to rational choice logic.

As an emotion, hope has two qualities, which make it both forward-looking and positive: *hoping*, the act of imagining a future desirable set of social circumstances and the ways to get there (that is, it supplies an eschatology), and *anticipation*, the internal feelings excited by the desirable end state being envisioned (that is, it elicits other positive emotions). Hoping and anticipation are indivisible, for the wished-for end state has to be one that is longed for, one that involves feelings of excitement and anticipation; only people outside the normal social bonds hope for something undesirable to happen to the social group and get excited by anticipating harm. This is why it is better to see hope as two complementary emotions rather than one – hoping–anticipation – much as with shame–guilt. Linking anticipating with hoping in this way accounts for why hope is inevitably positive and forward-looking and is associated with progress and optimism.

There is a global language of hope that picks up on these qualities. It was in order to tap into these associations that the USA named its peacekeeping campaign in Somalia 'Operation Restore Hope', and former US President Bush changed his language in his final address to Congress in January 2008 from 'the war on terror' to the campaign 'hope for freedom'; President Obama refers to the 'audacity of hope'. Rwandan health clinics servicing the needs of genocide victims are called Clinics of Hope; El Salvador's 'truth' commission report was subtitled 'from madness to hope'. These associations also explain why a few commercial corporations merchandise hope (on which see Drahos, 2004), with some multi-national companies invoking sentiments like hope for corporate ends – 'food, health and hope' is the slogan used by Monsanto to sell its genetically modified crops. Malign merchandising by Monsanto, of course, is coupled with the more benign marketing of hope done by marriage bureaux, dating agencies, plastic surgeons or fertility clinics and the like. The UK charity called HOPE (Helping Orphaned and Poor Exploited children across the world), puts the association of hope with positive forward-looking confidence and optimism to more beneficial use, stating on its website that 'the two most important aspirations for today's children are hope and imagination'. The mainline churches in Britain and Ireland, in conjunction with the Christian Enquiry Centre and United Christian Broadcasting, developed a programme called Hope 2008, especially designed for young people, church congregations and the press, to encourage people to use the web to share the good news of how religion is spreading hope around the world (see www.hopeinfo.co.uk). The language of hope is universal. This calls for a proper understanding of the concept.

In sociology, hope becomes conceptually a double-sided emotion (hoping–anticipating) that is public, in that cultural values can shape what it is that is hoped for and how it is achieved. It is an emotion affected by social conditions, something that can be constructed for societal goals by means of social change in the conditions that sustain it, with people's private perceptions open to management to enable the collectivity to imagine a desirable future and the means to achieve it. Hope and social change are in a symbiotic relationship: Courville and Piper (2004) stress the importance of hope in social change, while social change facilitates hope. Hope's envisioning of social change in the future may in situations of social conflict involve anticipating the ending of killings but also new identities, new political regimes and new forms of social relations. There are various social practices, technologies and public policies for this purpose, including museums that envision the future as much as record the past, such as the Holocaust Museum or Robben Island Museum (on which, see Shearing and Kempa, 2004), as well as use of the education curriculum in schools, media initiatives, public memorials and so on. Of course, some of these do not always work, for the idea of a museum to Northern Ireland's civil unrest at the former Maze prison was scuppered as too divisive, but hope is one way to harness the activism of NGOs and civil society groups (see Courville and Piper, 2004). Citizenship education programmes, for example, such as cross-community holiday schemes, summer camps for children from across the various divides, cross-community house-building initiatives, or specific lecture, seminar and workshop programmes, can place protagonists in settings where it is possible for them to begin hoping and anticipating.

Various social and cultural spaces for hoping can be developed in everyday life to complement citizenship education programmes, which place people in spaces that increase their sense of anticipation of the hoped-for end state. These can be cultural spaces (such as through poetry, drama and art exhibitions that envision a peaceful future and focus on hoping and anticipating the end state), political spaces (where groups and parties debate means–ends), religious spaces (through which the churches and para-church organizations stress the importance of hope), medical spaces (where welfare and medical care bring hope for health and cure) and so on. Public policies can be devised towards achieving this end state, which assist people and groups with the hoping and anticipating by improving the social conditions which sustain hope, such as by addressing issues of equality, justice and social redistribution. Ending the violence and dealing with the past via 'truth' recovery processes are important to hope, but hope needs the alleviation of the social ills that weaken it, which is why peace processes must address the tension between peace (normally seen as the ending of violence) and justice (the (re)introduction of equality, fairness and social redistribution). For all these reasons, while it may seem the most personal and individualized of emotions, hope is social. Of course, it remains still in part a cognitive process since hoping is an act of imagining (which is why social movement theory sees hope as part of the process of cognitive liberation that assists people in participating in movements of change), but the sociological context in which hope operates makes it an independent variable that exists also outside people's cognitive processes.

'Private hope' has been defined as the 'hopes an individual holds', while 'public hope' refers to the hopes of political actors in relation to societal goals (Drahos, 2004: 21); Rorty's notion of 'social hope' (1999) is nothing like 'public hope', since Rorty means by social hope the realization of utopian values through romantic notions of solidarity between humankind (Harvey, 2000, also uses the term 'hope' to describe utopianism). In these terms, public hopes can be those of powerful individuals and groups able to formulate and work towards societal goals as they construe them, as well as societal goals that are collectively held. In the first case, people buy into the vision of the future (and the route map to get there) of key political and group leaders; in the second, they absorb the means–ends of the collectivity. There are likely to be competing public hopes in the first case and consensus over means–ends in the second. Courville and Piper (2004: 39–61) discuss the potential for power imbalances to create competing hopes, but also highlight the way in which marginalized social groups can be empowered by buying into collective means–ends. But the potential for competing hopes means that in some situations public hope can be disabling or destructive for peace processes.

Valerie Braithwaite (2004: 128–51) employs the term 'collective hope' to emphasize the consensus over societal goals, and stresses the importance of transparent and social inclusionary procedures to ensure that the public is aware of their importance in the process by which public hopes are devised. This does not mean that public hope is only possible once the conflict is over and a consensus on societal means–ends is capable of emerging; the difference from many of the other emotional virtues that do require the war to be over first, such as 'truth' and shame–apology, is that those people who have *not* lost hope – who are still hoping and anticipating – are the only ones who have not closed their eyes to the violence and are able to see the horrors of conflict with clarity, as Vaclav Havel, the Czech human rights activist, put it in a prison letter to his wife (Havel, 1990: 1). Public hope, therefore, is important to conflict resolution as a strategy for stopping the violence. This is the reason why, as I wrote earlier, peace processes require a peace vocation, an emotional envisioning of the future and a sense of how to get there, for, even if there is no agreement yet on societal means–ends and these remain divisive, there is a consensus that before anything the fighting first has to stop. Public hope, in short, is a pre-requisite for peace and is one strategy to achieve it. Positive emotions like hope, therefore, need to be privileged in restorative peacemaking above shame–guilt.

If religion obscures the potential for a sociological perspective on hope, it shrouds forgiveness in even greater spiritual cloaks that limit further the immediate potential for the application of the sociological imagination to forgiveness. Nonetheless, it is a sign of the wide currency of the term that Griswold (2007) has written on the philosophy of forgiveness (see also Soyinka, 2000). There are, however, at least four genres in the history of the term. There is a huge literature in psychology (reviewed by Snells and Hargrave, 1998) that addresses, amongst other things, the personality traits associated with forgiveness (for example Kearns and Fincham, 2004; Zechmeister and Romero, 2002) and its therapeutic benefits to the offender and victim (see Pingleton, 1989; Snells and Hargrave, 1998). In feminist research, the term is associated with women's narratives of abuse and extending forgiveness towards the abusers (for example, see Clegg, 1999). The politics of forgiveness is another burgeoning field (for a review, see Digeser, 2001). Forgiveness has entered the debate about healing relations between nations (for example Amstutz, 2004), between warring ethnic groups (for example Shriver, 1995) and about the relationship between citizens and the government that abused them (for example Digeser, 1998). Theological exegesis in the area of forgiveness is not surprisingly the largest field (on the application of theology to forgiveness in politics, see G. Smyth, 2004; Torrance, 2006). Watts (2004: 180) noted that, amongst all this debate, there is no adequate sociology of forgiveness.

At first sight it seems extremely difficult to rescue the concept from Judeo-Christian theology; some of the social science attempts to debate forgiveness are written from a Christian perspective (notably Amstutz, 2004; Shriver, 1995; Torrance, 2006), invoke Christianity as a moral framework for the discussion of post-conflict emotions (notably Ure, 2008) or apply specific scriptural and sacred writings to flesh out the meaning of political forgiveness (see, with respect to South East Asian politics, Satha-Anand, 2002; more generally, see G. Smyth, 2004). At the heart of the Christian faith in particular stands an ethic of forgiveness that commands believers to forgive. The New Testament illustrates how Jesus forgave everybody, even his executioners, and is replete with exhortations to us to do likewise. St Augustine's instruction to Jesus' followers to hate the sin but love the sinner was an attempt to show how we might fulfil this commandment practically, and commentators since have debated the possibility for doing this in difficult circumstances; C.S. Lewis's (1952[1942]: 102) radio talk during the Second World War on how this might extend to the Gestapo is still quoted today. Forgiveness seems such a kernel of the Christian faith that the Revd Victor Griffin (2002: 11–12) once remarked that unconditional generosity to others, rather than enforcing one's own rights as a believer, is the heart of the Gospel (on the unconditionality of forgiveness, see Ricoeur, 2004a).

Forgiveness is invariably discussed using this kind of religious discourse. One consequence of this has been to place the term in the individual realm of private morality; and even though there are theologians who have specified the theological grounds for advocating forgiveness in the socio-political realm (for example Torrance, 2006), the debate is still conducted utilizing religious themes and vocabulary. Forgiveness, though, is another positive emotion essential to peace processes and is too important to be the sole preserve of the churches. The religious connotations of forgiveness, however, do not offer quite the same constraints on sociology as with hope.

The problem with hope when left to the churches is that religion pushes people's perspectives onto the world hereafter or into idealistic ideas about realizing the eternal world on earth. Forgiveness is forward-looking too, but focuses on future social relations. Forgiveness can be defined as intentional forbearance of the emotional and behavioural reactions that social action *might* otherwise deserve, in order to continue with or restore relationships. Even though notions about what is 'justly deserved' are relative, in this context one or both of the principal parties foreswear responses that they feel are justified, in order not to jeopardize the social relationship. The attention to repair of social relations by means of forgiveness firmly locates it in this world not the next. Of course, social repair may, if one's beliefs inclined in this direction, involve 'turning the other cheek', 'loving one's enemies', 'blessing those who persecute us' or 'embracing the evil doer in love', as Christian doctrine teaches, but sociologically it means release from the consequences of social action so that neither the action nor the responses to it become a barrier to on-going social relationships. This does not involve the offending action being sanitized, normalized or made excusable – no neutralization techniques are used to justify the action to oneself or others – and the responses it provokes are not denied, undervalued or diminished. Forgiveness means pardoning the action despite its wrongfulness (as the principal parties see it) and refusing to respond to it in ways that might otherwise be expected or deserved (although it may still involve the criminal justice system enforcing retribution under the law where this is taken out of the hands of the principal parties). This sociological approach is preferable to Pingleton's (1989: 27) definition in psychotherapy, where forgiveness is described as relinquishing the right to retaliate, which smacks too much of the Old Testament idea of an eye for an eye.

It needs to be emphasized that the moral deserts to forgiveness are the victims' not the perpetrators'. In order to support their claim that victims are morally entitled to anger and that too much can be made of forgiveness, Calhoun (1992: 78) and Muldoon (2008: 307) mistakenly suggest that advocates of the idea of redemption imply that perpetrators *deserve* to be forgiven. Muldoon (2008: 307–8) further warns that, under pressure (presumably from the rhetoric of forgiveness), victims can lose sight of perpetrators' culpability and deem themselves so lacking in esteem and moral worth that they fail to protest their victimhood. Nothing of the sort can be construed from the sociological approach adopted here, for the definition of forgiveness above makes clear that perpetrators are spared what is otherwise deserved and that no denial or denuding of the moral wrongfulness of the acts is implied by forgiving it. This is why Muldoon's 'paradox of forgiveness' (2008: 312, footnote 8) is no paradox at all but merely confusion of the moral obligations of forgiveness. The paradox supposedly is that forgiveness is only possible when it is deserved – that is, when the anger of victims is not well founded – and only necessary when it is not deserved – that is, when the anger of victims is well founded. The paradox collapses because it is the anger of victims that defines what are just deserts, not the feelings of perpetrators.

It is necessary to concede, however, that discussion about the moral obligations to forgiveness is complicated by three further sociological properties of forgiveness: the ability of perpetrators to forgive themselves independently of victims' sense of this being deserved; the existence of third-party forgiveness; and the possibility that some acts are so offensive to society's moral code that forgiving them ought to be forbidden. Let us deal with the latter condition first.

Drawing on her experience of the South African Truth and Reconciliation Commission, of which she was a member, Gobodo-Madikizela (2008) shows that some victims have had the magnanimity to forgive perpetrators heinous crimes because they recognized perpetrators' vulnerability. Irrespective of victims' remarkable willingness to forgive, however, she asks whether some acts are unforgiveable, redemption from which ought to be morally forbidden (2008: 334). The Holocaust is usually cited as an example (see Arendt, 1998[1958]). The idea of the unforgiveable, Gobodo-Madikizela writes (2008: 334–5), is no longer tenable in the light of the forgiveness witnessed in places like South Africa and Rwanda. Put another way, the political and moral landscape has been changed by some successful peace processes.

There is a philosophical discourse to support this pragmatic view. Jankélévitch (2005), for example, argues that the 'proper function' of forgiveness is precisely to forgive the otherwise inexcusable, a formula appropriated from Derrida (2002), who claimed that the essence of forgiveness is excusing the otherwise unforgiveable. In an interview, Derrida (1998) considered that, in the abstract, it was possible to conceive of circumstances where victims had lost the capacity to forgive. In practice, however, two caveats intrude in this simple formula: victims have shown a remarkable capacity to forgive even the most heinous crimes (Govier, 1999, considers no one sufficiently evil for victims not to see redeeming features); and forgiveness is not only the right of victims. Forgiveness has sociological properties that permit perpetrators to forgive themselves and for third parties to forgive on others' behalf. A sociological approach to forgiveness thus upholds Shriver's (1995) claim that there are no boundaries on the possibility of forgiveness. Let us expand on these two qualities of forgiveness.

Because people have the capacity to forgive themselves as well as others – to pardon themselves for what they have done and to foreswear responding to themselves as others might – forgiveness is not something that is only done to us by others. This might not be apparent at first sight because of the way forgiveness is understood religiously; even in psychology, the bulk of the literature is on inter-personal forgiveness rather than self-forgiveness (for an exception, see Hall and Finch, 2005). Religious discourse normally presents forgiveness as exogenous, coming from the outside, whether of God, the injured faction or both. This grants the power to forgive to the other party, equating forgiveness with the issuing of the pardon and the mercifulness shown in not responding in ways that otherwise would be justified, leaving the first party powerless, dependent on the other's magnanimity. This is what it means when believers are told to throw themselves naked upon God's mercy, as if powerless, defenceless, awaiting only His divine judgement. However, forgiveness ought properly to be seen as endogenous at the same time, coming from within, which is what forgiving oneself literally means (Hall and Finch, 2005: 621, define self-forgiving as abandonment of self-resentment). The plea for pardon, when genuine, thus already involves forgiveness, at least by the plea-makers themselves.

There is something of this in the distinction between passive and active responsibility (see Bovens, 1998). This was first applied by Bovens in relation to corporate responsibility for organizational crime, but the distinction has become popular in the restorative justice paradigm (see J. Braithwaite and Roche, 2001). As used by the criminological psychologists Maruna and Mann (2006: 167), passive responsibility involves the attribution by A of blame to B for what they have done in the past, while active responsibility involves B taking responsibility for putting things right in the future. B can decide to do this independently of A; indeed A's blaming may be an obstacle to them taking active responsibility. So it is with forgiveness. B is able to forgive themself separately from A's forgiveness, and can engage in repair independently of it. Even this kind of one-sided forgiveness assists in repair to social relationships, for it is necessary to distinguish between repair in the inter-personal relationship between offender and victim and in wider social relations with generalized others, which makes Shriver's idea of 'renewed community' (1995) a useful way of describing this second type of social repair (although Hutchinson and Bleiker, 2008: 389, remind us that restoration of senses of community is reconciliatory only insofar as the social bonds are inclusive not exclusive and these are not communities held together by fear or anger).

Social repair via forgiveness operates on the basis of the same two-party exchange as with shame apologies – the appeal for forgiveness by the first party, the offer of forgiveness by the second, and redemption for them both, redemption here being understood as repair in social relationships rather than spiritually. Unlike shame apologies, however, the two parts do not obligate each other: it is possible to petition for forgiveness from someone without them agreeing to it, and to offer forgiveness to someone when it is not asked for, although in each case only one party is redeemed. It is a moot point in Christian theology whether someone can be redeemed when others do not agree to their request for forgiveness, but if we consider redemption as it is understood in economics, as the final payment of a formal obligation, the offer of the first part (requesting forgiveness) seems all that the party can do to fulfil the obligation and to meet the payment (thus earning redemption). Forgiveness in social life involves a two-party exchange, only one part of which is necessary to achieve its purpose, for the obligation is not fulfilled reciprocally, with the two parties having to agree that the wording of the request is sufficient to consent to forgive. Economics is again useful in understanding this, for bonds and securities have redemptive value before their maturity date that can be greater than their face value, even if not as much as on maturity. Forgiveness is like this. Either party obtains redemption by fulfilment of their part of the obligation (either to seek or offer forgiveness), which, if it remains only one-sided, will not repair their inter-relationship, but the redeemed party will be able to take their redemption into other relationships in the wider community, the quality of which will therefore be improved.

Because forgiveness has value only when it results in redemption, to either one or both parties, it is best to conceive forgiveness as two emotions in one, forgiveness–redemption, similar to shame–guilt and hope–anticipation. However, forgiveness–redemption work together in fundamentally different ways from shame–guilt. It is possible to make a shame apology without it being accepted – indeed, most figurative shame apologies are of this kind – but there is no redemptive value attached to it when it is unaccepted. This is because shame apologies involve a reciprocal relationship and do not realize their purpose without successful completion of both parts. There is no redemptive value to the person offering a shame apology if it is not accepted; its acceptance *is* its value. One cannot apologize to oneself but we can forgive ourselves. The capacity to forgive yourself and to take this feeling of redemption into your future relationships with generalized others is a good demonstration of what I mean by the non-reciprocal nature of the exchange and shows that forgiveness has redemptive value irrespective of the other party. As the Catholic theologian Geraldine Smyth has noted (2004: 110) some people refuse to forgive because a relationship with the perpetrator cannot be countenanced; self-forgiveness, however, is redemptive.

Asking for forgiveness is redemptive to a wrongdoer even if the victim is unmoved to forgive, for the request itself liberates the person from the emotional burden and self-resentment their past actions have caused them. Forgiving oneself like this is often the foundation that begins the process of us forgiving those whom we have to, broadening further the scope of social repair. Redemption is available also to victims/survivors on a non-reciprocal basis, for by offering forgiveness without it being sought (or accepted) they are liberated from the emotional bitterness and feelings of anger and revenge that their victimhood might otherwise cause. This, too, can become the cornerstone for more general repair in social relations as they free themselves from the continual need to have others petition for repentance before relationship with them is permissible. They still take their grief and loss with them into the future but forgiveness gives them a measure of freedom from emotional bitterness. Most victims, of course, realize only a relative freedom, for, despite the enthusiasm of Christian commentators to claim forgiveness as the bolster against bitterness, experimental research in psychology invariably shows forgiveness to be easier for offenders than victims (for example, see Zechmeister and Romero, 2002). This highlights the importance of developing a co-ordinated approach to public policy in peace processes to ensure that victims are not overlooked, a topic addressed in the next chapter.

There is another fundamental difference between the way forgiveness and shame apologies work, for figurative forms work better than literal ones. If we take literal forgiveness to mean the two principal parties coming together in a face-to-face encounter (such as in a restorative case conference or before a 'truth' commission), it can be emotionally very difficult for specific parties to an atrocity to request/offer forgiveness because the intensity and urgency of the emotions get aroused again by the other's very presence, although there are obviously many cases where magnanimity of spirit rises above meanness. Redemptive value is more likely to be released when forgiveness is done in symbolic form, precisely because it is not dependent on the other party fulfilling their part face-to-face. Co-presence increases the reluctance of the parties to request forgiveness or agree to it, the emotional consequences of which when face-to-face can reduce dramatically the redemptive value experienced by the magnanimous party (making it difficult, for example, to forgive oneself). When co-presence reignites emotional feelings, making it harder to ask for or grant forgiveness, one or both parties can rile against the other's refusal, to the point where the exchange degenerates into mutual recriminations, with no knock-on effect for the quality of other relationships. For these reasons, figurative rather than literal forgiveness is always likely to be more redemptive.

Forgiveness in symbolic form is performed via public statements in the press, on television, at 'truth' recovery forums, such as public enquiries and 'truth' commissions; in civil society workshops, seminars or public lectures devoted to the topic; at citizenship education forums; during religious services, debates in parliament and political assemblies or in submissions at courts of law. These settings constitute what we might call public 'spaces of forgiveness', and they match the spaces of hoping–anticipating referred to above. Public spaces of forgiveness allow the emotions involved in forgiveness to be more easily managed because the absence of one party encourages the other to say what needs to be said. They can become spaces for the display of what Hochschild (1983) calls 'surface' emotions, irrespective of what people feel deeply; places for front-stage performances that might not be consistent with how they behave back-stage. Public 'forgiveness ceremonies' could be devised as part of cultural (and religious) practices, and policy makers could design special spaces of forgiveness for this purpose as part of the peace process.

Various interaction rituals could be invented by which forgiveness is standardized into various formulations of words and actions that people can perform in large numbers in covenants, petitions, newspaper advertisements or in specific acts and deeds, such as street marches or parades of forgiveness (similar to the 'redemption rituals' recommended by Maruna, 2001: 163, by which the state could 'graduate' young offenders leaving penal institutions). Some of these spaces and rituals could well be religious given the association of the process of forgiveness with religion, such as in liturgical settings, joint services, shared worship, in singing, public prayer and praise songs, in which forgiveness is made the theme and people are provided with opportunities for figurative forgiveness (whether by asking for or granting it publicly). The public theologies of forgiveness that are being developed (such as by Torrance, 2006) could be given focus in these religious ceremonies of forgiveness. Hymnody – whether Wesley's traditional hymns speaking of mercy for all, or modern praise songs with popular tunes – might reinforce the importance of believers practising forgiveness. Religious spaces of forgiveness seem especially important where the conflict was experienced as religious – once, that is, religious differences lose their political appeal.

However, secular spaces are more readily acceptable in late modernity, such as citizenship forums, other platforms in civil society, along with debates in political assemblies, in the media, as well as in the cultural and artistic life of the people through drama, poetry, novels, music and painting. Karl Jenkins's *The Armed Man: A Mass for Peace* was, according to the composer, devised during the massacres in Kosovo and is a good illustration of the point. 'What better way', the composer writes on his website (www.karljenkins.armedman.php), 'both to look back and reflect as we leave behind the most war-torn and destructive century in human history, and to look ahead with hope and commit ourselves to a new and more peaceful millennium'. As Reilly (2000: 162) notes, poets in Northern Ireland, for example, have borne witness to the society's worst atrocities in an attempt to capture and reflect their sense of people's emotional and moral sensibilities – and it is a small step further for artists to engage with the emotion of forgiveness. While poetry and classical music are minority interests, the broadcast media have greater opportunity to affect public emotions through programmes that address forgiveness. Reilly focuses on one in particular, broadcast on Radio Ulster and called *Legacy*, which ran as a five-minute slot every day throughout 1999, in which ordinary people spoke of the extraordinary events they had been caught up in, the effects of which Reilly, as a social work teacher, claimed were therapeutic for listeners (2000: 165).

Social spaces for figurative forgiveness like this make it much more efficacious than symbolic forms of shame apology. It is the *publicness* of the emotional display in figurative forgiveness that brings greatest redemptive value, for even if we can imagine a situation in which the injured party would prefer the request to be made face-to-face in order to agree to forgive, this repairs only the inter-personal relationship. The redemption earned by public statements, however, is experienced vicariously by many of the witnesses to them, for whom the statements speak to their own circumstances, garnering a 'community of forgivers'. Gordon Wilson's statement of forgiveness to the IRA after the murder of his daughter at the 1987 Poppy Day massacre in Enniskillen is an example of figurative forgiveness, which for a short time provided a 'moment of transcendence' (a term I owe to Larry Ray) that helped others forgive those they had to. Ignatieff's observation on Chile (1998: 28) illustrates the point better. When President Alywn appeared on Chilean television to seek forgiveness from the victims of Pinochet's crimes of repression, Ignatieff noted: 'he created the public climate in which a thousand acts of private repentance became possible'.

Figurative forms create a kind of third-party forgiveness, as it were, where third parties are other individuals, groups, generalized others and whole societies. This is not meant in the sense that the third party forgives on the offended person's behalf but that they themselves forgive on their own behalf for wrongs done to the collectivity that they experienced as personal. This does not involve the out-sourcing of forgiveness to a special body or commission whose responsibility it becomes to deal with forgiveness in the post-conflict setting in the way that happens with 'truth' recovery; this allows wrongdoers and victims/survivors to evade the personal responsibility for forgiveness that the process requires. What I mean here is that other parties for whom the conflict was experienced as personal can become forgivers with respect to their individual responsibilities as a result of the figurative forgiveness displayed by others. When this kind of forgiveness extends to whole groups, it is possible to conceive meaningfully of nations forgiving other nations as third parties. This is one of the ways in which political forgiveness works.

The claim that there is value in figurative, third-party forgiveness finds agreement in Prager's (2008: 416–17) idea of 'redressive community'. Drawing on Schaap's (2005) notion of 'political reconciliation', Prager argues that redressive communities offer spaces where forgiveness and apology are both spoken and performed. This is often an antagonistic process, but where guilty offenders (or victims) are unavailable or unwilling to occupy them, others with the authority to do so stand in for them. The redressive community thus is not constituted solely by the victim and perpetrator 'but rather by those willing, for the time being, to shorn themselves of their pre-existing positions, [and] with a preparedness toward forgiveness and apology, in the hope of reconstituting themselves and the social world into a life in common' (Prager, 2008: 417). Third-party forgiveness advances the potential to garner a culture of forgiveness in post-conflict societies, rather than a culture of shame–guilt. It is feasible to claim that, rather than shame–guilt being the master emotion after conflict, forgiveness–redemption is the principal emotion for it effectively absorbs shame–guilt and does away with the need for contrition, or, at least, makes contrition part of a broader set of emotional performances that automatically take us in a positive direction. In a post-violence setting where there is also hope, the problems of shame–guilt highlighted earlier can be solved by incorporating the contrition into a more positive range of emotions that are inherently forward-looking.

## Conclusion

Restorative justice is a fashionable idea because it works, even if it works best in post-violence societies with very specific kinds of social structure, such as Bougainville and Uganda. Its universal appeal attests to its popularity as well as its efficacy, although advocates tend to gloss over the cases where social structural arrangements are not conducive, such as Rwanda. The application of restorative justice principles to conflict resolution and post-violence adjustment problems is new but it is already clear that restorative peacemaking is a valuable contribution to the field. Restorative justice approaches to assisting the social reintegration of ex-combatants work well, since this most closely parallels its application to ordinary crime.

However, there are other features of the paradigm that do not work or do so less capably than advocates claim. The major weakness addressed in this chapter is its account of the emotional dynamics of post-violence societies, which is stymied by privileging shame–guilt. Shame–guilt *is* part of the emotional dynamics of post-violence societies but such are its problems that it is not an emotion that helps to realize peace: it is permissible only after peace has been stabilized – it comes at the end of the peace process, best expressed retrospectively, rather than at the beginning. Above all, the paradigm neglects the array of positive emotions that are needed to carry a peace process over its travails.

Positive psychology, so called, seems to suggest we can conjure up happy thoughts and positive emotions will flow, but, sociologically, hope and forgiveness are cognitive processes that can be socially constructed and manifested in social action. Their manufacture, however, needs to be worked at as hard as does the management of shame–guilt. Social spaces for hope and forgiveness can be constructed to encourage the forward-looking confidence and optimism associated with these emotions. Opportunities for hoping–anticipating and forgiving–redeeming, however, can be squeezed by political disputes over the peace settlement, by outbreaks of renewed violence and by on-going tensions arising from the continued social reproduction of relational distance. To help with this problem, hoping and forgiving need to be made objects of public policy, made as much a focus of peace negotiations as shame–guilt. They are also not one-off emotions, and their momentariness requires continual attention to their reproduction in people's cognitive processes as well as to the social conditions that sustain them. Their momentariness is more likely to be transcended when hope and forgiveness are made part of a co-ordinated policy programme that places them alongside shame–guilt, 'truth' recovery, victimhood, remembrance and citizenship education programmes. We turn to a consideration of these issues in the next chapter.

# 6

# Memory, 'truth' and victimhood

## Introduction

The notion of collective memory dominated sociology for generations and it inhibited intellectual innovation until very recently.
Contemporary formulations of the field now refer to memory as
'autobiographical' (Rubin, 1996), 'social' (Fentress and Wickham, 1992;
Misztal, 2003; Reading, 2003), 'cultural' (Sturken, 1997) and 'popular'
(P. Anderson, 1992). The new sociological interest in memory, 'truth'
and suffering can be attributed to the negative impact that several cases
of genocide have had on our notion of late modernity as enlightened
and progressive (on which, see Bauman, 1989). The rediscovery of
memory and 'truth' in sociology is really the return of genocide as a
contemporary experience.

However, they represent a challenge to the sociology of peace
processes in two senses: remembrance, commemoration and 'truth'
recovery are difficult peacemaking strategies, and memories of the
conflict and recovery of the 'truth' about it can be obstacles to reconciliation. Post-violence societies therefore need to find ways of dealing
with victims' experiences in such a way as to permit victimhood to be
recognized and victims honoured while moving them and the rest of
society beyond the memory. Peace processes thus need to manage two
problems: finding the balance between the need to know what happened in the past and moving forward, and encouraging people to see
the 'truth' from someone else's standpoint. This allows people to know
about the past in such a way as to avoid keeping them locked there.

The purpose of this chapter is to assess the pivotal role social
memory plays in peace processes. This involves attention to the
closely related issues of 'truth' recovery and victimhood for their
potential as strategies for healing. I will elaborate on the ways in

which memory can be used as a peace strategy and how 'socially functional victimhood', as I call it, can be made the subject of public policy. This involves making a distinction between 'personal' and 'public' victimhood and I address the ways in which public victimhood can be utilized to under-gird peace processes. The case study is Northern Ireland.

There are close ties between issues of memory, 'truth' and victimhood, which explain why they are being discussed together in one chapter. Most of the demand for 'truth' recovery comes from victims. Some of the insistence for 'truth' commissions and 'truth' recovery processes, of course, comes from combatants, in that the search for 'truth' feeds into the issue of amnesty and speeds their social reintegration. The ANC was in favour of the Truth and Reconciliation Commission on these grounds, as were some former members of the South African Police. Amnesty-through-truth was not a feature of Latin American peace processes, although security force personnel in Guatemala who have been 'born again' in their conversion to conservative evangelicalism have been keen to reinforce this wiping away of their past by also participating in 'truth' recovery (see Kaur, 2003). Governments can desire 'truth' recovery too, in order to try to give an official version of events. However, it is victims and victim groups who put these issues into high relief. How they remember what happened and find out the 'truth' of it is part of what makes up the victimhood experience, and victims take positions on remembrance and 'truth' recovery that raise their profile. These issues provoke considerable emotional intensity and are invariably politicized.

While memory, 'truth' recovery and victimhood clearly overlap in this way, they will be separated in this chapter in order to assist the argument. However, before we look at how memory is implicated in war and peace, it is worthwhile drawing attention to the particular way that memory is conceptualized in sociology, for the nature of memory affects the arguments considerably.

## Understanding memory

Sociology understands memory as having individual and social dimensions. Remembrance is something we all do as individuals all the time, and we all have our own personal stock of memories, unique in its constellation to us. What goes on in people's heads in the formation and use of individual memories is a question about individual remembrance. We might call this 'personal' or 'autobiographical' memory. What goes on in society in the formation and use of collective memory is a question of social remembrance, which we call 'social' memory.

Cognitive psychology teaches us a great deal about autobiographical memory that is relevant to sociological approaches to social memory. Summarizing this research, William Brewer (1996: 23–4) argued that memory imagery is dim, unclear, sketchy and simplified, and fades dramatically with time: on average people have 70 per cent recall of events after six months, dropping to 29 per cent after five years (W. Brewer, 1996: 49). Forgetting, therefore, is as much a part of memory as remembrance (see Connerton, 2008; Henderson, 1999; Ricoeur, 2004b). Yet for traumatic events, such as those surrounding communal violence and victimhood experiences, recall is improved. 'Emotion arousing events', as Christianson and Safer (1996: 219) describe them, are recalled with greater accuracy than everyday events. Emotions affect memory and negative emotions have saliency by being recalled with more intensity than positive emotions (1996: 220). So-called 'flashbulb memories', of shocking, emotionally negative public events, are recalled best of all (1996: 222–3). It is also the case that recall of emotionally arousing events are affected by people's mood state, in that feelings of sadness sharpen the recall of negative emotions and shocking events (1996: 229). Remembrance stirs up old emotions and our current emotions stir up old memories.

This sort of research bodes ill for the capacity of victims to move on in peacetime from bad personal memories or to recall with accuracy what their actual feelings were in the conflict. On the other hand, sociologists' understanding of social memory proffers more optimism for peace processes. The realization that societies remember as much as individuals has received renewed attention (see in particular Connerton, 1989; Misztal, 2003; Urry, 1996) as nostalgic notions of golden ages dominate collective memory in response to the contemporary feeling that societies nowadays seem to be more conflict-ridden, violent, vulnerable and subject to risk. People in the 'golden ages' themselves tended to look back to even earlier times, making the past seem a moving mirage of nostalgia, loss and regret (on nostalgia, see Davis, 1979). Sociologists have long recognized the power of collective memory, but the new term 'social memory' now dominates the field. There is a good reason for this change in nomenclature. Collective memories are understood as group memories, shared by a community, that help to bind that community together. Nations have collective memories as part of their narrative of nationhood; so can ethnic groups. Collective memories are thus shared images and representations of the past that assist in constructing social solidarity. Social memory as a term includes these dimensions, but it also incorporates the claim that individual remembrance or personal memory is itself social. Personal memory is clearly not collective but it is still social.

There are several reasons why memory is social (taken from J. D. Brewer, 2006: 215):

- People have personal and collective memories at the same time, the latter being those representations that are commonly shared by all
- Personal memories exist in relation to the social processes that occasion and shape them, such as language, nationalism, cultural and political symbols and the like
- Individual remembering takes place in a social context and memories can be occasioned by the context in which people live
- Remembering serves social purposes at the personal and public levels, being sociologically functional for individuals and societies
- Memories can affect the social behaviour of people and groups
- Memories supply individual and social sense-making processes, giving ways of understanding and comprehending the world and a set of values and beliefs about the world
- Memories help in the construction of collective identities and boundaries, whether these are national, cultural, ethnic, religious or otherwise
- Social processes like culture, nationhood and ethnicity are in part constituted by memory
- Memory is constructed by various social practices that encourage or discourage the remembrance and commemoration of particular things
- Forgetting is as social as remembrance and the denial or recasting of particular memories serves social purposes
- Memories are selective and therefore always open to change and can be affected by social change and changes which reinforce certain memories or encourage collective amnesia.

Social memory is more than just the social benefits or social aspects of personal memory, and social memory does not just work through people's personal memory as a set of consequences at the societal level deriving from individual remembrances. Social memory is all of these things, but it is also a set of specific public remembrances that are manipulated and constructed by various social practices and 'technologies of memory' (a term used by Sturken, 1997, and adapted to Ireland by Corcoran, 2000; on technologies of memory generally, see van House and Churchill, 2008). Various symbolic practices (emblems, dress codes, murals, photographs), cultural artefacts (parades, commemorations, memorial holidays, exhibitions), material objects (memorials, monuments, texts) and cultural and ideological enterprises (history books, school history curriculum, popular culture, the media, museums) furnish resources for the construction and reconstruction of selective versions of the past. Collins's (2004) discussion of 'interaction rituals' in sociology adds authority to these arguments. The emotions aroused in memory are encoded in symbols, objects and cultural artefacts and their repetition and reproduction helps in making short-term emotion-arousing memories continue into the long term, so that breaking the connection between short- and long-term memory can be facilitated by changing the symbols that encode them. This emphasis on technologies of memory production reinforces the view of memory as a social construction (see Sturken, 2008: 74–5).

'Facts' about the past are thus never neutral, for 'memories' are as much *interpretations* as they are *recollections* of the past. Arguments about how many Serbs were killed in Croatian concentration camps in the Second World War, for example, are not about the facts of the past, but how these events are interpreted in the present day and reconstructed as memories by various technologies of memory for contemporary purposes. It is not a question, as Hamber (1998a: 3) claims with respect to Northern Ireland, 'of setting up a process of remembering so that the past can be *properly* understood', since what the past 'means' is re-negotiated and re-evaluated in the present. Power relations affect these sorts of negotiations. Victors rather than the vanquished write history and construct the way the past is supposed to be officially recalled, against which survives a hidden narrative of history from the perspective of the defeated, making 'their' past a story of resistance and resentment, survival and suppression, heroism and harassment. Cultural annihilation can result in the vanquished internalizing the 'official history', but where they retain cultural capital, the hidden history is alive. Thus, what the victors come to forget over time is held on to tenaciously by the defeated. The past is thus often a series of parallel or divergent stories.

Time enters into the negotiations over the meaning of the past, for memories compress time. Present-day circumstances affect how the past is interpreted, and events long ago can cry to the present as if they were here and now. Societies do not experience their past in a serial ordering of time but a concurrent one, in which the distance between past and present is compressed into a simultaneous experience. This makes the past an eternal present. Remembering is guided by present ways of understanding, so that the past becomes like a moving target as its meaning gets negotiated and renegotiated under the impulse of the present day (see Robinson, 1996: 214). As Misztal (2003: 82) put it, 'frames of meaning, or ways in which we view the past, are generated in the present . . . Thus they change following social major shifts that affect entire mnemonic communities.' However, the past is also a critique of the present world (Schwartz, 2000: 253), in which frames of meaning from the past are used to construct a group's map of their current social world. Connerton (1989: 2) thus pointed out that it is almost impossible to disentangle the past from the present because present factors tend to distort recollections of the past, while past factors tend to distort our experience of the present. This constant traffic between the present and the past ensures that history is never closed and finished (a point made by Lane, 2001: 178) and social memories are never stable.

It is for this reason that remembering and forgetting are part of the same process in social memory. This is meant in a sense other than that remembering is unreliable owing to the fading of memory imagery, as cognitive psychology shows (for a comparison between sociological and psychological approaches to forgetting, see Connerton, 2008 and Erdelyi, 2008). Societies' preoccupations of today have a direct bearing on what they remember, which people and events are forgotten, and what is suppressed from the official history. It can be politically expedient to forget (Connerton, 2008, has distinguished seven types of forgetting, although what he mostly refers to is the different functions of forgetting). Cultural sanctions can suppress certain memories, such as in post-Franco Spain, and legal force can prohibit their practice and enactment; Argentina, for example, imposed legal restrictions on the pursuit of war criminals after the fall of the Junta as if to forget and to close the book on the past (or at least certain people's culpability during it). And silence can pass over the recollection of the past, preventing it being talked about in public space, as happened in post-independence India to the thousands of female victims raped during the chaos of partition (see Butalia, 2000). These silences can be dangerous, creating hidden and voiceless victims (see Cohen, 2001), although Barclay (1996: 122) reminds us that some victims are silenced because of unwillingness in others to listen to or believe the horrors.

But some things can be forgotten because they are just psychologically uncomfortable to recall, while others are because they undercut present-day narratives. Few Loyalists in Northern Ireland know – or choose to recall – that King William's defeat of the Catholic King James in 1690 was done with the support and assistance of the Pope; the newly independent Irish Free State suppressed the memory of the Irish Catholics who served in the colonial police force or fought on the side of the British in two world wars. Post-1945 Communist Yugoslavia repressed the history of inter-ethnic rivalry and conflict leading up to and during the Second World War, such that its re-emergence in the post-Communist era appeared to come out of the void and it took the international community by surprise. Conversely, Rwandans forgot that ethnic distinctions were a very recent phenomenon associated with Belgian colonialism and that inter-ethnic rivalries were imported from the outside.

## Memory and peace

Despite the close connection between memory and communal violence (see J. D. Brewer, 2006; Ray 1999, 2000), social memory can be used as a peace strategy. Indeed, it is precisely because social memory is socially constructed, subject to manipulation and change and affected by social change that various social practices that occasion and shape memory can be devised to garner peace, if not also reconciliation. As Lane (2001: 190) observed, 'the work of memory is a step on the road to reconciliation. Memory is not reconciliation but it can lead to reconciliation.' Social memory can be reconstructed to become a peace strategy and to help the maintenance of the peace process by revisiting, and where appropriate reconstituting, the past for the purpose of peace. There are a number of dimensions to this:

- forgetting to remember that which is divisive or inconvenient to the peace agreement;
- correction of the distortions of the past that once fuelled divided memories;
- historical re-envisioning of the conflict itself so that the way it is remembered changes;
- recovery of memories, perhaps formerly denied or avoided, that illustrate unity or peaceable co-existence in the past, rather than enmity;
- developing new narratives of nationhood and symbolic structures that legitimize the new post-violence regime;
- developing new forms of commemoration that celebrate peace and cultural diversity, which point towards the future;
- developing a pluralist approach to memory to incorporate other groups' memories;
- continually remembering to forget what needs to be discarded socially and to recollect what needs to be remembered.

Some of these will be developed below, but a brief comment seems necessary on collective amnesia since it is the oddest of the above notions. Amnesia is meant as a conscious decision to forget that usually involves *remembering* to forget. This is not denial. Denial is refuting the memory; forgetting requires the continuous remembering of the memory in order to be reminded to appear to forget it publicly. This was neatly captured by a Rwandan government official who, having lost seventeen relatives in the genocide, was asked if it were better he should remember or forget (see www.npr.org/templates/story/story.php?storyid=1127966). He replied: 'we must remember in order to keep it from happening again but it is only by forgetting that we are able to go on'. In ancient Athens, there was an annual ritual in the temple in which worshippers were reminded to continue to forget a defeat in war (see Connerton, 2008: 61–2). In Mozambique, for example, after sixteen years of civil war ended in 1992, ordinary people have resisted remembering (see Cobban, 2006; Hayner, 2002), and amnesia has been part of the nation-building project in many post-violence societies in the past, such as the USA after the War of Independence (on which, see Lane, 2001: 176), post-Franco Spain and post-war West Germany (on which, see Frei, 2002). Misztal (2003: 148–9) notes how after the Second World War, in nations like France and Italy, after initial legal attempts to account for past wrongdoings by collaborators, 'myths were constructed to gloss over the extent and depth of collaboration with the Nazi regime', while in West Germany 'it was a political necessity to adopt silence about the crimes of the past'. Only several decades later have Spain and the re-unified Germany begun culturally to address tentatively their fascist pasts, long after the emotional heat has dissipated and the people directly involved have died. Collective amnesia, it seems, makes re-remembering possible a long time later.

Mandela was famous for saying, in South Africa, that people needed to forget the past (some of his speeches are recorded in Hamber, 1998a: 2–3), as was Thomas Jefferson after the American War of Independence. The motto of the signatories to the Declaration of Independence in 1776, for example, was 'novus ordo saeclorum' ('the new order of ages') and was used to emphasize the nation's break with the past (I take this observation from Lane, 2001: 176). Jefferson, who became the third President, wrote in one of his letters in 1816 that 'the dead have no rights: they are nothing and nothing cannot own something' (cited in Lane, 2001: 176). The events of one generation should not bind another by vengeful memories; national renewal requires forgetting. This is the paradox to which the Rwandan victim referred.

### *The roles memory plays in peace processes*

It is necessary to focus on some technologies of memory by which social memory can be recast as a peace strategy. We can begin by identifying the different roles which memory performs in post-conflict societies. There are four:

- *Memory as restoration for perpetrators/collaborators.* This may be achieved through acknowledgement of perpetrators' culpability through personal memory work with them. It might take the form of 'truth' commissions or other 'truth' recovery processes, restorative justice policies and ex-offender/collaborator programmes.
- *Memory as healing for victims.* This may be achieved through the therapeutic effects that follow from remembering traumatic events and builds on work in cognitive psychology about the healing effects of releasing autobiographical memory. It might take the form of storytelling and other collations of personal narratives of suffering, such as oral history projects, as well as trauma counselling.

- *Memory as reconciling for inter-personal relations.* This can be addressed by sharing each other's memories, coming to learn of each other's experiences and views of history and of the conflict. It might take the form of cross-community work on issues around identity, history and memory and other inter-community interaction programmes. The intended outcome would either be respect for others' memories and the development of a pluralist approach to memory or the development of an agreed consensus about the past.
- *Memory as social transformation.* This may be achieved through change in social memory at the societal level.

I want to raise in more detail the last two. The sociological literature on memory as a concept emphasizes its connection to social interaction. It is true that talking about and making sense of our past is a major source of the self (Giddens, 1990), but the social self is intersubjective and dependent on social relationships. Recounting our past is a pervasive part of social interaction and many conversations with others involve recounting the past we share with them (Fivush, Haden and Reese, 1996: 341). Joint remembering serves to furnish a sense of shared history and to cement the social bond between those doing the memory work. Degnen (2005: 733) calls this 'memory talk', and through the web of social relationships in which it occurs, shared senses of place, experience and solidarity can be forged. These webs of social relations can in some circumstances become communities of memory, such that what is remembered and forgotten in the memory talk is to a large extent shaped by the social relationships in which the remembering and forgetting are embedded.

While there is no direct translation, so that by changing social relationships the memory talk automatically adjusts with it, old forms of memory talk can be undermined by new power relations, new senses of identity and nationhood and by different social contexts. It was for this reason that Thomas Jefferson recommended that revolutions occur every nineteen years so that people could be fully liberated from the shackles of the past (as noted in Lane, 2001: 176). Perhaps no less dramatically, it is possible to imagine that, where peace accords successfully change the dynamics of social relations, especially in settings where there is relational closeness rather than relational distance, a social context is developed in which new memory work can be attempted. In talking about their parallel narratives of the past, erstwhile opponents can begin to readjust the nature of their inter-personal relationship, success in which establishes a new social environment for yet further changes to the memory talk embedded therein.

As Geraldine Smyth put it (2004: 110), 'the duty to remember can easily become a wheel of no release'. She went on to quote Ricoeur (2004a: 15) to the effect that memories can make it hard to forgive.

However, joint remembrances of non-violent social life in the post-conflict phase, or perhaps of a peaceful pre-conflict period, can further consolidate new inter-personal relationships. Progressively over time, joint remembrances can achieve either a growing measure of consensus on how the past is to be understood or an agreement to adopt a pluralistic attitude towards the past in which the competing accounts are allowed to co-exist without antagonism. Teegar and Vinitzky-Seroussi (2007) describe this happening in the post-apartheid South Africa where new multi-vocal commemorations are taking place in which different meanings of an event (such as the annual Blood River commemorations) are able to be expressed without wider disagreement; Vinitzky-Seroussi (2002: 47) claimed this was the case also with the Vietnam Veterans Memorial in the USA. Teegar and Vinitzky-Seroussi (2007) referred to the potential for 'controlled consensus' emerging in South Africa, where the form and content of commemorative objects (like museums, memorials and new national holidays) were carefully presented and managed for the purposes of coming to agreement over the past. Hamber (1998b: 61) believes it is possible in Northern Ireland to embark on a remembering process that at least produces versions of the 'truth' that are broadly acceptable to as many people as possible.

Putting this sociologically, because memories exist in an eternal present, in which the past and present are compressed in time and experienced simultaneously, new power relations, changed social relationships, new identities and national narratives and, frankly, plain tolerance in the changed circumstances of the day encourage reinterpretations and re-evaluations of the past. Conditioned by changes to present circumstances, memories of the past can be readjusted to support and consolidate the new social context. The meaning attached to events in the past, including the conflict itself, can be re-addressed by the technologies of memory that manufacture it, and new sites of memory production can be created to construct new memories or to change the meaning of the old ones. Anwar Sadat once said that peace involves the rewriting of history: that he was assassinated for signing a peace agreement with Israel highlights the point that re-remembrance has to occur in the context of changing social relations. Re-remembrance is in part dependent on improved inter-personal relations between formerly warring parties as a result of the peace process, but new social relations following the peace settlement are also a consequence of the work done to reformulate divided memories. When this occurs, memory is socially transformative and it is to this role that we now turn.

Psychological healing and inter-personal relationship building have direct social benefits but, if it is to be transformative, social memory needs to become an object of policy management in its own right and to be addressed through various social practices that assist in its reconstruction. Civil society, which we saw in chapter 3 is a key agent of social change and foundational to peace processes, can be mobilized to achieve these policy objectives, so that there is not a sole reliance on the new state. Indeed, some of the social practices are best dealt with by community processes rather than national or governmental strategies. Five strategies for the social transformation of memory seem appropriate.

*Atonement strategies.* Theologians might rail against the word 'atonement' but it is used in a sociological sense to describe reflexivity about the past, such as through the 'sorry day' in Australia, Guatemala's Day of the Dead (which is actually two days, 1–2 November) or Holocaust Day, which are earmarked as special Days of Atonement, Days of Pardon or Reflection; the development of public 'narratives of mourning' that help deal with the loss and grief (such as texts, images, photographs, exhibitions and story-telling that capture a society's cultural mourning); programmes to facilitate reflexivity amongst communities, institutions and organizations about the conflict; the provision of mechanisms for making public apologies, like formal 'truth' commissions; concerted campaigns to address the issue of forgiveness and redemption; the signing of covenants and participation in other forms of public declaration, such as marches, parades and rallies, designed for mass acts of atonement (a good example of which is the One Small Step Campaign in Northern Ireland, which urges people to sign a peace pledge, see www.onesmallstep.org); and the provision of special public sites of atonement, like parks and gardens, memorials and places of quiet, where people from all sides can come together for personal acts of atonement, which parallel the 'public spaces of forgiving' referred to in the last chapter. The 'peace trains' that used to trundle between Northern and Southern Ireland, or the 'peace buses' between New Delhi and Lahore, could be reused in the post-violence phase as 'atonement trips' or 'sorry sojourns', designed to get travellers to commit to new social memories. For example, Cyclists Pedalling for Peace, part of the One Small Step Campaign in Northern Ireland, involved 100 people from the Catholic and Protestant parts of West Belfast making a cycle journey of reconciliation together as a public act of atonement.

*Citizenship education programmes.* These involve civil society and the state developing education programmes that help people acquire the knowledge and learn the skills for tolerance (peace activists in Northern Ireland refer to this quaintly as 'the public practice of manners'), such as adult education programmes; teaching respect for tolerance, civic responsibility and cultural diversity in schools; the establishment of bridge-building forums in war-torn areas and the like. Post-conflict wish fulfilment does not have to re-fight the war, and popular culture could be reoriented to help establish the peace by the garnering of hope–anticipation and forgiveness–redemption.

*Re-remembering strategies.* These capture hidden memories that are now functional to peace and revisit the distorted memories of the past through various story-telling procedures, 'truth' recovery projects, changes to the history curriculum, to the content of history textbooks and to the mass media's cultural mediation of history in directions which help us to re-remember the past. They include public mechanisms to garner and support new frames of meaning and sense-making through re-remembering, such as memory workshops held by civil society groups, television and radio programmes, novels, films, the arts and the like. Public memories can be recast and reconstructed by means of historical re-envisioning of the conflict (in which, for example, it might be denuded of its ethnic origins, blamed on third parties – normally colonizers – or shown to have affected all groups equally rather than one victim group alone). There are even cases where memories have been publicly recovered (and people's personal memories now publicly acknowledged) when they pertain to a pre-conflict past or become convenient as part of the reconciliation of social divisions, as in the new public recognition of Tamil contributions to Sinhalese culture in Sri Lanka, or Irish Catholics who served in the British armed forces (on which, see N. Johnson, 2003; Rigney, 2008) or in the colonial Royal Irish Constabulary (on which see J. D. Brewer, 1990). This might also involve re-remembering that the ex-prisoners in Northern Ireland are not demons, even that on release (or perhaps even from the inside) some played a significant part in persuading colleagues to lay down their arms (on the positive role of ex-prisoners from all sides in Northern Ireland's peace process, see Shirlow and McEvoy, 2008).

*Re-memorializing strategies.* Examples are museums, exhibitions and memorials that celebrate peace, either through a focus on the pain of the past enmity, such as the several Holocaust museums, or by pointing towards a new shared future, such as the Robben Island museum (on which see Shearing and Kempa, 2004); the development of new symbols of commemoration, such as new flags, public rituals and national holidays; and new sites for memorializing, such as Centres for Remembrance or Reconciliation (buildings, places, heritage centres, even forests or parks devoted to peace). Ahmed Kathrada's comment on Robben Island museum, as a former inmate of the prison, sums up the point of re-memorialization: 'While we will not forget the brutality of apartheid, we will not want Robben Island to be a monument of our hardship and suffering. We would want it to be a triumph of the human spirit against the forces of evil; a triumph of wisdom and largeness of spirit against small minds and pettiness' (quoted in Shearing and Kempa, 2004: 66). Re-memorialization can involve making official the many hitherto 'unofficial' community-based memorials and refurbishing and smartening them up. The commodification of the former conflict – through films, novels, poetry, art, exhibitions, tourism, heritage centres, museums and the like – re-memorializes the events by packaging them for consumption either one-step-removed from the real events or in fantasy form, both of which tend to reduce the emotional intensity of the past. This commodification allows people to perceive how the conflict was experienced by others, perhaps for the first time, and can be the initial step towards the critical interrogation of their own memories and the development of tolerance (see Davis, 1979, for analysis of how people are said to reflect critically on their feelings of nostalgia, and Strangleman, 2004, for an application of Davis's work to railwaymen).

*Forgetting strategies*. Here conscious decisions are made to exclude from the public sphere socially dysfunctional memory talk – what Paris calls 'hate speech' (2004: 196–9). Information that is encoded in long-term memory will still be available but it is no longer made accessible in the public sphere (on the distinction between memory availability and accessibility, see Singer and Conway, 2008: 280–1). Cultural, political and legal constraints could be imposed on those who want to exploit the normally open access to the public sphere to engage in memory talk that is destabilizing or threatening to the peace agreement (this can include some victim groups that use their victimhood to undermine peace). However, the value of amnesia depends on what is being forgotten and why; this is its paradox referred to earlier. Forgetting can be problematic when it leaves hidden suffering and voiceless, unrecognized victims. Victim experiences need to be addressed at a social policy level even when forgetting strategies are adopted, so as to avoid hidden victimhood. There are some things, indeed, that ought *not* to be forgotten, since they serve as a lesson for the future about what global society should never let happen again. However, forgetting strategies need to be deployed in order to let go of the enmity and bitterness surrounding divided histories, old group loyalties and identities, and relational distance. As Ahmed Kathrada said (cited in Shearing and Kempa, 2004: 66), South Africans should not forget apartheid but it should be remembered selectively for ways that facilitate consensus over their shared future.

These strategies of social memory transformation require direction through public policy, civil society engagement and media participation, and the case study of Northern Ireland addressed at the end of this chapter demonstrates how some of these strategies can be implemented in practice. However, in order to be successful, culturally organized re-remembering and forgetting also needs new technologies of memory, or for existing technologies to be redeployed for different ideological goals. I have in mind particularly the positive contribution of the media in enhancing and supporting the encouragement of new identities, new patterns of social relationships and power relations as the context within which social memory works. As important producers of social memory, television, for example, 'is not a vessel in which people's memories passively reside but a technology that selects and organises images, sounds, voices, landscapes, text, colours and motion into new patterns' (Corcoran, 2000: 28). Memories are produced through the media, disseminated and shared collectively, and can be given new meaning (on memory and the media, see Sturken, 2008). A partisan media, therefore, is very problematic for peace processes; a media wedded to old shibboleths, unreconstructed identities and exclusive ethnic nationalism, still supportive of the former regime, and with a narrow market restricted to one grouping can resist the transformation of social memory to very damaging effect.

## 'Truth' recovery

These strategies of memory transformation are likely to be more effective in conjunction with public policies that address 'truth' recovery and victimization, and it is to these concerns we now turn. Hayner (2002) has pointed to the common elements of 'truth' commissions: they focus on the past (and in ways that try to separate it from its eternal present); they aim to provide a comprehensive picture of human rights abuses; they exist for a limited period (ending in publication of a report, which tends to close official interest in 'truth' recovery); and they have (varying) authority to access information. To which we might add that they 'professionalize' the process and separate it from communal 'truth' recovery. Nonetheless, Ray (1999) and Wilson (2001: 17–18) argue that 'truth' recovery is a useful alternative to the legal system and can help the legitimation crisis of weak states. However, a lot of the demand for 'truth' recovery comes from victims' groups who want an opportunity for their suffering to be publicly acknowledged, to discover those responsible for their pain and to expose the general atrocities of the perpetrators. One might use the common alliteration of the three 'R's to understand this: victims approach 'truth' recovery procedures from the point of recognition (of their victimhood), responsibility (discovering who is to blame) and retribution (exposing the perpetrators). Whether or not we add a fourth 'R' to the alliteration – reconciliation – depends upon whether the victimhood experience becomes psychologically healing and sociologically functional. I will explain later what is meant by socially functional public victimhood.

Recognition, responsibility and retribution are motivations that easily resonate with the experience of victimhood. The three – or four – 'Rs', however, are difficult to achieve, or at least, to do so in ways that meet the competing demands placed on 'truth' recovery by different sections in post-violence society. There is a general problem with 'truth' recovery, for the idea of 'truth' is problematic (see Rotberg and Thompson, 2000). Common sense renders the idea of 'truth' as objective, unaffected by partisan standpoints (for a history of the idea of 'truth', see Shapin, 1994), so that victims think it is easy to find out what happened and who was responsible, and believe that these 'facts' about the past represent the one 'true' account. They tend not to accept that 'truth' is selective and interpreted from one standpoint (see Cohen, 2001: 227ff. for different kinds of 'truth' and their associated speech codes). As identified earlier, peace processes therefore need to manage two problems: finding the balance between the need to know what happened in the past and moving forward, and encouraging victims to see the 'truth' from someone else's standpoint. This kind of balance allows victims to know about the past in such a way as to avoid keeping them locked there. However, this balance requires modification of the way victims common-sensically understand the idea of 'truth'.

## Why 'truth' is important

'Truth' commissions have been used for a long time (for summaries of many examples, see Hayner, 1994, 2002), particularly in Latin America – seventeen countries established them in the twenty years up to 2000 (Wilson, 2001: xviii) – and the universalization of South Africa's Truth and Reconciliation Commission has made the demand for one part of the rhetoric of several peace negotiations since. It is easy to see why. There are at least four reasons that make 'truth' important.

- recognition of victimhood via 'truth' recovery, particularly of unacknowledged suffering, is therapeutic for victims;
- assigning responsibility for incidents can be healing for victims and their relatives, as well as restorative for perpetrators;
- 'truth' recovery is a way of managing the emotional dynamics of post-violence adjustments and of dealing with the problem of memory;
- 'truth' recovery offers procedures for making 'shame apologies'.

Brendon Hamber (2001) argues that 'truth' is healing (see also Tombs, 2005: 3). The South African Truth and Reconciliation Commission saw its deliberations as achieving 'reconciliation through truth' (Wilson, 2001: 6; the Commission's official website is: www.doj.gov.za/trc/index.html).

For my purposes here, however, I want to focus on the negative case in order to illustrate that 'truth' recovery is not a simple panacea. There have been many different complaints made about the specific 'truth' recovery processes deployed in the past, but these essentially break down into three sorts of problem, which we can briefly look at in turn:

- those around how the claims to 'truth' are received in the recovery process;
- concern around the partiality of the truths disclosed by the process;
- and anxieties over the selective use to which truths are put.

What matters for the effectiveness of 'truth' recovery is how the claims to 'truth' are received. They have to be heard by participants as accurate descriptions of events, despite no such thing being possible. The South African Truth and Reconciliation Commission set up an investigation unit to test the veracity of 'truth' claims – a huge task when it is recalled that it received 20,000 statements – only to discover that most things could not be proved unless the perpetrator claimed responsibility – as most did not. The readiness to hear what is disclosed as somehow 'true' is diminished when what is disclosed does not fit with what the victim or relatives expected or wanted. Uncomfortable truths are often explained away as inadequate or, indeed, as untrue, especially if the 'truth' recovery process that disclosed it lacks community legitimacy. Judicial or governmental enquiries as specific 'truth' recovery procedures often lack legitimacy because of poor levels of local involvement. Afrikaners saw the South African Truth and Reconciliation Commission as a witch hunt against them and mostly refused to participate. Only one senior member of the apartheid security forces sought amnesty; oddly enough, the individual concerned, Eugene de Kock, despite disclosing horrible crimes, was loudly applauded when he did so by Black people present in the court at the time. This tendency to see 'truth' as what you believe or authorize it to be is reflected in a survey of 3,700 South African respondents on the success of the South African Truth and Reconciliation Commission (Gibson, 2004). In a remarkable example of circular argument, he found that those who accept the 'truth' about the country's apartheid past have more 'reconciled' racial attitudes, which is like saying that 'truth' contributes to reconciliation when it tells you what you want to hear about apartheid. If it is to serve its purposes, in other words, 'truth' has to be perceived as plausible; if not, it is difficult to see what purpose it serves (for varying positions on the relationship between 'truth' recovery and reconciliation, see the debate between Borneman, 2002, and Sampson, 2003).

Even where shame apologies are made as part of 'truth' recovery, by which ex-combatants acknowledge culpability, apologies have to be heard by the former enemy to be authentic, the key to which, according to the restorative justice paradigm, is hearing the shame–guilt as genuine. In the last chapter I discussed some of the problems around shame–guilt as emotions, and some of the difficulties in eliciting shame apologies; all that needs to be repeated here is that some perpetrators have difficulties in saying precisely what victims want, and victims in accepting what is actually said. Quite often, however, the response of the military and members of government paramilitary forces is to deny alleged evidence rather than own up. Some of the Black translators used by the South African Truth and Reconciliation Commission who had themselves been political prisoners knew that what they were transcribing was lies, and Steve Biko's family – Biko being one of the most celebrated victims of apartheid oppression – later described the 'truth' recovery process in South Africa as imperfect (quoted in the *Scotsman*, 21 May 2006). Ten years on from the establishment of the Commission, a group of survivors known as Khulumani (with membership of 48,000) took out an unsuccessful class action in New York against corporate backers of apartheid in an attempt to get justice and Tutu was forced to admit that the Commission dealt with 'truth' only in a symbolic way (quoted in the *Irish Times*, 15 April 2006). Walaza (2003) saw South Africa's problem as both partial truths and contradictory versions of the same 'truth', to an extent that there was no 'true reconciliation' (see also Asmal, 2000; Jeffrey, 1999; for more optimistic analyses, see Burton, 1998; Gibson, 2004; Leman-Langlois and Shearing, 2003; Villa-Vicencio and Vervoerd, 2000).

The partial nature of the truths disclosed is both cause and effect of the problems around how 'truth' claims are received. Some people can simply refuse to participate in the recovery process, ensuring a one-sided or selective recovery of 'truth'. There can be vested interests trying to limit what is disclosed. 'Truth' recovery processes have sometimes been designed by states, governments or political groups to disguise their own culpability or partisanly expose that of their opponents. This is most likely to happen in post-violence settings where the former regime retains some capacity to dictate the disclosure of its activities and thus in those peace accords where there has not been an outright winner. For example, in Guatemala's case, the Recovery of Historical Memory project was told by the government that it could not individualize responsibility and its recommendations would not have any legal implications (see Wilson, 1998: 184–5), and it was only some years later, in February 2008, that the new President of Guatemala opened up the files of the military that earlier post-conflict regimes had decided to keep closed.

The terms of reference of the 'truth' recovery process can sometimes be under the control of powerful groups who limit the range of activities to be addressed. The South African Commission focused on 'gross violations of human rights' that took place between March 1960 and

May 1994. It had the widest remit of any commission to date, being able to investigate: the killing, abduction or severe ill-treatment of any person; and any attempt, conspiracy, incitement, instigation, command or procurement to commit an act referred to above (see Wilson, 2001: 34). This was impressive enough but it addressed actual incidents and thus excluded what we might call the 'structural violence' of the apartheid regime itself, the 'mundane bureaucratic enforcement of apartheid' (Wilson, 2001: 34) and its institutional racism. It has been noted, for example, that despite women bearing the brunt of the oppression, through forced removals, the pass laws, 'domestic' violence and broken families, they were not recognized as a special category of victim beyond specific incidents that involved them. Given the gendered nature of victimhood, referred to in chapter 4, women tend to be over-represented as witnesses before most 'truth' commissions, which compounds the failure to recognize the special victim status of women.

Other 'truth' commissions have been less generous in handling memory and 'truth' recovery. The Chilean Commission, for example, focused only on the disappearances and not on Chilean human rights abuses, although the El Salvadorian commission had a very broad mandate to address 'serious acts of violence' (for a comparison of the two, see Ensalaco, 1994). The United Nations' Commission on the Truth for El Salvador took the decision to name over forty military officers and eleven members of the main anti-government guerrilla group who were responsible for ordering, carrying out and covering up abuses (see Hayner, 2002: 38), but within twenty-four hours of publication of the report the government introduced a blanket amnesty; this included amnesty for the government minister whom the report identified as ordering the murder of Fr Ignacio Ellacuria, a Jesuit liberation-theology priest (on whom see Burke, 2001). The same minister appeared on national television, flanked by chiefs from the El Salvadorian military, and denounced the report as untrue and unfair; he was 'retired' three months later with full pension and praised laudably by the President. The Northern Irish Victims Commission, not strictly a 'truth' recovery process but which was set up as part of the peace accord, published a report entitled *We Will Remember Them* (see K. Bloomfield, 1998a), which completely excluded victims of state violence (for an account from the Chair of the Commission, see Bloomfield, 1998b).

One response to control on the 'truth' recovery process from above is to have community-based processes. However, these are mostly localized and focus on 'truth' recovery in a particular neighbourhood or group, and thus tend to be unapologetically one-sided. One notable exception was the Recovery of Historical Memory Project (1999; see also Cabrera, 1998; Hayes and Tombs, 2001; Kaur, 2003). This was set up by the grassroots and civil society in Guatemala under the aegis of the Catholic Church as a popular response to the weakness of the UN's commission established under the 1994 Oslo Peace Accord, known as the Commission for Historical Clarification (although the Report of the 'official' Commission was hard-hitting enough – see Kaur, 2003: 38). The Project's Report was launched in 1998 to great controversy – the co-ordinator of the project, Bishop Juan Gerardi, was assassinated two days later (for details, see Wright, 2001). The project addressed country-wide cases of murder and managed to be popularly acclaimed by local communities, demonstrating the viability of democratic and grassroots approaches to 'truth' recovery; but even so, it lacked legal powers to compel participation. Information collected could not be used in pros-ecutions, and it lacked resources; only minor ranks in the military gave evidence and did so in ways that protected their anonymity (Levy, 2001: 109). The paradox is that the more local the 'truth' recovery process is, the greater is its legitimacy and the more limited its effect.

If 'truth' recovery mostly discloses only partial truths, it is hardly surprising that its disclosures can be selectively used. Indeed, people often have pre-determined preferences in the way they intend to use so-called 'truths', which limit their capacity to receive as genuine what-ever the recovery process reveals. 'Truth' may merely be a bludgeon with which to beat the other side, to criticize their position as elected representatives or dispute their place in new political institutions. 'Truth' in these settings may lead to revenge killings rather than emotional recovery. This is especially likely to occur under three con-ditions: where victimhood is widely dispersed throughout the society so that most people can claim status as victim and perpetrator at the same time; where moral notions of culpability are confused by some ex-combatants being kidnapped and forced into that role; and where the peace accord is fragile so that 'truth' recovery is used intentionally to oppose a settlement.

With respect to the first condition, as we saw in chapter 5, victim-hood in Rwanda, for example, is complicated by the large number of revenge attacks on Hutus by Tutsi soldiers once Hutu-led killings were stopped, so that not only do the Hutus fear revenge for the genocide of Tutsis, Tutsis live in fear of reprisals for the revenge they inflicted. Multiple victimhood like this leads to no easy truth and reconciliation process, since the moral obligation to reveal the 'truth' is everyone's and the potentially damaging political consequences of disclosing it are experienced by all – which may explain why Rwanda and Northern Ireland, where victimhood is also widely dispersed, have avoided a formal 'truth' recovery process. Multiple victimhood increases the temptation to deny the culpability by one's own group and to impose a hierarchy of victim experiences in which one's own group suffered the worse. Collective memory may well try to present one group as the 'real' victim and as morally superior to another. Where victimhood is multiple, the one-sidedness of 'truth' recovery is intensified.

'Truth' recovery is also more problematic, and its purposes morally ambiguous, when combatant roles were forced on some perpetrators. In Sierra Leone, for example, child soldiers were commonly abducted and kept 'loyal' by making them addicted to drugs, and women were kidnapped and used as sex slaves and forced to commit some of the worst atrocities against other women. Culpability needs to be handled differently when such people come before 'truth' recovery processes. In Sierra Leone's case, for example, the process of 'truth' recovery was managed in such a way as to allow special status to women perpetrators-*cum*-victims, giving them ample opportunity to tell their stories without threat of shame. The risk of legal prosecution was removed by the government granting 'an absolute and free pardon and reprieve'. However, the one-sidedness of this absolution did not endear the 'truth' recovery process to their victims – some of whom had hands and limbs chopped off by the very child and women soldiers given free pardon. We have already seen in chapter 4 that, with regard to the ambiguous culpability of child soldiers in Sierra Leone, it was agreed that child soldiers should not be forced to give public testimony before the Commission, that they not be required to seek forgiveness or be publicly shamed and humiliated, and that the local press not sensationalize their role in the war. The final condition is self-explanatory: 'truth' recovery can be used to motivate 'spoiler violence' in those states sufficiently weak to prevent war lords mounting resistance to the peace agreement. The spoiler violence is used either to prevent any form of 'truth' recovery or to limit the participation by some groups in order to distort the reliability of the disclosures.

---

## Vignette: Sierra Leone's truth and reconciliation commission

The civil war in Sierra Leone was notorious for the forced involvement of child soldiers, the level of gendered atrocities and its barbarous punishments. By 1996, five years after the violence began, the Abidja Peace Agreement was signed and quickly abandoned. In 1999, the Lomé Accord was agreed between the government and the main rebel group (which had been responsible for well over half the violations), setting up a truth and reconciliation commission under the chair of Bishop Humper, although on-going violence delayed it until 2003; it reported in 2004 (see www.trcsierraleone.org/drwebsite/publish/index.shtml). 'Truth' recovery was enthusiastically encouraged by civil society groups, utilizing the international discourse of 'truth', reconciliation and memory, linking with international peacemaking and humanitarian networks. UNICEF and

UNIFEM acted as advisors in view of the many child and female victims (there was a separate children's version of the Report, witness videos and a schools programme to disseminate the process widely). The initiative was funded by the UN, EU and a wealth of Western governments. Local civil society groups championing the idea included the Campaign for Good Governance, the National Forum for Human Rights and the Inter-Religious Council.

The terms of reference of the Commission were expansive: to examine human rights violations and abuses *related to the armed conflict* as defined in international humanitarian law (it was barred from commenting on structural violence inherent in the organiza- tion of Sierra Leone society); to create an accurate historical record of the conflict; to accord human dignity to victims; and to facilitate a constructive interchange between victims and perpetrators. While the first two drew heavily on international discourses around memory and human rights, the latter was conditioned by local reli- gious rhetoric. Humper, like Tutu in South Africa, gave the process a quasi-sacred tone, telling victims at the opening launch that they should expect to forgive and perpetrators to confess, express remorse and receive forgiveness (cited in *Religion and Ethics Newsweekly*, 10 January 2003). The commission conducted its activities within the midst of localized violence. Of the country's 149 districts, 9 were not visited by commissioners due to the security situation. Even so, it heard evidence of 40,242 'human rights violations and abuses' from 14,995 victims (see the Report's Statistical Appendix 1: 12–13). Women and child victims were given special attention, including child ex-combatants, despite the evidence that male victims outnum- bered female ones by 3:1. Women tended to report rape and sexual slavery, men forced recruitment, forced labour and disablement of limbs. Half of males reporting forced recruitment were under four- teen years of age, 25 per cent under eleven. A quarter of the rape victims were under thirteen years of age (Statistical Appendix 1: 15).

The Revolutionary United Front insisted on blanket amnesty before it would agree to the Lomé Accord. The government reluc- tantly consented, against Western opinion. However, it restricted this to offences committed between the two peace agreements (1996–9) and the Special Court of Sierra Leone was established at the same time to pursue, in parallel, prosecutions of the main perpetra- tors. The court agreed to give amnesty to child soldiers – to universal acclaim – but has been slow in bringing the chief organizers to trial; former President Charles Taylor, who conducted a vicious cam- paign of government-led spoiler violence, only appeared before it in 2008, with the proceedings (restricted and still on-going at the time of writing) quickly adjourned until 2009. Sierra Leone's transitional justice mechanisms thus divide between retribution and reconciliation, revenge and restoration. The Truth and Reconciliation Commission and the Special Court sit uneasily together. Information is not shared between them (Dougherty, 2004: 50) and their reconstruction of the national narrative potentially differs as they struggle over 'truth' recovery and the management of social memory (Martin Shaw, 2007: 183ff.).

The truth commission jealously protects what it sees as its specialism in reconciliation via 'truth' recovery. 'The truth will be known', it declared in its Report, 'it will be complete and publicly exposed'. Two ethnographic studies of the 'truth' recovery process in local districts, however, are disbelieving (Kelsall, 2005; R. Shaw, 2005). R. Shaw (2005) described selective engagement with the Commission. Whole communities determined not to give evidence in order to protect the child ex-combatants of neighbours; people concealed knowledge or felt intimidated by reprisals and did not appear. Kelsall was blunter: people told lies (2005: 361ff.). Shaw's interviewees talked of being caught between retribution and reconciliation, and found some sort of peace in the idea that God should deal with such matters, not them or the Commission. Some went as far as to say that the truth commission was socially destructive and what matters is not perpetrators' past behaviour but how they conduct themselves in the present. This illustrates the friction over memory in local spaces she later emphasized (R. Shaw, 2007). This ambiguity over the purposes of 'truth' recovery is reproduced in the government, newly elected in 2007, which contains some cabinet ministers opposed to the President's reform agenda and critical of the Commission's recommendations for reparations to victims (which began in 2008). It may or may not be relevant here that Sierra Leone remains riddled with corruption and has discovered government officials linked to drug trafficking and siphoning aid.

With such a weak economy – Sierra Leone is one of the world's poorest countries – ordinary people are also more focused on material issues than symbolic ones like 'truth'. It is worth noting further that Sierra Leone's peace process has so far been largely successful and some people express the views of ordinary Mozambiqueans that the past should be let go (R. Shaw, 2007). Two elections have been fought peacefully since Lomé, the UN peacekeepers were withdrawn in 2008, and thousands of child ex-combatants have, according to Dougherty (2004: 50), been successfully reintegrated into society. Sierra Leone benefitted from cultural continuity as traditional forms of authority survived the war. In her ethnography, R. Shaw (2005) observed a 'cooling the heart' ceremony in rural areas for child soldiers (similar to those in Northern Uganda referred to in chapter 5), in which local communities tried to undo the work of the combatant groups by using traditional forms of healing, restoration of relationships through ceremonies of confession, forgiveness and prayer, and traditional cleansing practices. Thus Dougherty (2004) argued that, while reconciliation via 'truth recovery' was promulgated most vigorously by civil society groups in Sierra Leone, it has had little impact on the rest of society, especially in rural areas, where traditional forms of restorative justice were employed in preference.

On the basis of the foregoing arguments it is reasonable to claim that 'truth' recovery works best, if at all, as part of a successful settlement that has already stopped the killing, not as a mechanism itself to end the violence. This claim is not intended to belittle 'truth' recovery – it questions its status as universal panacea. In some cases where 'truth' recovery has been used, 'truth' itself becomes the major casualty as partial, selective and one-sided truths are disclosed. The management of disclosure (such as by limiting the damage through non-attendance, imposing procedural and legal restrictions, and downright deceit by witnesses) can take precedence over the moral obligation to victims and society's need for reconciliation. Victims can find a kind of closure in the proceedings but more are left bereft at the floppy gesture towards 'truth' and the failure to receive justice. But if not by means of 'truth' recovery, what is the best way to manage the experience of victimhood?

## Victimhood

In previous chapters I have described the ontological costs of peace for victims. What makes their adjustment worse is that victimhood is highly politicized, for it encapsulates the moral virtues of the groups involved in the conflict and addresses their separate claims to moral justification for the war. What victimhood is and who gets to define it are thus key questions in peace processes.

These questions turn victimhood into a public process. There are three dimensions to its publicness. First, communal violence is very public behaviour; people are normally not victims as a result of their private behaviour but as a result of the immense public investment in their attributes of group identity. People are killed or injured for their group membership according to how this is understood and displayed in public (by where they live, their 'race' and skin colour, the cultural symbols they wear, how they talk, religious practices and so on; and the fact that these are stereotypical cues means that sometimes the 'wrong' people can be killed or injured).

Second, people are mostly killed or injured in highly dramatic public events or in events that quickly become public by their cultural resonances. While this is not always the case, targeted assassinations of single people in private are normally of high-profile public figures or of people whose death is designed for its public effect because of the cultural symbolism associated with this category of victim. Private deaths and injury are public events in communal violence. The publicness of victimhood, therefore, is achieved either by the kind of harm inflicted or the type of person attacked.

Third, while victims' relatives and survivors do enormous amounts of grieving and suffering in the private sphere of family and home, which we can call 'private victimhood', when these victim experiences are taken into the public sphere we have 'public victimhood'. Victims/survivors make their experience public when, for example, they complain to the press and politicians or on television that the death of their loved one or their own injuries seem forgotten by the rest of society and are not marked in a public way. Public campaigns by mothers of the disappeared, for example, the parading done by ex-service associations, or campaigns by victims/survivors for justice through the courts continue their victimhood as public performance. When victims/survivors come together unofficially to mark the anniversary of an incident or establish a local memorial, victimhood is again made public; and this is done by the state when commemorations or monuments are official and marked by public commemoration rituals. The state also makes victimhood public when it designs public policies to address the needs and interests of victims/survivors. There is invariably also public discourse on victimhood utilized by the churches, politicians and civil society groups which lay claim to speak about or on behalf of victims in the public sphere.

Perhaps the most obvious practice for performing public victimhood is mobilization by victims' groups. Such groups tend to dominate the debate about victimhood and to affect our perception of who the victims are and what experiences they suffered. Some victims' groups almost constitute themselves as 'professional victims' (a term borrowed from M. Smyth, 2003), at the centre-stage of the debate about the harm caused by the conflict and attributing to themselves a power of veto when it comes to discussion of the future. An important feature of public victimhood, therefore, is contestation by victims' groups over who has the right to the status of victim.

In an important sense, everyone who has lived amidst communal conflict is a victim of different degrees of harm. Some conflicts involve multiple victimhood, where the lines of responsibility are blurred because some social groups were perpetrators and victims at the same time. This is why the discussion of victims in transitional societies by Elster (2004: 166–87) is naïve. It assumes no moral ambiguity around victimhood by portraying victims as passive recipients of harm from others rather than as also simultaneously inflicting it. While Elster thus categorizes types of harm (2004: 168ff.) in order to get away from the moral complexity of distinguishing kinds of victim/survivor, Amstutz (2004) defines victims as 'primary' (direct), 'secondary' (bystander-indirect) and 'tertiary' (the collectivity as a whole), a typology he uses to argue that primary victims do not have the monopoly on suffering nor the sole voice when it comes to forgiveness.

While some victims/survivors recognize that everyone shares the experience of victimhood in different ways, others operate a hierarchy of suffering and attach to themselves and their kind a special victimhood. Levels of harm can be differentiated medically and victimhood is not equal (as emphasized by M. Smyth, 1998: 34, 38; see also Morrissey and Smyth, 2002), but hierarchies of suffering are often employed politically to place the experience of one's own group at the apex. This is perhaps the most distasteful feature of public victimhood for it can involve some victims' groups decrying the suffering and harm of others; this is made worse morally when the harm others experienced was done in the name of, or on behalf of, those who now decry it.

There is one further negative feature of public victimhood as practised by victim groups, for there are individuals with profound feelings of harm and suffering who are not in victims' groups, who thus get ignored inasmuch as victims' groups attribute to themselves the moral right to articulate victims'/survivors' interests. Victimhood is a more general experience than victims' groups imply and needs to become recognized as a moral claim everyone can reasonably invoke.

However, victims' groups serve several functions, not all of which are negative for the peace process. In contexts where victims suffered human rights abuses, victims' groups double up as human rights groups, notably many indigenous Indian victims' groups in Latin America. Victim groups provide support structures, from counselling through to shared story-telling. They can act as campaigners on behalf of victims, mobilizing for material resources and public attention. Many voluntary groups, charities and social movements in civil society similarly work in this positive way for their client groups. The main problem arises when victims' groups act as forms of political mobilization, either as political alternatives to conventional groups, or more likely, as surrogates on behalf of political parties. Victims' groups that ally themselves with anti-peace groups and political parties opposed to the deal use their suffering as a brake on the negotiated settlement by accusations that their suffering is being neglected or undervalued. Particular commemorations get used as political platforms to resist the negotiated peace settlement or to abuse politically erstwhile colleagues now making the new institutions work. It is hard to respond to such claims because of their moral tenor; victims/survivors have special status in a society where the damage caused is so unnatural, and they can all too readily render criticism of their antics as dishonouring the dead. Victimhood can thus remain politically divisive in peace processes. Equality of victimhood is denied, so that victimhood is not a uniting experience amongst people who share the same emotional and physical suffering. Victim groups in these circumstances thus tend to cohere around the lines of division, easily reproducing the old dysfunctional passions.

What makes victimhood so problematic for peace processes is that even though victimhood is politicized and morally manipulated, post-violence societies cannot afford to neglect victims. Finding a pathway to psychological healing for the individual should form part of all post-violence adjustments. However, victimhood is more than a psychological state; it is also a sociological process. That is to say, victimhood has ramifications at the level of society. It can distort society by introducing what has been called 'bad civil society' (Chambers and Kopstein, 2001), that is, voluntary and community groups whose practice and effects destabilize the social structure, perpetuate ancient hatreds and reproduce the conflict. Victimhood at the public level can keep vivid the emotional dynamics associated with the former conflict, inhibiting the transformation from emotion/identity politics to democratic/class politics. A post-violence society thus needs to find pathways to healing for the society as well as for the individual.

### Sociologically functional public victimhood

Sociologically functional public victimhood requires, first, a change in social attitude towards victimhood that releases society from the 'cult of the dead' (Ignatieff, 1998); and, second, the introduction of social policies designed carefully to address the separate needs of individual victims and society as a whole.

It seems almost impossible sociologically to evade the living weight of the dead. Societies are made up of the dead as well as the living, (and the yet unborn) and tradition, such a central concept in sociology, involves the past being continually reproduced. Abraham Lincoln summed up the impact of the slain of the American Civil War in his speech at the dedication of the cemetery at Gettysburg on 19 November 1863, when he said that the living are obliged to honour the dead. This is unimpeachable as a moral principle. Honouring the sacrifice of the dead/survivors, however, does not involve them becoming such a weight that they preclude the living from moving on. The needs of victims/survivors must be managed through public policy but, at the societal level, a redirection of society's public gaze seems appropriate, with sights set determinedly on the future not the past. Looking forward not backwards is not just something that victims/survivors themselves have to do; it is society's responsibility too. Cultural and media critiques of public victimhood, via civil society, the churches and political parties, for example, should try to assist society in moving on from the dead weight of the slaughtered by showing how the cult of the dead harbours conflict not peace. Post-violence societies need to look at the future through the eyes of their children not their ancestors, and they should not be made prisoner of victims'/survivors' unforgivingness. Victims should be made as accountable for the future as the rest of society.

This does not mean individual victims/survivors should be silenced or hidden, or that victims' groups should not be supported by public policies and money, but neither should victims' groups become like parasites feeding off the dead and injured. Victims' groups can wittingly keep the cult of the dead alive. Michael Gallagher, twice traumatized in Northern Ireland's violence by the murder of close relatives, the second his son in the 1998 Omagh bombing, observed in Northern Ireland 'the lot of little groups looking for grants who are like vultures feeding on the dead and injured' (quoted in *The Sunday Times*, 31 October 2004). Marie Smyth (2003) has referred to what she calls 'professional victims', who cannot relinquish victimhood for fear of losing what attention and resources have been offered. Public policies need to lessen the monopolization of public victimhood by professional victims' groups as much as focus on psychological and social healing for individual victims/survivors. The public exchequer, for example, should be used to make professional victims' groups accountable to the future with the risk of having their financial support withdrawn.

Geraldine Smyth (2004: 113ff.) has recommended the development of a victims forum in Northern Ireland as a space for healing, where victims of every kind can be given a voice, where their memory narratives can be heard and acknowledgement made of their loss and suffering, as a precursor to reconciliation with the 'other'. Her nomenclature of healing rather than 'truth' is significant. She does not envisage this as a 'truth' commission, but a 'forum of healing' as the 'first necessary stage in a wider process of reconciliation' (2004: 128). 'Truth' can be divisive, healing has an opposite effect. For this reason Hutchinson and Bleiker (2008: 396) urge politicians, diplomats and mediators in peace processes to 'create a space where grievances can be freely expressed and emotions worked through', although the creation of these spaces of healing seems far better the responsibility of civil society working in conjunction with the grassroots. Prager (2008: 417ff.) thus refers to 'communities of redress', where bottom-up rather than top-down spaces for speaking and listening are constituted by ordinary people with a preparedness towards 'forgiveness and apology in the hope of reconstituting themselves and the social world into a common future-in-the-making, to a life in common'. This describes better than I the outcome of socially functional victimhood.

The following seem relevant public policies to achieve socially functional public victimhood, although they are hardly comprehensive.

- Society needs to find ways in which victimhood can be honoured as an experience in public ways (in acts of remembrance and commemoration, sites of memorial, recovered memory projects, 'truth' recovery projects and the like).
- Victims' groups need to be recast as 'healing groups', in which victims are encouraged to release themselves from the past and look to the future, by which victims' groups maintain their positive functions (support structures and resource campaigning) but shed their political ones, a transformation that society reinforces financially, materially and symbolically.
- Society should materially and symbolically discourage burdens of grief for the individual being used by victims' groups to prevent the rest of society moving on.
- Forums of public accountability need to be developed in which victims and victims' groups are required to take responsibility, along with the rest of society, for the future rather than just commiserating in their suffering.
- Financial and material resources should be deployed by the state to manage the practice and functions of victims' groups, using public money to manage their aims and objectives.
- A pluralist attitude towards victimhood should be facilitated and supported in which the victimhood of everyone is morally upheld and hierarchies of victimhood challenged.
- If not equality in death and suffering, victimhood can be presented as a shared experience, with tolerance shown towards the others' pain and loss.
- Cultural adjustments in the long term should stress the unity of victimhood as an experience across the divide, something reinforced in the short term by citizenship education programmes, adjustments to school curricula, publicity campaigns and acts of public remembrance and commemoration, and in sites of memorial.
- Special sites of healing should be developed in parallel to sites of remembrance, being those places, events, moments or experiences that bring together victims from across the divide.
- Commemorations must be made socially inclusive; not honouring 'our dead' at the exclusion of 'your dead', but all those who died. 'Official' commemorations, funded from the public purse, should make no distinction in the colour or hue of the dead and even 'unofficial' commemorations should be as inclusive as possible in terms of opening up invitations to attend to all sides.

Not only is this kind of public victimhood healing for society generally, many of these policy initiatives seem relevant also for psychological healing of individual victims.

## Case study: Northern Ireland

Northern Ireland's conflict is such that all can assume the status of victim – Catholics of four centuries of social exclusion, Protestants and Catholics of thirty years of terrorism – and all portray the other as perpetrator, complicating peacemaking. Its interest as a case study, however, is due to the prominent place history and memory have in the construction of group identities. Perhaps because history was so much a part of the symbolic form of 'the Troubles', considerable attention has been placed on memory, 'truth' recovery and victimhood as part of Northern Ireland's post-violence recovery, with substantial sums of money thrown at the problems they pose. Amongst contemporary post-violence societies, Northern Ireland is perhaps the most advanced in dealing with these issues, as well as the wealthiest.

Northern Ireland is rare in having a First-World economy that is capable of spending vast amounts of money to address post-conflict readjustment. Three national governments – of Britain, Ireland and the USA – and the European Union underwrite the peace process. Civil society is large and active; money is no obstacle. By 2008, ten years after the signing of the 1998 Good Friday Agreement (which was the first of three iterations of the peace accord), upwards of £400 million of public money has been spent on the official enquiry into Bloody Sunday, £20 million has been given to victims' support services and £33 million to finance the work of the victims commission, and £8.4 million to the Police Service of Northern Ireland (PSNI) to conduct enquiries into unsolved murders from the past. The third stage of the European Union's Peace Programme is funded to the scale of €267 million, this coming after two previous initiatives, the three programmes estimated to have totalled between £754 million and £1.3 billion. According to an economic audit by the *Regional Monitor*, a further £575 million has been allocated to Northern Ireland and the six bordering counties in the Irish Republic by the EU under the Transitional Objectives I programme. Other post-violence societies in the globalized Third World must envy these sums; the resources devoted to peace in Northern Ireland exceed the GDP of most other countries undergoing similar post-conflict transitions. Post-conflict adjustment in Northern Ireland has the cash, if cash were all that were needed.

History was something that gave form to the conflict (although in substance it was about much more material things). Sir Kenneth Bloomfield's report on victims (Bloomfield, 1998a) noted that the first stirrings of the last phase of the four centuries-old conflict, which was its most intense, began in 1966 with rival fiftieth-anniversary commemorations of the Easter Uprising and the Battle of the Somme. Divided histories ensured that competing interpretations of the past were part of the identity construction process that resulted in two antagonistic, zero-sum notions of group boundaries. Catholic and Protestant communities both have their separate 'sad celebrations' of defeat, resistance and betrayal, and of hard-won victories fought at the cost of their martyrs' blood, that go back centuries (the catalogue of which can be found in Faith and Politics Group, 1998: 7–8). The final thirty years of conflict are thus rendered as part of a historical struggle that weaves backwards far in time. Now, in the post-violence phase, people have no choice but to remember; the past is an eternal present and memories get recalled daily.

The 1998 Good Friday Agreement left these matters vague but made gestures to them when it stated that victims 'had a right to remember', that remembrance generally was part of the 'wider promotion of a culture of tolerance at every level of society' and that it is part of reconciliation to 'acknowledge and address the suffering of victims of violence' (these quotations are taken from Lundy and McGovern, 2005: 6). It did not, however, argue for a formal 'truth' commission and one has not been established since; the ministerial trips taken to visit South Africa in 2005 to discuss 'truth' recovery did not persuade the government of its value. However, the popular enthusiasm that accompanied the proceedings in South Africa led to some grassroots support for one in Northern Ireland (for a selection of the academic debate, see Gawn, 2007; Hamber, 1998c: 79–86; Rolston, 1996; M. Smyth, 2003; Tombs, 2005). People's motives were diverse. Rolston (1996, 2000) wished to expose the culpability of the British security forces, not fearing that this would jeopardize Republicans (for Sinn Fein's position, see www.sinnfein.ie/news/detail/1370); Loyalists opposed one for fear of exposing their own vulnerability, arguing that it would serve only to reinforce what they allege is the criminalization and demonization of Loyalism (see EPIC, n.d.: 6–7; the rhetoric of 'Protestant alienation' has been subjected to academic analysis and partly reinforced by it: see Dunn and Morgan, 1994; Hennessey, 2007). So did the Retired Police Officers' Association.

The Bloomfield Report, *We Will Remember Them* (Bloomfield, 1998a: Appendix 1), acknowledged that many ordinary witnesses counselled for the establishment of a South African-style commission, although the Report itself did not, observing that 'truth' could be used in Northern Ireland as a weapon of attack as well as a shield to hide behind (Bloomfield, 1998a: 38). Some civil society groups, notably those connected to ex-offenders and victims, invited the Deputy Chair of the South African Truth and Reconciliation Commission, Alex

Boraine, to Belfast in 1999 to speak of the virtues of a similar process in Northern Ireland (see Boraine, 2001, for his 'insider' account of the South African Commission); Boraine doubted it could work in the North of Ireland because of lack of agreement (see Northern Ireland Association for the Care and Resettlement of Offenders, 2000). In a wonderfully adept phrase, Marie Smyth (2003: 213), who supports the idea of a 'truth' commission for Northern Ireland, summed up the problem: 'the appetite for truth far outstrips the supply of truth available; there are more wishing to hear the truth than there are those who wish to tell it'.

Consequently, 'truth' recovery and memory work has not been delegated to a 'professional' body, to be closed as an issue once the report has been published. Instead it has been diffused to diverse initiatives and local programmes spread across several social groups and locations, and made part of on-going structures and activities. The Northern Irish response has not been to doubt that society should remember, it has pondered on how and what to remember. We can analyse how this is being thought through in terms of the three core issues of this chapter – victimhood, 'truth' recovery and memory.

### Victimhood

The public discourse on victimhood in Northern Ireland speaks volumes about the centrality of victims to the future stability of its peace process. Churches, political parties, human rights NGOs, other civil society bodies and victims' groups contribute to a debate that makes victimhood one of the last unresolved issues arising from the peace settlement. The main vehicle for moving forward on 'private victimhood' has been the Bloomfield Report (1998a). Its title, *We Will Remember Them*, evoked symbolism from the First World War, being the recurring line from the poem that is read as part of every state commemoration on Armistice Day. This was perhaps not an auspicious start for Republicans, especially given Bloomfield's refusal to address victims of state violence, and some critics have not overcome their recoil (for example Lundy and McGovern, 2005: 7). If, however, we extend what was recommended to all victims, as should be the case, and see references to local communities as describing both sides, the Report is a sensible starting place for addressing private victimhood. The recommendations (summarized in Bloomfield, 1998a: 66–8) contain the following highlights.

- Local community developments in areas of high violence, often led by people who have been severely traumatized themselves, should be supported as part of an overall co-ordinated response to the needs of victims.

- Crisis support teams should be made available to all traumatized individuals, and the location of services should ensure they are accessible to everyone. A 24-hour confidential help-line should be established for victims/survivors.
- Improvement in counselling training should become the object of social policy and a consultation process should be initiated amongst relevant groups to co-ordinate training programmes. Professional accreditation is vital for counsellors.
- Local health trusts and statutory social service boards should compile and maintain a register of services for victims/survivors, which they should advertise in accessible and readable ways.
- Legal assistance should be available for victims/survivors seeking compensation.

The opportunity lost in the Report was that of addressing 'public victimhood'. While the British government accepted the recommendations in full, its public policies towards victims fortunately went considerably beyond them. Public victimhood is much more than provision for counselling, and over time Northern Ireland has seen the establishment of a government minister for victims to oversee the state's responsibility and to formulate a programme of public policies that deal with both private and public victimhood, as well as appointment of four victim commissioners to ensure independently that the needs and interests of victims/survivors are promoted. The Human Rights Commission, set up under the peace accord, published a report which argued that victims' rights were integral to the future of Northern Ireland (Northern Ireland Human Rights Commission, 2001: 7) and this has been taken seriously. Both the UK national and Northern Irish local-devolved governments have mechanisms to advance the needs and interests of victims. In 1998 the British government established the Victims Liaison Unit in the Northern Ireland Office, which is one of two main organizations dealing with victims/survivors. It has overall responsibility for co-ordinating government funding for the full range of government schemes and programmes devoted to victims. The Northern Ireland Office outlines its programme of activities for victims as follows:

- financial support for victims' groups;
- the establishment of a Memorial Fund to which individuals can apply for help;
- the establishment of two trauma centres;
- an analysis of the needs of victims and survivors who live in Great Britain;
- the development and rolling out of a strategy to deliver practical help and services to victims and survivors (see www.nio.gov/ issues/victims.htm).

The Memorial Fund, with a budget of £7 million (see www.nimf.org. uk/), concentrates on financial support for chronic pain management, funding short holiday breaks for victims and carers, re-education and re-training schemes and a discretionary hardship fund. According to the Final Report of the Interim Commissioner for Victims (www.cvsni. org/final-reportnew-2.pdf, p. v), between 1998 and 2008, the Northern Ireland Office channelled £36.4 million to victims. In addition to funding its own programme, the unit disburses money to civil society groups, mainly co-ordinated through the Community Foundation for Northern Ireland (formerly the Northern Ireland Voluntary Trust). The first round of the Foundation's funding amounted to £3.1 million and its primary focus has been on the delivery of practical needs-based services (Lundy and McGovern, 2005: 8).

The other official body delegated with responsibility for victims is the Victims Unit within the devolved Northern Ireland government, established in 2000 and located in the Office of the First Minister and Deputy First Minister (see its website at: www.ofmdfmni.gov.uk/victims. htm). The Victims Unit funded the 'Healing Through Remembering Project', which we shall consider shortly, but is primarily responsible for co-ordinating victims' schemes and policies across all the ministerial departments of the devolved government and for managing the funding for victims provisioned under the EU Peace Programme. The sums from the EU programmes have been extensive. In a written answer in the House of Lords on 11 January 2006 (Hansard, 11 January 2006, column WA70), Lord Rooker, Minister of State for Northern Ireland, confirmed that approaching £670,000 was devoted to victims and victim support groups from the first two phases of the programme. This compared with just over £400,000 given to ex-prisoner groups.

These sums are complemented by the money spent by the local health trusts and local district councils in responding to victims'/ survivors' medical and practical needs, especially for physiotherapy and support groups. There is also a compensation scheme for victims, with no limit on the maximum sum, and the government-funded Community Relations Council has its own special fund for victims/survivors, with £3 million available to fund the core activities of victims' groups, and sums up to £750,000 available for programmes of activities and support schemes for individual victims/survivors. As Marie Smyth (2003) recounts, however, public money is used to encourage victims/survivors to move beyond a 'victim identity', or a sense of themselves as 'professional victims'. This might seem tautological, in that public resources are the key attraction in developing an identity as a professional victim, but policy documents now stress the need for rebuilding, reshaping, self-help and practical support for the life ahead. This transition is supported by social policies directed towards addressing public victimhood. Victims' representatives have been co-opted onto several political bodies and civil society groups. The Civic Forum, for example, is a consultative body of sixty people and one chair established under the peace settlement, and represents the main sectors of civil society. Victims are represented by two people, Alan McBride, a youth worker with the WAVE Trauma Centre and Patricia MacBride, Manager of the Bloody Sunday Centre. MacBride was subsequently appointed as one of four Victim and Survivor Commissioners under the terms of the 2006 Victim and Survivors Order (details can be found at www.opsi.gov. uk/si/si2006/20062953.htm).

On appointment in February 2008, the Interim Commissioner was joined by three others, the decision to expand to four being explained as reflecting the need for them to be trusted by respective constituencies – which is tantamount to accepting that Northern Ireland has not changed enough to enable everyone to trust the same person. Under the terms of the Statutory Instrument, Commissioners promote an awareness of matters relating to the interests of victims and survivors and of the need to safeguard them. They keep under review the adequacy and effectiveness of law and practice affecting the interests of victims and survivors, and practical services for them. They also advise the Secretary of State, the Executive Committee of the Assembly and bodies providing services for victims and survivors on matters concerning their interests. Commissioners are expected to consult amongst victims on the exercise of their duties, for example providing special forums for consultation and discussion with victims and survivors. They have the power to undertake, commission or provide financial or other assistance for research or educational activities concerning the interests of victims and survivors, and to issue guidance on best practice in relation to any matter concerning their interests. Commissioners have yet to develop their programme of work but these terms of reference bode well for taking victims beyond personal grief (see the Commissioners' home page at www.cvsni.org/). The final report of the Interim Commissioner (see www.cvsni.org/final-reportnew-2.pdf) in January 2007 might set a tone; its chief recommendation concerned the development of policies to address young people from areas of high conflict (who are not necessarily 'direct' victims) and to establish a forum for victims so that they can set their own agenda of issues, to be a platform for victims and survivors to come together and to have a voice on aspects that they believe are not being dealt with, and to be an 'independent, inclusive and accountable' alternative means to 'share their experiences' with the rest of society. The devolved government has since set up a consultation exercise on the forum (for example see www.cvsni.org/forumoption.doc).

The Commissioners are joined by a large number of victims' groups in the public sphere with responsibility for public victimhood. There are at least sixty victims' groups registered under various funding schemes (for details of a selection, see Lundy and McGovern, 2005: 11–13) and thus considered active. They come from a wide span of political positions, some of which are opposed to the Good Friday Agreement (but willing to accept monies made available because of it), and thus some resist the transition Northern Ireland needs to make from victims' personal grief towards a new beginning. The most politically active anti-peace victims' group is Willie Frazer's Families Acting for Innocent Relatives (FAIR). Five members of Frazer's close family were killed as members of the security forces and he has stood unsuccessfully for election on several occasions campaigning against the Good Friday Agreement for its betrayal of victims and, in a reference to Sinn Fein, 'against terrorists in government' (on FAIR, see www.victims.org.uk). Nonetheless, this did not prevent FAIR seeking £10,000 from the EU Peace I and II Programmes for core funding. Once courted by Paisley and the DUP when in opposition as part of their critique of the peace process, Frazer exemplifies the dangers of parties politicizing victim issues, for he vehemently opposes Paisley now that the DUP has joined Sinn Fein in power sharing. Frazer was arrested by the Kent police at the time of the Leeds Castle talks (which refined the initial peace agreement).

## 'Truth' recovery

In the absence of a formal process, 'truth' recovery has become the responsibility of diverse organizations and initiatives. The distinction between 'official' and 'unofficial' processes still holds, for the state recognizes its responsibilities and has funded some of them. There is, for example, the little-known Independent Commission for the Location of Victims' Remains, colloquially known as 'the disappeared' – relatively unknown because there are few victims that fit this category: fifteen are known about, nine admitted to by the IRA and four bodies have been located. Most were killed by Republican paramilitaries for alleged spying. The Commission was established by the Irish and British governments in 1999. Evidence obtained on their location is considered inadmissible in a court of law under the terms of the treaty that established the Commission, and bodies are not allowed to undergo forensic investigation. What 'truth' recovery there is in this initiative, therefore, is about giving comfort to relatives to bury their dead. Republicans are eager to assist in locating bodies but the passage of time has defeated several searches; well-publicized searches, assisted by Republicans, did not give up the dead. Gerry Adams, President of Sinn Fein, quoted in the Republican newspaper *Saoirse32* (3 August 2006), urged the governments to move speedily to ensure that, where practical, digs took place: 'The suffering of these families has gone on too long. They have been victims of a grievous injustice done by Republicans. The IRA has acknowledged this and its engagement with the forensic expert, and the report he has now produced, is evidence of its determination to right this wrong.' Digs have not taken place recently, however.

Another 'official' initiative on much the same lines is the PSNI's historical enquiries (see www.psni.police.uk/departments/histori-cal_enquiries_team.htm); similar in that 'truth' is being interpreted in its 'official' meaning as rediscovery of features of the past, with little likelihood of new legal proceedings and the primary purpose being to give comfort to relatives. Set up on the initiative of the Chief Constable, Sir Hugh Orde, in January 2006, and headed by Commander David Cox from the London Metropolitan Police, the Historical Enquiries Team is the first of its kind in post-violence societies (see Lundy, 2008). It has a two-fold role: to investigate unsolved murders committed as part of the political conflict between 1968 and the signing of the peace accord in 1998; and to explain to relatives, where this is not already known, some of the circumstances surrounding the unsolved death. There are 3,268 unsolved deaths as a result of 'the Troubles', and in its first year of operation the Team opened investigations into 10 per cent of them. It operates on strict chronological order and all cases are sup-posed to be assessed by 2011. Figures vary widely over the resources it has been given to undertake this immense task, estimates ranging between £4 million and £32 million; in Hansard (29 October 2007, column WA142), Lord Rooker confirmed a budget of £8.4 million and personnel of 204. The Team's website states a staff of 84; in response to a question in parliament in February 2008, Hansard reported 175 staff, dealing with 3,268 cases, with 1,039 rolled out at that point (25 February 2008, column 1143W). This includes an investigative team composed of personnel from outside Northern Ireland and one of serving and retired officers from Northern Ireland (some of whom had thus failed to solve the cases first time round). Staff skilled in family liaison are also employed to work with relatives. In March 2008 it was revealed that there had been a 40 per cent turnover in staff within the first year of its operation, slowing down its activities.

New judicial proceedings are not guaranteed – and most cases would be covered under the terms of the Good Friday Agreement anyway, permitting perpetrators release under licence. Expectations are unrealistic amongst the PSNI – where 40 cases per month are sup-posed to be closed, increasing to 60 in subsequent years – and amongst the public, who envisage criminal proceedings. The Chief Constable dampens these expectations but does not rein in his own, leading to disquiet, mainly amongst Unionist politicians, at the slow progress; the Team did not meet its target of closing 40 cases a month in any of its first 48 months (see Lundy, 2008). Some Unionists hope for smoking guns to condemn Sinn Fein but 'truth' is many-sided, and, reporting in November 2006, a separate independent panel of international legal experts, in reviewing 76 murders by Loyalist paramilitaries between 1972 and 1977, found evidence of collusion with the RUC or British army in all but 2. The independent panel that produced the report was composed of: Professor Douglass Cassel of Notre Dame Law School; Susie Kemp, an international lawyer based in The Hague; Piers Pigou, an investigator for the South African Truth and Reconciliation Commission; and Stephen Sawyer of Northwestern University School of Law. In January 2008 it was announced that the Historical Enquiries Team (HET) would reopen files on the 124 deaths for which the British army was responsible. This is a stab in the direction of non-partiality and independence, but critics are unconvinced that it will close the door on the past; it cannot be judged yet whether relatives find closure.

To epitomize the HET's difficulties, its report on the Aidan McAnespie case in January 2008, where the victim was killed at an army checkpoint, concluded that the soldier's claim that his hands were wet and the gun misfired was the 'least likely version of what happened', but the charge of manslaughter was dropped. RUC officers involved in the original investigation of the 16 deaths at McGurk's Bar in 1971, which was claimed as an IRA 'own goal' (meaning the bomb exploded prematurely), for example, could not be persuaded to co-operate with the HET, and its report concluded that the original version of events was largely correct. Only in one case has a trial ensued from their report, involving two brothers who were charged in December 2008 with allegedly murdering Tommy English in a Loyalist paramilitary feud in 2000.

Another 'official' public 'truth' recovery process is judicial enquiries. These include the Stevens Enquiry, by Sir John Stevens, at the time Chief Constable of the London Metropolitan Police, into collusion between the security forces and Loyalist paramilitary organizations (see Stevens, 2003). The parts of the Report that were published in April 2003 provided incontrovertible evidence of collusion, leaving people wondering what the confidential parts contained. Collusion was an issue Republicans tried to exploit to readdress Unionist focus on IRA violence but they did not really succeed and the Stevens Report did not receive the public attention it deserved. The British government and Unionist politicians formed a strong lobby that was able to manage the media agenda, although it was not long until the Northern Bank raid and Robert McCartney's murder, both with suspicion of Republican involvement, which made the Stevens Report old news. Collusion was revisited, however, in the Cory Report, conducted by retired Canadian Supreme Court Judge Peter Cory (see Cory, 2005). The Report was into alleged collusion with Loyalists over the murders of Robert Hamill, while police in vehicles allegedly looked on and did nothing, and Rosemary Nelson and Pat Finucane, human rights lawyers from the Nationalist community (the Pat Finucane Centre for Human Rights and Social Change, at www.serve.com/pfc/ offers access to several web resources connected to collusion). Cory also investigated security force collusion with Republicans in the Maze Prison over the murder of leading Loyalist killer Billy Wright (so-called 'King Rat', on whom see J. D. Brewer, 1998: 160–1). The report, published in April 2005, supported claims of collusion in all four murders and recommended separate public enquiries, which occurred in the cases of Nelson and Finucane. Someone was later found guilty of the Finucane murder, delaying the enquiry, and both enquires are still underway. No prosecutions took place of police or army personnel for colluding in the murders, leading to accusations of state cover-ups.

The British government's appetite for public enquiries is weak – it consistently refuses to open one for the London 7/7 bombings – but it is unable to resist the pressure for them in some high-profile murders in Northern Ireland. This is not done benevolently, for in response to the Cory Report the government passed the 2005 Inquiries Act which seriously curtails exposure of state crimes; the Act is not restricted to Northern Ireland. The Act stipulates that the terms of reference of all future enquiries would be decided by the executive; no independent parliamentary scrutiny of these decisions would be allowed; the chair of the inquiry would be appointed by the executive and the executive would have the discretion to dismiss any member of the inquiry; the decision on whether the inquiry, or any individual hearings, would be held in public or private would be taken by the executive; the decision to issue restrictive notices to block disclosure of evidence would be taken by the executive. There are few costs, save embarrassment, to the government in holding enquiries under this legislation.

Costs of another kind weaken their appetite as well. Lord Justice Saville's enquiry into Bloody Sunday has been flagrantly profligate. Tessa Jowell, former cabinet minister, let slip that the 'true costs' of the enquiry approached £400 million (*Daily Telegraph*, 5 July 2006); lower estimates place it at about a quarter of this. The government's official estimate, so far, is £163 million. Opening in 1998, the Enquiry has completed evidence-gathering but, ten years on, its report is still awaited. Transcripts are available online (www.bloody-sunday-inquiry.org/index.htm), however we already know from public comments that it will dismiss the veracity of the account of the event in the 1972 Widgery Tribunal which completely exonerated the British army of the thirteen killings (and of injuries to thirteen others). Saville has publicly condemned the 2005 Inquiries Act, stating that he would not be prepared to be appointed again under these terms, so his report is eagerly anticipated by Republicans as part of the word-war over 'truth'. First expected in 2005, the report is now promised for late 2009. The Enquiry has thrown up some legal issues (see Walsh, 2000), but it is drowning under its own weight. On 6 November 2008, *The Times* recorded that there were 2,500 witness statements, 160 volumes of evidence, amounting to between 20 and 30 million words, plus 121 audio tapes and 110 video tapes.

'Unofficial' 'truth' recovery processes exist in parallel to those of the state. 'Truth' in these instances tends to mean 'story-telling' about the past rather than a serious intention to rediscover 'facts' about it. Of course, all 'truth', as I have emphasized, is partisan. What distinguishes 'unofficial' 'truth recovery from the state's version is that there is no attempt to disguise that it is from the standpoint of the persons whose stories about the past are being captured. Neither version of 'truth' is any more or less 'true' or factual than the other, but story-gatherers collecting unofficial truths know this to be the case. The methodological reflections, for example, of the researchers involved in the Ardoyne Commemoration Project (Lundy and McGovern, 2006a, 2006b), perhaps the best example of its type in the North of Ireland, are honest about this. Lundy and McGovern (2006a: 83) state that 'while the truth presented might be partial (in both the sense that it is incomplete and reflects a particular perspective) the word mattered because it had a resonance that other terms lacked'. The tension between 'truth' and 'partiality', they noted, was a theme that recurred in their interviews as people became aware of the standpoint through which the past was being recounted in their stories.

The Project itself (for details see Lundy and McGovern, 2002, 2005) took four years and was financed by the Community Relations Council, a government-funded but autonomous civil society organization designed to promote better community relations in Northern Ireland. The Project was originally conceived, however, in response to a local demand for the voices of hidden victims in the war to be heard. The area of North Belfast where it was based, the Ardoyne, is 'mixed', with Catholics and Protestants living cheek by jowl, and in consequence it experienced one of the highest murder rates in the conflict; it is also one of the most economically deprived areas. The Project conducted 300 interviews, and 99 victims' case studies are retold by the researchers. In the report to the Community Relations Council, Lundy and McGovern (2005: xv–xvi) recommend that other local '"truth-telling" processes' be developed alongside state-led ones. They stressed the need to make these inclusive in order to represent what they described as the essential 'equality of victimhood', and suggested that some 'truth' recovery initiatives should be intentionally cross-community in order for competing or divided truths to be shared. 'Truth' telling in this way could be both therapeutic to the victims and potentially healing of sectarian divisions.

The Ardoyne Project is not the only local 'truth' recovery process focused on collecting personal stories of 'the Troubles'. Founded in 1994, An Crann/The Tree is a civil society organization dedicated to providing a space in which people can tell their personal stories of the violence. The core of its work is the collection of an ever-expanding archive of personal stories, memories and feelings about the conflict, expressed in story form, art, music and drama (some of this record is contained in An Crann/The Tree, 2000; see also Holliday, 1997 and M. Smyth and Fay, 2000, for other collections of personal accounts). It is An Crann/The Tree's belief that it is 'only by embracing all perspectives of "the troubles" that we can, as a society, break through prejudice and suspicion, rediscover our similarities, respect our differences, and chart a fresh course for our future together' (quoted in J. D. Brewer, Bishop and Higgins, 2001: 48). As a voluntary group, An Crann/The Tree faces many problems in its work, not least funding. In general the membership is secular, but it is interesting that many of the stories people tell involve the importance of a 'God-like' figure helping them to come to terms with the personal feelings of loss and suffering. A similar initiative is the Duchas Living History Project, set up in the Falls area of Catholic West Belfast by local people, and it is concerned to document only the personal accounts of 'Nationalist West Belfast' who are excluded from 'official and establishment versions of history' (cited in Lundy and McGovern, 2005: 13). On the other hand, there is also the Eolas Network (*eolas* being the Irish word for guidance, training or knowledge), which was founded in 2002 by a variety of grassroots and civil society groups working with Republican victims/survivors and ex-prisoners, and which supports a formal 'truth' commission, so long as it is bottom-up and community-orientated (see Eolas, 2002).

It is noteworthy that these examples concern victims in mainly Republican areas, or 'truth' from a Republican's perspective – which is not surprising for newly empowered minority groups. It is not that Loyalists are poor at telling the 'truth', but that they see 'truth' recovery as a political conspiracy against them and the British state to which they are loyal, a loyalty which undergoes strain whenever they perceive the British government itself initiating 'truth' recovery (see EPIC, n.d.: 10). Lundy and McGovern (2005: 75–7) note that, even for mainstream Unionists, 'truth' recovery is not a major priority. Therefore, whatever local spaces are provided in Northern Ireland for 'truth' telling as part of society's wider attempts to deal with the past, Loyalists in particular will not occupy them. Regretfully this will make 'truth' even more partial and one of the major casualties of 'the Troubles'. If a pluralistic attitude is to be developed towards the past (or even consensus on an agreed view of the past) as part of the transformation of social memory in Northern Ireland, Loyalist and Unionist versions of 'truth' need to be heard.

### Social memory

The distinction between 'official' and 'unofficial' memory work is sustained in Northern Ireland's manifold initiatives for remembering the conflict and the historical past in which it was embedded. State initiatives have tended to address remembrance of 'the Troubles', which is what many local communities and civil society schemes have also done – or at least unofficial remembrance of some localized aspects of the violence – but some civil society groups have addressed the re-envisioning of Irish history as a whole. We will deal first with the problem of how to remember the conflict.

The British government has plainly taken the view that history is not for the professional historian to determine; it has not 'parked' the issue of Northern Ireland's difficult past until this is picked up by academics some time in the future. Its principal initiative to confront history's eternal present is the Consultation Group on the Past. Established in June 2007 by the then Secretary of State for Northern Ireland, Peter Hain, the Group is under the dual chairmanship of Lord Eames, former Archbishop and Primate of the Anglican Church of Ireland, and Denis Bradley, from the Nationalist community, vice-chair of the Policing Board and a former priest. Matching the traditions was also the criterion in selecting the membership. The full membership of the Group is: Jarlath Burns, former GAA Captain of Armagh; Revd Lesley Carroll, one of the first female Presbyterian ministers; Willie John McBride, former captain of the British and Irish Lions rugby team; James Mackey, Professor Emeritus in Philosophy at Queen's University Belfast and Visiting Professor at Trinity College Dublin; Elaine Moore, alcohol and drugs counsellor at Northlands, based at Magilligan Prison; and David Porter, Director of the Centre for Contemporary Christianity in Ireland. In addition, Martti Ahtisaari and Brian Currin act as international advisors to the panel to offer impartial advice on any lessons that might be learned for Northern Ireland from their wide-ranging experience of addressing the aftermath of conflict in other countries – Ahtisaari is former President of Finland, a UN Envoy to Kosovo and a recognized diplomat, and Currin is South African, founder of the Lawyers for Human Rights organization that was active in the South African peace process, a member of the Northern Ireland Sentence Review Panel and mediator in several local disputes in Northern Ireland and Sri Lanka. Hain established its terms of reference as follows: to consult across the community on how Northern Irish society can best approach the legacy of the events of the past forty years; and to make recommendations, as appropriate, on any steps that might be taken to support Northern Irish society in building a shared future that is not overshadowed by the events of the past.

At its launch, the government's rhetoric could be faulted only for its optimism. The Group was to 'come up with a formula by which Northern Ireland can address its past in a way that heals rather than poisons . . . no society can develop a shared future if it is always looking backward over its shoulder to the divisions of the past' (Peter Hain, quoted in the *Belfast Telegraph*, 23 June 2007). Loyalists opposed the initiative for the reasons they criticize all 'truth' recovery procedures, while Republicans saw it as too closely allied to the state. Loyalists, however, met with the Group; the IRA refused, saying it was set up on the Brits' 'own terms', a suspicion of one-sidedness that by default became self-fulfilling. It held meetings with Lord Stevens over collusion and MI5 and Loyalist paramilitaries exploring the British army's 'dirty war'.

Its Report was published on 28 January 2009 (and is reproduced in full at www.cgpni.org). The recommendations went under several key headings, which disclose the breadth of issues they saw as relevant to social memory. They are worth noting at length because of their potential value to other post-violence societies:

*Dealing with the past*: An independent Legacy Commission should be established to deal with the legacy of the past by combining processes of reconciliation, justice and information recovery. A Reconciliation Forum should be established through which the Legacy Commission and the Commission for Victims and Survivors for Northern Ireland (CVSNI) would liaise to tackle certain society issues relating to the conflict. The Legacy Commission should be given a bursary of £100m to tackle them.

*Victims and survivors*: The suffering of families was recognized by giving the nearest relative an *ex-gratia* payment of £12,000, including the families of combatants. The CVSNI should take account of, and address in their work programme, the present and future needs and concerns of victims and survivors, devoting attention to provision of services, funding, health-care needs and compensation. The Reconciliation Forum would also have a mandate to promote the improvement of services for health-care issues attributable to the conflict, such as trauma, suicide and addiction.

*The Legacy Commission*: The mandate of the Legacy Commission would consist of four strands: helping society towards a shared and reconciled future, through a process of engagement with community issues arising from the conflict; reviewing and investigating historical cases; conducting a process of information recovery; and examining linked or thematic cases emerging from the conflict. The Legacy Commission's mandate would be for a fixed period of five years.

*Society issues*: Issues arising from the conflict in need of tackling include: addressing sectarianism; promoting remembering activities; working with young people; providing improved services for health-care needs; ensuring an even spread of economic benefits; and helping those exiled from Northern Ireland during the conflict to return. The Legacy Commission should act as a champion for these society issues. The Legacy Commission should engage specifically with the Christian churches in Northern Ireland to encourage them to review and rethink their contribution to a non-sectarian future in the light of their past, particularly in the area of education. Policies to outlaw discrimination against those with conflict-related convictions should be incorporated into statute and made applicable to the provision of goods, facilities and services as well as recruitment.

*Processes of justice and information recovery*: A new independent unit dealing with historical cases would be created within the Legacy Commission, which would continue to review and investigate historical cases, backed by police powers, taking over the work of the Historical Enquiries Team and the Police Ombudsman's Unit. The Legacy Commission would examine themes arising from the conflict which remain of public concern, such as specific areas of paramilitary activity, or alleged collusion. This thematic examination would take place without public hearings. This would facilitate more open and frank disclosure and avoid the constant publicity of present inquiry proceedings. There would be no new public inquiries. The question whether to proceed with the promised Finucane Inquiry is a matter for the British government but the issues raised by this case could be dealt with by the Legacy Commission. The outstanding Inquests would remain with the Coroners Service. Criminal case reviews would continue to be pursued through the Criminal Cases Review Commission. The Group is not proposing an amnesty but recommends that the Legacy Commission itself make recommendations on how a line might be drawn at the end of its five-year mandate.

*Remembering*: The Legacy Commission should support, facilitate and encourage the telling of stories, including by young people, about the impact of the conflict on individuals and communities. CVSNI should also be supported in developing the existing ways in which the conflict and its impact are remembered. This should include the development of educational projects; providing support and guidance for those facilitating remembering projects; and promoting the value of remembering across society. Full support should be given by government, the private and voluntary sector, including the churches, to the continuation of the annual Day of Reflection, initiated by Healing Through Remembering, on 21 June each year. Consideration should be given to renaming the event a Day of Reflection and Reconciliation. Each year, on or around the Day of Reflection and Reconciliation, the First Minister and Deputy First Minister should together make a keynote address to the Northern Ireland Assembly and invited guests, reflecting on the past in a positive way and confirming their commitment to leading Northern Ireland society towards a shared and reconciled future. The Reconciliation Forum should take the lead in implementing an initiative, at the end of the five-year mandate of the Legacy Commission, whereby Northern Ireland should conduct a ceremony remembering the past and all those who suffered during the conflict. The Group therefore recommends that the Commission should, at the end of its work, challenge the people of Northern Ireland, political parties and whatever remnants of paramilitary groups remain to sign a declaration that they will never again kill or injure others on political grounds. A shared memorial to remember the conflict should be kept under consideration by the Reconciliation Forum.

(Executive Summary Report, www.cgpni.org).

This is an impressive set of recommendations, with an even-handedness that seems suitable for the purpose and instructive for elsewhere. Responses to it diverged, however, along sectarian lines, profiling the controversy of social memory when history remains divided. The public launch of the Report was disrupted by hardline Unionists objecting to its alleged pro-Republican ethos, moderate Unionists baulked at the moral equivalence of victimhood and harangued the Consultative Group for recommending financial compensation to the families of Republican combatants, while Sinn Fein queried the value of a Legacy Commission under the direction of the British government. The government may have wished it had left history to historians, although an editorial comment on 2 February 2009 in the *Belfast Telegraph*, a cross-community newspaper with moderate sympathies, contained the view that:

> The Eames-Bradley Report is not without its flaws and detractors, but the blunt truth remains that it may help all of us, however painfully, to confront those things which we may not want to face, and in the process to inch ourselves forward together. The alternative, as Eames and Bradley so chillingly pointed out, is to perpetuate the divisions which will confront future generations who need to be freed from the past. The Eames-Bradley Report still provides the best basis for moving forward.

A few weeks later, on 25 February 2009, the government announced its support for the Report except for the recommendation of financial compensation, which it said proved too divisive. Unionists might reflect that their objection to compensation for the families of Republican combatants means that all families of victims now lose.

Other memory work on the conflict is not directly state-sponsored and is less divisive as a result, although some of it is only one stage removed and still in receipt of state finance. The Community Relations Council, for example, funded a project on how best to memorialize the conflict, which reported in the wake of the ceasefires (see Leonard, 1997). The Report noted that the ceasefires had inaugurated a vigorous public debate on suitable forms of commemoration of the casualties. For example, a national memorial was proposed within a few days of the IRA cessation of violence in August 1994 and some journalists and politicians argued that the statue of Lord Carson on the driveway at Stormont should be replaced by a new peace sculpture. Leonard records that early proposals included a wall monument honouring the names of victims in date order, similar to the Vietnam Veterans Memorial in Washington DC. The precedent of Berlin in 1990 produced suggestions that such a memorial could be constructed from material out of Belfast's peace walls, from the sentry towers that overlooked border crossings or the boulders which had closed minor roads. Leonard noted that the post-Communist approach to public sculpture in Eastern Europe was invoked in suggestions that the Carson statue and other Unionist figures outside Belfast City Hall be removed to sculpture parks, to be replaced with more inclusive monuments. However, Leonard made no recommendation for how the conflict should be remembered, preferring instead to review the nature of the memorialization that had occurred up to 1997.

This difficult task was not side-stepped by the Healing Through Remembering Project, established in 2000 under the auspices of the local devolved government's Victims Unit (for its Report, see Healing Through Remembering Project, 2002). Lundy and McGovern (2005: 7) argue that this was subterfuge on the part of the Office of the First Minister and Deputy First Minister, which funds the Victims Unit, in order to defer delicate issues of 'truth' recovery, although this also ensured it was delegated to specialists in the topic of remembrance. It also successfully introduced some distance between the problems of remembrance and victimhood. The Project was chaired by Professor Roy McClelland, a mental health expert from Queen's University Belfast. There was an eighteen-person Project Board, all from Northern Ireland and covering key civil society groupings, victims, academics and ex-service personnel, as well as a team of consultants including specialists like Alex Boraine and Brandon Hamber. It received 108 submissions (identified in Healing Through Remembering Project, 2002: Appendixes F–J), reflecting widespread public interest in the issues of remembrance and memorialization. (This level of public interest was also picked up on in the 2003 Northern Ireland Life and Times Survey, which revealed that two-thirds of respondents felt there should be a special memorial for victims of 'the Troubles', although only 49 per cent felt it should be for every victim: see Hamber, 2004: 5.)

The Project was intended to document possible mechanisms for remembrance that would be healing for those affected by the conflict and for society in Northern Ireland as a whole. This was remarkably far-sighted in seeing social memory as a strategy for reconciliation. The final Report was visionary also in locating remembrance in people rather than in symbolic or material monuments, more specifically in people's personal accounts of the conflict. Submissions recommended a range of remembering processes (see Healing Through Remembering Project, 2002: iv–v), including: story-telling and oral history, public memorials, museums and exhibitions, public and collective commemorations, 'truth' recovery procedures, legal and judicial enquiries, a purpose-built Centre for Remembrance, public apologies and other institutional self-examination. The Project supported an approach that was consistent with several local initiatives that focused on the collection of oral history about the conflict, and its chief recommendation was to develop a network that linked the diverse forms of story-telling and archiving of stories already underway. Making this inclusive of all sections of Northern Irish society was seen as foundational to healing at the societal level (a point stressed by M. Smyth, 2003: 215, who was a member of the Project Board). It also proposed an annual Day of Reflection as a universal gesture of acknowledgement and atonement, and a permanent living memorial museum, both of which would give structural focus and aid to remembering. It further recommended that a dedicated NGO on remembrance be established to oversee these recommendations, equivalent to that for victims. By 2008 none of the recommendations had been implemented and what oral history is done is still locally based. It remains the case, therefore, that most memorialization and remembering of the conflict is conventional in being monument based.

While they are only one technology of memory, memorials and monuments are, as we have seen, the principal form of memory work after conflict, and Jane Leonard's Community Relations Council Report (1997) notes the dominance of traditional forms of memorialization. Some of these are official state monuments, others unofficial responses by the communities affected. The names of police officers and soldiers killed while on duty are often added to state-built world war memorials in Northern Ireland, but there are also dedicated memorials to members of the security forces killed in 'the Troubles', as well as to regiments that served. These can be found in various public spaces (as distinct from inside police and army buildings), such as churches, hospitals, schools, civic buildings and government offices. There is a spatial dimension to this local memorialization, however, which reflects the religious geography of the conflict. For obvious reasons, public monuments and plaques tend not to be built outside and few of the spaces where they can be found are shared between Catholic and Protestant communities; not surprisingly, official memorials tend to adorn public buildings in Protestant areas. Republican areas have their local and unofficial memorials to volunteers killed on active service, including the Hunger Strikers, as a permanent and formal presence in Catholic areas, sometimes at the spot where death occurred. These can be murals and paintings on walls, stone obelisks, statues and cemetery plots – even graves are turned into political displays commemorating militant Republicanism, with accompanying flag poles and appropriate wording on flagstones to mark the fact of their death during wartime. Republican murals tend to absorb the death into a history of resistance and Celtic mythology, while Loyalist ones usually evoke continuity with the sons of Ulster dying on the Somme. Republicans have tended to memorialize in stone to a greater extent than Loyalists because state-built monuments invariably honour the soldiers and police killed defending the Union, although this also holds true for members of Loyalist paramilitary organizations killed on duty. These people tend to be memorialized in wall murals rather than stone obelisks or plaques (hence the umbilical connection between space, territory, Orange Order parading and Loyalist wall murals, to which Jarman, 2001, refers).

Local and official memorials to civilians killed in the violence tend to occur in Republican and Loyalist areas at the site of the atrocity itself or very close nearby, such as obelisks, plaques, memorial gardens, stained glass memorials in churches and the like. These, too, have a strong spatial dimension as sites of memory directly tied to the place of death (as is the case, of course, with roadside memorials to victims of traffic accidents, which are particularly evident throughout Ireland because of the strong senses of place in Irish culture). These give focus to com-memoration rituals every anniversary. The Bloody Sunday Memorial in Derry (on which see Conway, 2003, 2008) and the memorial that honours those killed in the Enniskillen Armistice Sunday bombing are examples of monuments to civilians, although, since security force per-sonnel were also killed in the latter, the monument is state-built. Some civilian deaths are memorialized in poetry (such as James Simmons's *Ballad of Claudy*), songs (for example Bono's *Song for Omagh*), murals and paintings. The banners of Orange Flute Bands, knitted remembrance quilts and exhibitions of photographs are other symbolic memorials to the dead that can be used as specific commemoration rituals when linked to anniversaries. Loyalist and Republican marching bands are sometimes named after particular victims (that there is a Republican marching tradition may come as a surprise given the association of parading with Protestantism, but see Fraser, 2000).

Since a few of these local spaces of memorialization are residen-tially mixed, or the public places in which local memorials get built are shared, there can be contention over the one-sidedness of unof-ficial memorials. Conway (2003: 315–16) notes, for example, political objections to the Bloody Sunday Memorial from local Protestants and the Presbyterian Church of Ireland in its first years, which reproduced the traditional divisions that spurred what was then still the on-going communal violence. Conversely, it is now the case that the memorial has been desensitized, in part by the inclusivity that has accompa-nied the peace process but mostly because it has been neglected by Protestants in Derry, who are content to allow a pluralistic approach to memory by default as a trade-off for their own commemorations (especially the Apprentice Boys' marches in Derry, which now take place peacefully). Other potential battles over history remain there under the surface, however, especially over a possible change of the city's name (Londonderry/Derry), nomenclature which encapsulates the divergent histories that exist in Northern Ireland as a backcloth to all contemporary memory work on the conflict. This emphasizes the importance of ensuring that memory work is not restricted to remembering 'the Troubles' but also incorporates the historical re-envisioning of the past, a type of memory work to which we now turn.

Re-remembering and re-memorialization are part of the transformation of social memory necessary in peace processes and this type of memory work lags well behind that of remembering the conflict, and yet the latter will not fully succeed unless it is accompanied by the re-remembering of Irish history. This is one of the fundamental weaknesses of the Eames-Bradley Consultation Group on the Past – the 'past' is interpreted to mean the last forty years, not the previous four centuries. In addressing the contentious issue of remembrance of 'the Troubles', it has reproduced all the sectarian divisions to be expected in a context where divergent histories and senses of the past frame how the conflict is seen. Consensus about the immediate past can be developed properly only by addressing divergences over the distant past.

Very little memory work of this kind is being done in Northern Ireland. The British state has eschewed this kind of memory work entirely and it is left to a scattering of civil society groups, private individuals and random political initiatives to address the broader historical framework. Referring back to the earlier discussion of the five strategies for the transformation of social memory, joint remembrances are one approach, either by recalling formerly hidden events that permit shared remembrances and which were forgotten during the conflict or by re-remembering joint events in order to display what can now be recalled as shared experiences. Joint remembrances of shared Catholic and Protestant service in the former Royal Irish Constabulary come to mind as an example; so does service in two world wars. In the early period of the new Irish state, it proved premature to build a memorial garden commemorating the Irish dead in Britain's wars, and it was left unkempt and ignored, save for a few unofficial ceremonies by ex-servicemen (see Rigney, 2008).

However, the peace process made joint remembrance feasible in the late 1990s. The Irish government, for example, contributed a substantial financial sum in 1997 towards purchase of a Peace Park and the construction of a Round Tower at Messines Ridge, West Flanders, to commemorate the 50,000 or so Irishmen, from North and South, Catholic and Protestant, who perished in the First World War, seeing this as a powerful symbol of reconciliation in the lead-up to the 1998 Good Friday Agreement that might consolidate the new patterns of social relationships that the accord was intended to create. Sinn Fein's first Lord Mayor of Belfast, Alex Maskey, made similar overtures in 2002 on the occasion of his first speech marking the annual commemoration of the 1916 Battle of the Somme. Not only did he break Nationalist silence, on both sides of the border, about Catholic participation in

Britain's world wars, he acknowledged the symbolism of the carnage to Protestant-Unionist identity. He saw memory of the event as means for 'seeking common ground' (Maskey, 2002: 2). On the day itself, in laying the wreath, in a significant gesture of reconciliation, he remarked that his objective had been 'to seek to identify common ground for all of us in this generation'. The last act of Taoiseach Bertie Ahearn and First Minister Ian Paisley before they resigned in May 2008 was to cut the ribbon at the opening ceremony of a new museum in the Irish Republic to commemorate the 1690 Battle of the Boyne, the decisive moment in Irish history when Ulster Protestants saw themselves liberated from popery, which by 2008 was used as an opportunity to signal the unity of purpose between North and South in recasting Irish history. The history of Ireland has generally been written as one of division between two zero-sum identities – British/Protestant, Irish/Catholic – with little attempt to examine what people of different identities may have to share and to commemorate together. Joint remembrances such as these can readdress outdated shibboleths.

Re-remembrance is another strategy for re-envisioning Irish history. Underlying the construction of group identities in the North are different, sometimes contradictory, histories of key events, and some civil society groups have begun to challenge the way certain key moments are historically understood. This is best exemplified by the Inter-Church Faith and Politics Group. Established in 1983, this is an ecumenical and cross-border group whose activities include producing pamphlets on critical topical issues from the perspective of a faith-based approach to peace and reconciliation, and hosting regular consultative meetings with political and religious leaders. Members represent some of the sharpest minds and most committed peace activists from amongst the churches, such as Johnston McMaster, Geraldine Smyth, John Morrow, Trevor Williams and David Stevens. Ecumenical bodies like the Corrymeela Community, the Irish School of Ecumenics and the Irish Council of Churches are well represented amongst the membership, although the group is unaffiliated to any denomination. In the first of its pamphlets on history (see Faith and Politics Group, 1991), the group tried to place in a new light remembrance of the key events of 1690 (the victory of the Protestant King William over the Catholic King James, dear to Protestants) and 1916 (Dublin Easter Rising by Republicans, dear to Catholics) by helping groups to realize what each affair means to others and correcting some of the mythology which surrounds them. Recent commemorations of these events have also encouraged some critical self-examination. The ninetieth anniversary of the 1916 Easter Rising, for example, provoked reflexivity in the Irish press, and, in a debate in the *Irish Independent Review* on 15 April 2006, on whether rebels were heroes or villains, one of the journalists arguing the latter wrote that the Easter Rising initiated the bloodthirsty trail that ended up in 'the Troubles' and those who praised them should be ashamed. Re-remembrances of events in Irish history like this are only to be encouraged, if done on all sides. Protestants in the Faith and Politics Group come closest to the reflexivity required from that tradition. The call by the Group for re-remembrance was significantly extended when in 1998 it recognized that the Good Friday Agreement of that year would require a new approach to remembrance and forgetting (Faith and Politics Group, 1998). Showing extraordinary foresight, they argued that building a future for Northern Ireland required that Irish history be reckoned with, rather than having a line drawn underneath it (1998: 3), by recovering certain memories, and forgetting or re-remembering others.

It is possible to give one example of how this was put into practice by a Sinn Fein councillor and former Mayor of Limavady, Anne Brolly. In August 2005 she publicly announced in the press that her father had been a decorated British soldier who had died some years later from injuries sustained in the Second World War. One of his brothers, her uncle, had been a volunteer in the IRA and interned during the 1950s, and it was felt possible only now to acknowledge memories that had formerly to be concealed. She told the local press:

> We need to look at and acknowledge where we came from. My father was proud of what he did. The fact he fought for the British doesn't make me any less a republican. We need new relationships in our communities. Unionists need to form new relationships with the rest of Ireland, while nationalists need to form new relationships with England and the rest of Britain.
>
> (*Derry Journal*, 26 August 2006)

Re-remembrances, in other words, can be used to sustain new patterns of relationship that better fit the post-conflict society in the North of Ireland.

In a society where religion is the form through which the conflict has been experienced and is perceived to be part of the problem, it is difficult for the churches to be seen as contributing to the solution. The Faith and Politics Group's prescience went wholly unheeded and it never returned to this theme again. The public discourse on victimhood drowns out that on social memory and in the clatter one of the most important re-memorialization strategies for dealing with divisions over Irish history has been rejected. Museums are an important site of memory and one of the foremost technologies by which memories are socially constructed and changed. The several Holocaust Museums and Robben Island Museum are exemplars of how divided and painful histories can be repackaged for the purposes of peace (for the Holocaust Memorial Museum, see www.ushmm.org/). In their account of Robben Island Museum, Shearing and Kempa (2004) have shown how the museum designers and managers have sought to promote what they call 'a hope sensibility' through exhibits and interactive work programmes for children, and by the commentary and notes used in the tours. They claim this to be inspirational to South Africans in tackling the 'very difficult tasks they face in building a new South Africa' (2004: 64). There is also the Apartheid Museum which states that it is not just an institution informing historical accounts of apartheid but a resource re-informing history as a way of promoting hope (see www.apartheidmuseum.org). There are smaller museums marking particular historical events, issues or locales, such as the District Six Museum in Cape Town which uses the example of the forced population relocation of Black people from District Six in 1966 to address contemporary issues around diasporas and refugees. Perhaps the best example is the Museum of Tolerance (www.museumoftoler-ance.com/) in Los Angeles. It features the Holocaust and the histories of slavery and racism in the USA to draw lessons from the past, turning history into an education resource to ensure it is not repeated.

The demand for a similar museum in Northern Ireland was voiced by the Report of the Healing Through Remembering Project (2002: 26–8), which pointed out that thirty-two submissions had recom-mended one, with none against. Private individuals have advanced the case. Marie Smyth, for example, based on her experience of the costs of 'the Troubles' study (see Fay, Morrissey and Smyth 1999; M. Smyth and Fay, 2000), urged the idea of a museum in her submission to the Victims Commission (see http://cain.ulst.ac.uk/cts/smyth97a.htm). She saw it acting as an archive and as an educational and research resource that would be open to the public and to schools. A variety of civil society groups have separately campaigned for a museum, such as An Crann/ The Tree and Coiste na n-Iarchimi. The latter is a Republican ex-pris-oner network which has promoted the idea of turning the former Maze Prison, where the infamous H-Blocks were housed, into a museum (see Coiste na n-Iarchimi, 2003). This idea is supported strongly by Sinn Fein. So far it has been rejected by the devolved government in Northern Ireland. The problem in part is its location, which leads to fears that if it were based at the Maze (and no other sites have so far been mentioned) it might be used to glorify the activities that resulted in the men (and they were all men) being incarcerated there. What makes the former prison on Robben Island work as a technology for transforming social memory is its forward-looking gaze, the intention to assist in the cultivation of hope for the future and its design features that help in the construction of new identities by repackaging South African history in more inclusive ways. Plans have developed so modestly on the Maze Museum that it is difficult to gauge whether this is its ambi-tion (although comments in Coiste na n-Iarchimi, 2003, are reassuring on this point). This describes another of its problems, in that the idea is being driven by Republicans who as yet are not generally trusted; were the British or local devolved governments to develop their own plans on a different site it can be anticipated that Republicans would also object. This disagreement is deeply paradoxical, for divided histories produce lack of trust, preventing the building of a museum that could help to re-remember Irish history and thus end the mistrust.

The success of the Doagh Island Famine Village Museum in Inishowen, Donegal (see www.doaghfaminevillage.com/), offers a lesson to close neighbours over the border in how to deal with difficult history through museums. It entered its eleventh year in 2008, and its motto is 'looking forward to the past'. It traverses the eternal present of history by re-remembering the past and using the new memories to look to the future. For example, it represents social life at the time of the Great Famine in the 1840s in less divisive terms than how this is sometimes portrayed in folk narratives, popular history and what some professional historians (for example Kennedy, 1996) call the 'MOPE' (most oppressed people ever) mythology, pointing to the inter-denominational features of Irish village life and the co-operation between Catholic and Protestant farmers and parading organizations. It refers to those Protestant landowners who were benign or supportive of their Catholic tenants during the starvation and uses the event to get visitors to reflect on world hunger today. The commentary and notes are inclusive and the design of exhibits is used to reinforce this message. The Great Famine may well exemplify some of the worst features of English laissez-faire policy in the nineteenth century, but the features the Museum chooses to forget and remember are intended to re-remember Irish history for purposes of the future. Were a similar museum to be developed in the North it would assist in the commodification of the past – making 'the Troubles' into heritage and a huge tourist attraction – which was noted earlier as an advantage in exposing people to others' histories and thus beneficial to developing pluralist attitudes to memory.

## Conclusion

Memory is a pivotal notion in any sociology of peace processes. For one thing it takes us back to the chapter on emotions, for we have seen how remembrance after conflict is best connected with positive emotions like hope and forgiveness. But memory is a central cog for another reason. As we have argued in this chapter, memory, 'truth' and communal violence can be an unholy trinity. However, the sociological nature of memory permits it to become an object of social reconstruction through dedicated public policies, in which various social practices and technologies of memory can be deployed to make memory functional for post-violence societies. Subsidiary issues like 'truth' recovery and victimhood, if also dealt with in the process of re-remembering, turn the past into something pivotal for the future. The policy management of this triumvirate, however, is not easy: this is the cautionary tale of this chapter.

As Elster (2004: 171–2) argues, when closing the book on the past it is important not to replace one injustice with another: whatever is done in repairing past injustices should not make them worse. The management of victimhood in peace processes risks this happening. Victims can feel forgotten and ignored, leaving them open to mobilization by spoiler groups wanting to undermine the peace accord. Social policies are needed that address the interests and needs of victims, but public victimhood also needs to be made sociologically functional for the new society. This means, as I have argued, that post-violence societies, while sensitive to private victimhood, need to look at their future through the eyes of their children not their ancestors and should not allow themselves be held prisoner of victims' unforgivingness.

Policies directed towards managing private and public victimhood, however, should not be in isolation from those addressing 'truth' recovery and social memory. Some people want 'truth' for retribution, others for redemption of themselves or to get repentance from others, and some for reconciliation. 'Truth' recovery, while not a panacea, seems in one form or another an inevitable condition for the stabilization of peace processes. Finding out the 'truth' of the past, however, is not about collecting 'facts' but primarily coming to the realization that there is no single 'truth' and accepting that all truths are from a standpoint. With this awareness it is possible to develop a pluralist attitude towards memory, if not an agreed understanding on the past. In this way, the re-envisioning of the past will help to ensure the peace is consolidated.

# Conclusion
# *A sociological approach to peace processes*

## Introduction

I have climbed a foothill and left a mountain still to be scaled. In a lecture on dignity, equality and inalienable rights, Archbishop Tutu remarked that South Africa had experienced a negotiated revolution (2001: 14); all successful peace accords are like that. They demand a great deal from their negotiators and pose a considerable challenge for the people subject to them. The paradox in Tutu's remark is worth emphasizing: peace can be as costly as violence, as cataclysmic as conflict, and a peace process as protracted and difficult as the conduct of war. Giving up preferred first-choice options for the sake of a negotiated agreement asks as much of the protagonists as the original decision to fight. To die in war is a sacrifice; to live to make the peace an even greater one. In looking at some of the sociological features of second-best compromise peace settlements that make them work or not, I am aware that I have left much more to be said – and perhaps said better – by others. From the top of my small summit, I can see the ranges ahead and the potential for further sociological explorations of peace processes. But like all small achievers, I want to celebrate the panorama from the height I have conquered.

My purpose in writing this book was two-fold: to introduce specialists in peace processes to sociology's special perspective; and to highlight for sociologists the subject's contribution to the stabilization and long-term success of peace processes. I came to it aware that sociologists on the whole knew little about the substantive topic of peace processes, and believing that other disciplinary approaches, which eschew sociology, would be enriched by its distinctive imagination. I do not want to repeat the detailed arguments of earlier chapters in shortened or truncated form but rather to strike home these ambitions by summarizing the arguments in answering two questions. What is distinctly sociological about my account? What can sociology add to our understanding of peace processes? The second is obviously the more significant question but let me get the first out of the way.

## What has been distinctly sociological?

I have throughout contrasted my arguments with those of the 'good governance' approach to peace processes. International Relations theorists know this approach better as liberal internationalism (Paris, 1997), Wilsonianism (Paris, 2004), political realism or Westphalianism (Atack, 2005). It began to be called 'good governance' in the 1990s precisely around the time of the collapse of various authoritarian societies, when it was felt a generous dose of democracy was needed to consolidate the change. This was a time when neo-conservatives in the USA were forecasting the end of history (as in the 1960s they did for the end of ideology, see Bell, 1962). Fukuyama (1992) predicted the universalization of Western liberal democracy as the final form of government, and Kagan and Kristol (2000) urged that US military power should be used to reorder global strategic relations by promoting democratic changes and good governance reforms in dictatorial regimes. While Kagan (2008) has come to realize that these were utopian dreams and that history has returned with a vengeance – as, incidentally, did ideology – the good governance rhetoric survives. The research institute that appropriates Wilson's name, the Woodrow Wilson International Center for Scholars, is chief amongst many in utilizing the new discourse. The Wilson Center, to which the institute is affiliated, lists its primary research theme to be 'governance, including such issues as the key features of the development of democratic institutions, democratic society, civil society, and citizen participation', www.wilsoncenter. org/index.cfm?fuseaction=fellowship.welcome). The features of good governance are clear, however, whatever the approach is called.

Good governance approaches address the political, economic and justice aspects of conflict, and see peace processes as about institutional reform to introduce a democratic polity, market economy and human rights law. Paris's realization that Wilsonianism is not a 'miracle cure' (2004: ix) still prevents his modernization from prioritizing political and economic reform (2004). In reproducing Western notions of market democracy, the Western-based governments, research centres, philanthropic foundations and INGOs which push good governance proffer the West as the model for the solution to communal violence. Leaving aside those conflicts that are motivated by or involve rejection of the West, this Westernization of peace is sometimes problematic. Three conditions make it so: when good governance rhetoric is blurred by colonial memories of Western imperialism, to the point where peace groups sometimes have to distance themselves from the West, as we saw in Sri Lanka; when the demand for economic redistribution after communal violence is something the new market economy cannot deliver or deliver quickly enough, leaving swathes of poverty and economic marginalization as potential threats for renewed conflict, as is the case in many African countries and Latin America – the deaths of fifty or so African foreign migrants in Johannesburg in May 2008 can be attributed to competition over jobs, housing and services in a context where local people have not had their socio-economic expectations of reform met; and when traditional notions of justice, while having strong restorative elements, nonetheless infringe Western notions of law and are criticized for the extent of their departure from modern legal norms, as Rwanda's *gacaca* courts exemplify.

The good governance approach to peace processes is overwhelmingly desirable in its emphasis on reform in these key areas. The conflict is likely to have been motivated by undemocratic notions of politics, economic inequality and unfairness and human rights abuses, and institutional reform that corrects the original causes cannot be criticized. Sometimes the new structures are implemented partisanly by in-coming regimes and their operation of the principles of good governance tests the level of genuine reform, but this impugns the democratic quality of the new state not the desirability of good governance structures. I am not perverse enough to claim good governance is unnecessary; it is insufficient.

The sociological approach adopted here demonstrates that good governance does not go far enough in conceptualizing the range of issues that peace processes need to tackle. None of the concepts at play in this volume are exclusively sociological, however. To describe my approach as sociological might therefore appear to represent the return of the nineteenth-century arrogance of Comte, who argued that everything is sociological since the discipline is at the apex of the intellectual hierarchy as the Queen of the Sciences. Such aggrandizement is not intended. I believe that there is nothing yet imagined that *cannot* be approached sociologically but I also recognize that sociology often asks the *least* important questions about many of the things to which it is applied. However, peace processes are one of the areas where sociological questions are worth asking. There are two grounds to describing my arguments as sociological and for claiming that the questions sociology raises about peace processes are complementary to good governance approaches.

First, this volume has neglected mention of voting systems, constitutional rearrangements, economic reforms, the structure and composition of new representative assemblies, the contents of Bills of Human Rights and so on, because their value to peace processes has been taken for granted. The sorts of concepts I have been concerned with, like 'truth', memory, masculinity, hope, forgiveness, reconciliation, restorative justice, victimhood, civil society, gender and so on, circulate around and across disciplinary boundaries. Sometimes these concepts are by tradition the domain of one discipline – theology tends to take privilege in the elaboration of 'truth' and forgiveness, psychology for victimhood and criminology for restorative justice. They are given intellectual refreshment, however, when they travel through unfamiliar disciplines. New insights can arise when 'strange others' take novel perspectives on these topics in order to expand their meaning and application, as with the contemporary emphasis on 'political forgiveness' in International Relations, restorative justice in Peace Studies, and Religious Studies' interest in civil society. These new disciplinary approaches are often highly illuminating by changing the light in which familiar concepts are seen, and give value to what we popularly call multidisciplinarity (see J. D. Brewer, 2007, for sociology's relationship with a selection of relatively unfamiliar disciplines). Sociology is able to flesh out the interdisciplinarity of these travelling concepts as much as any other discipline. This leads me to a second more significant point.

In introductory sections to most chapters, I outlined sociology's perspective on the subject under discussion in order to bring to life the discipline's relevance for subsequent arguments. In this way we were introduced, for example, to the sociology of emotions and the sociology of gender, whose very nomenclature signals that they form a sub-field of the discipline, but also to sociology's understanding of memory, hope, forgiveness, civil society, 'truth' and the like. While this served the purpose of acquainting non-specialists with the discipline, the chief intention was to highlight what of significance emerges out of sociology for peace processes and their stabilization. The chapters tried to elaborate on this relevance by identifying the public policies they require and assessing the viability of whatever policy responses have been implemented to this point.

The popularity of some public policies has been called into question, such as restorative justice in Rwanda's *gacaca* courts and 'official' truth and reconciliation commissions, while gaps in policy have been stressed, such as, for example, the neglect of the need for male ex-combatants to develop non-violent masculinities and of the plight of many women victims/survivors or child soldiers, the relative absence of public spaces for hoping/anticipating and forgiving/redeeming and associated social ceremonies, the need to recast social memory in the public sphere, the limited capacity of minority churches to occupy key political spaces and the restricted space for women to be social transformers in patriarchal societies. Successful cases, however, also featured, such as, for example, the role of religion in Poland's transition from Communism, Northern

Ireland's forms of new memory work, restorative justice in Bougainville, women's empowerment in Sudan and Rwanda, the shift away from militarism amongst some of Liberia's warlords and the development of global civil society in several countries.

Only the skill of my prose will be able to persuade the reader that the management of these sociological issues is as necessary for the stability of peace processes as is institutional reform. If I have succeeded in the ascent of this small summit, the vista will show that the good governance approach to peace processes needs to be supplemented. Sociology can reasonably stake a claim to provide this.

## What can sociology add?

Sociology helps us to understand the nature of the communal conflict that necessitates peace processes. As explained in the Introduction, even in the accomplished hands of someone like Charles Tilly (2003), collective violence loses its connection to the social structure of the societies in which it occurs, for the collectivity involved can be as few as three and the violence they perpetrate can be random. Pub brawls, football hooliganism or 'domestic' or child abuse are not the sorts of violence that concern peace processes, but rather that which is located in the society's social structure as an on-going conflict between its communities and which coheres around fairly rigid social cleavages (such as 'race', ethnicity, national origin, religion, language and the like). Or, at least, pub brawls, football hooliganism and 'domestic' abuse become relevant only if they are related to wider social structural conflicts – as they can often be in divided societies.

This is why the term 'communal violence' has been used throughout, since it distinguishes itself from random violence between ad hoc collections of people and makes plain that the sort of violence requiring peace processes is built on social fissures inherent in particular social structures. Ethnic and racial violence, genocide, sectarianism and nationalist conflicts are zero-sum social cleavages and create mutually exclusive interests that result in a distorted form of politics based on deep identity concerns. The 'politics of identity', however, becomes problematic only because it reproduces rigid social structural cleavages and zero-sum notions of group identity. The impact of particular kinds of political formation on the propensity to collective violence (as discussed by McAdam, Tarrow and Tilly, 2001) can thus be reduced to sociological concerns around inbuilt social structural divisions. Distorted identity politics are a mirror of distorted social structures and thus come within the provenance of sociology.

The nature of communal violence has profound negative effects for peace processes, however, for it severely complicates the post-conflict adjustment problems. Embedding communal violence in the social structure of the societies in which it occurs helps to explain why peace processes are fragile, for second-best negotiated compromises have either to eliminate the social cleavages that once provoked the violence or to allow their continued social reproduction in non-violent ways. There are all sorts of factors that make peace difficult, including spoiler violence, the psychological and ontological costs of peace and the financial incentives for conflict arising from the war economy, as we saw in chapter 2, but as a backdrop to all these problems with peace is the basic challenge: namely, that communal violence is difficult to transcend because it is so effortlessly reproduced as part of cultural continuity – part of the traditions, history and institutions of society as sociology terms it. Structural divisions that lend themselves to communal violence are socially reproduced, such that successful peace processes have to involve profound social change (along with governance reform in the polity, economy and legal system). Sometimes this change is created by means of conquest or cartography, as we saw in our typology of post-violence societies in chapter 1, but this is merely an unsatisfactory negative peace. Where partition, repression or cultural annihilation cannot be applied or do not work in the longer term, negotiated peace settlements have to presage a deeper transition towards positive peace.

Positive peace is not met simply by parties agreeing to the accord itself. Ironically, signing the accord is the beginning not the end of a peace process (which is why sociology's nomenclature should emphasize 'peace building' rather than 'conflict resolution'). If they are to effect positive peace, peace processes must, through social change: reduce the saliency of the social cleavages that marked the social structure in the past, either through elimination of the divisions or by transcending them to allow them to be reproduced in non-violent ways; address the sociological issues that encourage people to develop senses of flourishing and well being; and (re)introduce public policies that deliver fairness, justice and social redistribution. It is the difficulty of doing this that marks compromise post-violence societies as they were defined in chapter 1, for negative peace through conquest or cartography is not possible and positive peace is not easy to implement. The three axes by which types of post-violence societies were categorized – relational closeness versus distance, cultural capital versus annihilation, and territorial integrity versus separation – simultaneously encapsulate the problems faced by compromise negotiated peace accords and reinforce the importance of social structural change to the stability of positive peace. In compromise post-violence societies where territorial integrity has been preserved and groups retain their cultural capital and co-exist in a context of relational distance, peace processes have hard ground to plough in nurturing positive peace. This is why so many stumble along at the bottom, go through various iterations, or are eventually abandoned or replaced by military strategies.

Yet some peace processes succeed in realizing positive peace. Social change is paradoxical in that it is easier where there is a sense of accompanying continuity in both norms and affective relations. Relational closeness, which facilitates cultural continuity, may already exist between the erstwhile opponents or can be rediscovered by the reimagining and re-remembering of history. The heat can be taken out of group boundary markers by the development of cross-cutting cleavages and each group's cultural capital can be used as bridging social capital to establish common links in this way. The nation, while remaining intact territorially, can embark internally on a nation-building project based on a new inclusive national narrative, and public policies can be devised which address some or all of the key sociological issues thrown up by the transition. There are no perfect peace processes but I have deployed throughout case studies which demonstrate how, in a few, some of the sociological issues are being worked through.

So important are these sociological issues to the success or failure of peace accords that it is worthwhile drawing the distinction between political and social peace processes. A political peace process describes the negotiation process that culminates in the accord and which regulates conformity to the good governance reforms in the post-conflict phase. The diplomatic and conflict-resolution skills that make for successful negotiations have been taken for granted here, as have the party political manoeuvrings, inventive voting systems and electoral and constituency changes that encourage successful political deals afterwards. Rwanda, South Africa and Northern Ireland exemplify the success of political peace processes, and the catalogue of failed or abandoned political peace processes serves to reinforce the importance of this range of issues to post-agreement stability. There is a massive literature on conflict resolution and negotiation skills, some by successful negotiators disclosing their personal contribution (for Northern Ireland, see Mitchell, 2000). Handbooks for negotiators flourish, trying to distil these skills into easily accessible advice (for a selection, see: Bercovitch, Kremenyuk and Zarman, 2008; Cleary, 2000; Deutsch, Coleman and Marcus, 2006). The UN High Commission for Human Rights recently published a toolkit of practical advice for dealing with transitional justice issues (OHCHR, 2006). This has not been my focus.

My concern has been with what we can now call the social peace process. Existing alongside the political negotiations and post-violence good governance reforms must be a social peace process, requiring as many resources and as much attention as other reforms. The social peace process is about the repair and rebuilding of social relationships, interpersonal and inter-group reconciliation, the restoration of community and the social bond, and social and personal healing. Defined in this way, the social peace process realizes positive not negative peace. What this means in practice for specific post-violence societies, in terms of new social relationships and new sources of identity and community, depends on local circumstances, history and tradition, the nature of pre-conflict social relations and the level of the violence, amongst other things. It is impossible to predict what exactly is necessary for social peace in each case. However, social peace processes are largely realized through attention to the issues that have dominated here, such as civil society engagement with peace, the development of non-violent masculinities for ex-combatants, managing negative emotions and promoting positive ones, re-remembering and historical re-imagining strategies, 'truth' recovery, socially functional public victimhood and the rest. This sort of peace work can be done before and after the signed peace agreement. It is thus both a pre-requisite for the political process and an outcome of it.

It is important to stress, however, that the pre-agreement social peace process often has limited space for reconciliation, repair and restoration, although many examples can be cited to illustrate how peace groups have tried valiantly amidst the communal violence to ply their work (for histories of peace movements, see Adolf, 2009; Cortright, 2008). It is feasible before a political peace process to try to develop shared value orientations amongst protagonists and to discuss their expectations of a peaceful future. The communication of expectations and discussion of the potential for the development of agreed normative standards are very useful forms of pre-agreement social peace work. Social peace processes can, in advance of the political peace process, therefore establish whether there is a community of ends and normative consensus over means, leaving it to the negotiators to establish a discursive resolution of these disagreements in an accord. As Rex (1981: 18) discussed with respect to the sociology of conflict generally, a settlement can only be achieved when protagonists are persuaded that the costs of continuing the struggle are greater than any gain that might be realized from continuing it; and social peace processes ahead of political agreements can assist in this. For this reason it can be argued that a social peace process opens up back-channels of communication that prepare the foundations for a political peace process.

It is a moot point, however, how far, for example, the well-developed ecumenism of some minority churches and para-church groups in Northern Ireland contributed to the political peace process that resulted in the Good Friday Agreement or succeeded in breaking out from their self-contained ecumenical constituency to persuade hardliners of their errors. The rapid rise in popularity of ecumenical activity since the 1990s is largely a religious response to developments in the political peace process, with shifts in politics opening up spaces within the churches that were resisted before the political peace process. It is also doubtful, for example, that women's groups can be empowered sufficiently to realize peace without there first being a political peace process. The case of Southern Sudanese women highlights the point that, without a peace settlement, or rather one that the parties adhere to, the empowerment of women enhances their own capabilities without much advancing the general society towards a stable political peace process. The failure of women's groups in Southern Sudan to stem the violence in Darfur, despite the heavy involvement of UNIFEM, Hunt Alternatives and the global women's movement, needs to be contrasted with the contribution women's groups are making in Rwanda now that a stable peace settlement has been negotiated. It was noted in chapter 4 that many women's groups in Southern Sudan are based in neighbour- ing states because of the difficulties their presence inside the country creates for local women.

There is, thus, no sickly sentimentality for peace movements here. The global peace movement against an invasion of Iraq, for example, never witnessed before or since in its scale and spread, failed to prevent the war. By February 2009, Sri Lanka's social peace process had col- lapsed in an attempt by government forces to squash Tamil rights militarily, and the Real IRA continues to murder soldiers and police- men in March 2009, eleven years after the Good Friday Agreement. In the pre-agreement phase, the social peace process is highly constrained in the critical social spaces it can occupy within civil society and mostly restricts itself to localized efforts, to relatively safe forms of passive peace work (on the distinction between active and passive peacemak- ing, see J. D. Brewer, 2003b: 73; Brewer, Bishop and Higgins, 2001: 15–16), like ritualized denunciations of the violence, or to mobilization of the constituency of already converted peace activists.

There are many 'moments of transcendence' that occur in the pre- agreement phase that give the social peace process a spur. Some are strategically planned, most are spontaneous. They erupt, for example, as a result of widespread public outrage at an atrocity (the Northern Irish Peace People organization, for example, sprang up unprompted in response to the death of two children), following dramatic public statements of figurative forgiveness (such as by Nelson Mandela) or after significant public gestures towards tolerance and reconciliation. They can be released during large protest marches against violence or after individual acts of martyred self-sacrifice. But who now remem- bers the protester setting himself alight in front of the tanks in Beijing's Tiananmen Square or recalls the words of Gordon Wilson forgiving the IRA the Sunday morning they murdered his daughter? Moments of transcendence are just that – momentary – and their effects rarely last very long; the Peace People organization collapsed under internal dis- sension within a few years. Or, at least, they tend not to be permanent until the final throes when, paradoxically, moments of transcendence are thought to have made all the difference.

A thoroughgoing social peace process is therefore largely enabled by the political one. A political accord opens up spaces for managing the sociological issues that define the social peace process, allows the new or reformed state to combine with civil society and the grassroots in transforming private troubles into public issues, and encourages ordinary people to contemplate the necessary social change for living together peacefully with difference. Memory work, 'truth' recovery, socially functional public victimhood, the management of negative emotions and the proselytizing of positive emotions are all post-agreement concerns or better dealt with once the violence has stopped. Indeed, in several places this volume has sought to downplay the popular enthusiasm that surrounds peace initiatives like shame apologies, 'truth' commissions, restorative case conferences and cross-community work when I argued that, to be most effective, these first required the ending of violence (and thus a political peace process): they were initiatives for the post-conflict phase not a strategy to end the killings.

However, the relationship between the social and political peace processes is recursive, so that they enable and facilitate each other. While the social peace process fully blossoms only in the post-agreement stage, the political peace process will not be sustained unless the social peace process is addressed simultaneously to good governance. Sociology's chief contribution is in helping us identify that there is such a thing as the social peace process and in assisting us to understand both how it unfolds and how it can be managed in policy terms. A sociological approach to peace processes does not subvert good governance approaches but complements them by revealing what else needs to be tackled if the political peace process is to be accompanied by a successful social peace process. The sociological approach adopted here shows that, while the social peace process is largely predicated on a political peace process, the latter will not endure into the long term unless the social peace process is also successful. Political peace processes that are, in effect, drawn games, with neither side winning an outright victory in a compromise settlement, seem in particular need of having their sociological dynamic resolved, making the success of the social peace process a precursor to stability of the political one. Roland Paris's (2004: 194–6) recognition of the importance of healthy civil societies to the stability of good governance structures is a nod in the direction of sociology's more open approach.

It is a common observation in peace processes that the agreement displayed by parties to the negotiations is in advance of the reconciliation in society, leaving most peace processes as elite compromises at the top with little coming together at the bottom. This is in part because, as we have seen, there is little space for a social peace process in the

pre-agreement phase – which was the case even with the two most successful political peace processes in recent history, Northern Ireland and
South Africa, although the pre-accord social peace process was more
advanced in the former than the latter. The observation is grounded in
the fact that social peace processes are harder to cement than political
ones in the post-agreement period; the evidence of several failed political agreements should not disguise the fact that reconciliation in society
is an even harder task, for the reasons outlined in this book.

Progress in some areas of the social peace process is easier than
in others (both in the pre- and post-agreement phases), depending
upon local circumstances, the history of social relations and the nature
and level of the violence, amongst other things. Progress in the social
peace process can also seem to lag behind developments in the post-
agreement elite political compromise, leading to public frustration and
disappointment, which only makes advance in the social peace process
appear slower and less successful. This is a dangerous perception, for
it can encourage ordinary people to lose faith in the possibility of a successful social peace process. This reinforces the importance of garnering
positive emotions like hope–anticipation to overcome the travails. And
yet the recursive relationship between the two kinds of peace process
means that the stability of the political peace process is predicated on
progress in the social peace process. The elite political compromise will
not be sustained into the long term unless there is a policy initiative to
try to effect reconciliation in society. This is the importance of a sociological approach to peace processes.

## What are the lessons of this book?

I hesitate in developing a list of policy guidelines or tips to peacemakers.
This has already been done many times by others. Nonetheless, some
clear injunctions follow from the preceding pages. It is clear that peace
processes must be both top-down *and* bottom-up. Elite compromises
at the top table, if they are to last, must have a reality underneath in
the desire amongst ordinary people for peace and a willingness in civil
society to engage with the terms of a negotiated peace settlement. Peace
processes must have both a political *and* social dimension, with the
social peace process being treated as equally as important as the political
one by policy makers, negotiators, third party mediators and new good
governance structures. A social peace process has three tiers – the state,
civil society and grassroots – and is more likely to succeed when policy
issues are managed in a combination of all three. The new state can only
do so much, especially if it is weak or unable to engage in economic
redistribution; civil society and the grassroots need to work in conjunction with the state in taking responsibility for tackling the social peace

process in areas of their competence and remit. This means that there have to be local, national and global spaces of peace – spaces where the violence is moderated, where the social peace process is advanced in the pre-agreement phase, and where, post-agreement, the social peace process is accelerated apace by the provision of spaces of hoping, forgiving and apologizing, spaces for memory work, for 'truth' recovery and for socially functional public victimhood. Spaces can be opened up for social reintegration of former combatants, for restorative justice, citizenship education and so on. It is necessary for the state and civil society to provide these spaces and for the grassroots to occupy them.

This returns us to the starting point of this book. It is not only with respect to organized violence that globalization is an important consideration in late modernity. While the sad truth remains that some communal conflicts cannot be resolved in the lifetimes of several generations, globalization mediates new forms of peace work and has intensified the international focus on local wars, extended the reach and impact of civil society and INGOs, and empowered the grassroots through means of global networks. INGOs are more prevalent and powerful as a result of globalization; indeed their expansion contributes to the process of globalization itself. Philanthropic foundations devoted to peace now abound as part of a global financial investment in peace, and various international regulatory frameworks, mostly based around the United Nations, mediate the international community's interest in peacemaking. Global civil society, working in a glocal way through indigenous civil society groups and local grassroots bodies, is an actuality. While this term has it critics (Keane, 2003), and some observers have complained that there has been little empirical research on global civil society (Holton, 2005: 24), I have, hopefully, demonstrated that global civil society furnishes the cosmopolitan virtues that form the basis of the moral imagination for peace, it has the resources and skills that local groups can appropriate in order to turn private troubles into public issues on a global arena, it has the international networks that empower national civil society and the grassroots into working for peace locally and globally, and it has the force of numbers, the international connections and humanitarian regulatory frameworks to make a difference by turning localized wars into successful peace processes.

The social peace process is inextricably bound up with global civil society and exemplifies all three of the meanings given to the term in sociology (see Holton, 2005: 133). We can see with respect to its involvement in social peacemaking that global civil society is: a distinct transnational sphere or space, in between the state and the market, that is glocal in its character, exploited by local groups seeking to place themselves on a global stage and by INGOs working in localized areas in conjunction with them; a form of social activism transnational in its reach and motivated by humanitarian and cosmopolitan virtues; and a set of autonomous organizations and networks that consider global society the space for their activities, whether these be research, relief and charity work, local empowerment, peacemaking or the monitoring and regulation of behaviour.

Global civil society is largely Western in its values and reproduces the hegemony of the West despite the anti-Westernism of some elements of global civil society; this is the paradox of the anti-globalization movement, for its global activities, values and networks reproduce the very thing they rail against. And some elements of global civil society are full of loathing, hatred, xenophobia, ethnic and national exclusivism and racism towards everybody but themselves, including towards the West. Israel–Palestine is fought over by Mullahs, ultra-orthodox Jews and conservative evangelical Christians who all exemplify what Chambers and Kopstein (2001) term 'bad civil society', and although this example might seem to evince the vigour of national identities, the groups involved are determinedly global in the way they act. For these reasons, Holton (2005: 139) refers not to one global civil society but several, as different parts occupy distinct global spaces.

The fissures in global civil society reproduce themselves glocally in specific peace processes in two ways. Leaving aside those regressive parts of global civil society that oppose peace, firstly, progressive groups can be divided over means. Civil society is a politically contested space in Sri Lanka; and we saw in the case of Rwanda, for example, that global human rights groups and the global women's movement took different positions on the viability of reconstruction in the country, illustrating that parts of progressive global civil society can differ in strategy, ideology and practice, resulting in them occupying different – even opposed – spaces locally. Global human rights groups criticize transitional justice in Rwanda, while global women's groups applaud the reconstruction for empowering women; and both are right if we conceive of global civil society as containing fractures which differentiate groups glocally within particular peace processes.

Secondly, progressive groups can be divided over ends. There is no discord over commitment to peace, but peace can mean different things. One notable disagreement is over commitment to negative peace (the ending of killings) or positive peace (the wholesale reordering of social relations). The latter requires more than just agreement to a negotiated settlement. I have throughout stressed another division, contrasting those parts of global civil society that occupy spaces where good governance is the solution to communal violence, essentially advocating a political peace process that reproduces Western notions of democracy, market economics and justice, with those that work to realize a social peace process, seeing healing, reconciliation and the restoration of the social bond as the goal. The latter, for example, is achieved by confronting the negative effects of communal violence on gender identities by empowering local women's groups and working to rid male ex-combatants of socially destructive violent masculinities; by facilitating local groups to manage 'truth' recovery, social memory work and victimhood experiences; by the provision of spaces of peace, places where hoping, forgiving, apologizing, remembrance and re-remembrances and the like can be done, amongst other things. Social peace processes thus put in high relief the global–local connections that mark the complexity of globalization in late modernity and seem to represent one way in which glocalization as a process is socially reproduced.

Charles Wright Mills once said that sociology cannot save the world – adding the caveat, however, that he saw no harm in trying (2000[1959]: 193). I take his observation to mean that, if sociology cannot solve problems, it offers, nonetheless, an informed, wise and enlightened commentary on current experiences, widening our horizons beyond usual perspectives. Putting this in a different way, as another grandee of sociology wrote, 'the fascination of sociology lies in the fact that its perspective makes us see in a new light the very world in which we have lived our lives' (Berger, 1963: 32–3). The small foothill this book has climbed hopefully opens up such a vista, in which sociology guides us towards a more holistic account of peace processes. We must now triumph beyond base camp.

# References

Abu-Nimer, M. (2004) 'Education for Coexistence and Arab–Jewish Encounters in Israel: Potential and Challenges', *Journal of Social Issues*, 60: 405–22.

Adelman, H. and Suhrke, A. (1999) *Paths to Genocide*. New Brunswick: Transaction Books.

Adolf, A. (2009) *Peace: A World History*. Cambridge: Polity Press.

Ahmed, E., Nathan, H., Braithwaite, J. and Braithwaite, V. (2001) *Shame Management through Reintegration*. Cambridge: Cambridge University Press.

Akenson, D. (1988) *Small Difference*. Dublin: Gill and Macmillan.

Alexander, J. (2004a) 'Toward a Theory of Cultural Trauma', in Alexander et al. (2004).

—— (2004b) 'On the Social Construction of Moral Universals: The "Holocaust" from War Crime to Trauma Drama', in Alexander et al. (2004).

Alexander, J., Eyerman, R., Giesen, B., Smelser, N. and Sztompka, P. (2004) *Cultural Trauma and Collective Identity*. Berkeley: University of California Press.

Alonso, H. H. (1993) *Peace as a Women's Issue*. Syracuse: Syracuse University Press.

Amnesty International (2004) *The Impact of Armed Conflict on Girls*, at www.amnesty.org/pages/svaw_militarisation.php.

—— (2005) *Shield the Women of Darfur*, at www/amnestyusa.org/shield-the-women-of-darfur/shield-the-women-of-darfur/.

Amstutz, M. (2004) *The Healing of Nations*. London: Rowman and Littlefield.

An Crann/The Tree (2000) *Bear in Mind: Stories of the Troubles*. Belfast: Lagan Press.

Anderson, K. and Rieff, D. (2005) 'Global Civil Society: A Sceptical

View', in Anheier, Glasius and Kaldor (2005).

Anderson, P. (1992) *Imagined Communities*. London: Verso.

Anheier, H. and Daly, S. (2005) 'Philanthropic Foundations: A New Global Force?' in Anheier, Glasius and Kaldor (2005).

Anheier, H. and Simmons, A. (2004) *The Role of Philanthropy in Globalisation*. International Network on Strategy Philanthropy. Gutersloh: Bertlesmann Foundation.

Anheier, H., Glasius, M. and Kaldor, M. (eds) (2005) *Global Civil Society 2004/5*. London: Sage.

Appiah, K. A. (2007) *Cosmopolitanism*. New York: W. W. Norton.

Appleby, S. R. (2000) *The Ambivalence of the Sacred*. Lanham, MD: Rowman and Littlefield.

Arendt, H. (1998[1958]) *The Human Condition*. Chicago: University of Chicago Press.

Armstrong, K. (2007) *The Bible: The Biography*. London: Atlantic Books.

Arnson, C. J. (1999) *Comparative Peace Processes in Latin America*. Washington, DC: Woodrow Wilson Center Press.

Ashford, M. W. and Huet-Vaughn, Y. (2000) 'The Impact of War on Women', in B. Levy and V. Sidel (eds), *War and Public Health*. Washington, DC: American Public Health Association.

Asmal, K. (2000) 'Truth, Reconciliation and Justice: The South African Experience in Perspective', *Modern Law Review*, 63: 1–24.

Atack, I. (2005) *The Ethics of Peace and War*. Edinburgh: Edinburgh University Press.

Audi, R. and Wolterstorff, N. (1996) *Religion in the Public Square*. Lanham, MD: Rowman and Littlefield.

Bairner, A. (1999) 'Masculinity, Violence and the Irish Peace Process', *Capital and Class*, 69: 125–44.

Bandura, A. (1989) 'Human Agency in Social Cognitive Theory', *American Psychologist*, 44: 1175–84.

Barash, D. and Webel, C. (2009) *Peace and Conflict Studies*. London: Sage.

Barclay, C. (1996) 'Autobiographical Remembering', in Rubin (1996).

Barnes, C. and Polzer, T. (2000) *Sierra Leone Peace Process: Learning from the Past to Address Current Challenges*. London: Conciliation Resources.

Bar-Tal, D. (2001) 'Why Does Fear Override Hope in Societies Engulfed by Intractable Conflict, as It Does in the Israeli Society?' *Political Psychology*, 22: 601–27.

Baubock, R. (1999) 'Liberal Justifications for Ethnic Group Rights', in C. Joppke and S. Lukes (eds), *Multi-Cultural Questions*. Oxford: Oxford University Press.

Bauman, Z. (1989) *Modernity and the Holocaust*. Cambridge: Polity Press.

———— (1998) *Globalization: The Human Consequences*. Cambridge: Polity Press.

Becker, L. (1980) 'The Obligation to Work', *Ethics*, 9: 35–49.

Bell, D. (1962) *The End of Ideology*. Cambridge, MA: Harvard University Press.

Bercovitch, J., Kremenyuk, V. and Zartman, I. (2008) *Sage Handbook of Conflict Resolution*. London: Sage.

Berger, P. (1963) *Invitation to Sociology*. Harmondsworth: Penguin.

———— (2005) 'Religion and Global Civil Society', in Juergensmeyer (2005).

Bloomfield, K. (1998a) *We Will Remember Them: Report of the Northern Ireland Victims Commissioner*. Belfast: HMSO. Accessible at http:// cain.ulst.ac.uk/issues/victims/docs/bloomfield98.pdf.

———— (1998b) 'How Should We Remember?: The Work of the Northern Ireland Victims Commission', in Hamber (1998c).

Bloomfield, S. (2006) 'Power of Forgiveness Offers Hope for Peace in War-Torn Uganda', *The Independent*, 25 September.

Boraine, A. (2001) *A Country Unmasked: Inside South Africa's Truth and Reconciliation Commission*. Oxford: Oxford University Press.

Borneman, J. (2002) 'Reconciliation after Ethnic Cleansing', *Public Culture*, 14: 281–304.

Bovens, M. (1998) *The Quest for Responsibility*. Cambridge: Cambridge University Press.

Braithwaite, J. (2002) *Restorative Justice and Responsive Regulation*. Oxford: Oxford University Press.

Braithwaite, J. and Mugford, S. (1994) 'Conditions of Successful Reintegration Ceremonies', *British Journal of Criminology*, 34: 139–71.

Braithwaite, J. and Roche, D. (2001) 'Responsibility and Restorative Justice', in G. Bazemore and M. Schiff (eds), *Restorative Community Justice: Repairing Harm and Transforming Communities*. Cincinnati, OH: Anderson Publishing.

Braithwaite, V. (2004) 'The Hope Process and Social Inclusion', *Annals of the American Academy of Political and Social Science*, 592: 128–51.

Brewer, J. D. (1990) *The Royal Irish Constabulary: An Oral History*. Belfast: Institute of Irish Studies.

———— (1998) *Anti-Catholicism in Ireland 1600–1998*. Basingstoke: Macmillan.

———— (2000) *Ethnography*. Buckingham: Open University Press.

———— (2003a) *C. Wright Mills and the Ending of Violence*. Basingstoke: Palgrave.

———— (2003b) 'Northern Ireland', in Cjeka and Bamat (2003).

———— (2003c) 'Are There Any Christians in Northern Ireland?', in A.M. Gray, K. Lloyd, P. Devine, G. Robinson and D. Heenan (eds), *Social Attitudes in Northern Ireland: The Eighth Report*. London: Pluto Press.

—— (2006) 'Memory, Truth and Victimhood in Post-Trauma Societies', in G. Delanty and K. Kumar (eds), *The SAGE Handbook of Nations and Nationalism*. London: Sage.

—— (guest Ed.) (2007) Special issue on 'Sociology and its Strange "Others"', *History of Human Sciences*, 20, 2: 1–175.

Brewer, J. D., Bishop, K. and Higgins, G. (2001) *Peacemaking among Protestants and Catholics in Northern Ireland*. Belfast: Centre for the Social Study of Religion, Queen's University of Belfast.

Brewer, W. F. (1996) 'What is Recollective Memory?' in Rubin (1996).

Brown Childs, J. (2003a) *Transcommunality: From the Politics of Conversion to the Ethics of Respect*. Philadelphia: Temple University Press.

—— (2003b) 'United States', in Cejka and Bamat (2003).

Brubaker, R. (2002) 'Ethnicity without Groups', *Archives Européennes de Sociologie*, 43: 163–89.

Bruce, S. (2007) *Paisley*. Oxford: Oxford University Press.

Burke, K. F. (2001) 'Memory and Martyrdom', in Hayes and Tombs (2001).

Burnett, R. and Maruna, S. (2004) 'So "Prison Works" Does It?' *The Howard Journal of Criminal Justice*, 43: 390–404.

Burton, M. (1998) 'The South African Truth and Reconciliation Commission', in Hamber (1998c).

Butalia, U. (1997) 'A Question of Silence: Partition, Women and the State', in Lentin (1997)

—— (2000) *The Other Side of Silence*. London: Hurst.

—— (2002) *Speaking Peace: Women's Voices in Kashmir*. London: Zed Books.

Cabrera, R. (1998) 'Should We Remember? Recovering Historical Memory in Guatemala', in Hamber (1998c).

Caesar, E. (2009) 'Living with the Enemy', *Sunday Times Magazine*, 4 January.

Calhoun, C. (1992) 'Changing One's Heart', *Ethics*, 103: 76–96.

Campbell, C. (1992) 'Learning to Kill? Masculinity, the Family and Violence in Natal', *Journal of Southern African Studies*, 18: 614–28.

Carothers, T. and Ottaway, M. (2000) *Funding Virtue: Civil Society Aid and Democracy Promotion*. Washington, DC: Carnegie Endowment for International Peace.

Casanova, J. (1994) *Public Religions in the Modern World*. Chicago: University of Chicago Press.

Catholic Relief Service (2005) *In Solidarity with Colombia*. Baltimore, MD: Catholic Relief Services.

Cejka, M. (2003) 'God, Justice, Gender and the Family', in Cejka and Bamat (2003).

Cejka, M. and Bamat, T. (eds) (2003) *Artisans for Peace*. Maryknoll, NY: Orbis Books.

Chakravarty, A. (2006) '*Gacaca* Courts in Rwanda: Explaining Divisions within the Human Rights Community', *Yale Journal of International Affairs*, 1: 132–45.

Chambers, S. and Kopstein, J. (2001) 'Bad Civil Society', *Political Theory*, 29: 837–65.

Chapman, A. and Ball, D. (2001) 'The Truth about Truth Commissions: Comparative Lessons from Haiti, South Africa and Guatemala', *Human Rights Quarterly*, 23: 1–43.

Christianson, S. A. and Safer, M. (1996) 'Emotional Events and Emotions in Autobiographical Memories', in Rubin (1996).

Church of Ireland (1996) *Brokenness, Forgiveness, Healing and Peace in Northern Ireland.* Lectures at St Anne's 1996. Belfast.

Ciabattari, J. (2000) 'Rwanda Gambles on Renewal not Revenge', *Women's E News*. Accessible at www.womensenews.org/article.cfm/dyn/aid/301/context.

Clapham, C. (1998) 'Rwanda: The Perils of Peacemaking', *Journal of Peace Research*, 35: 193–210.

Cleary, P. (2000) *The Negotiation Handbook.* Armonk, NY: M. E. Sharpe.

Clegg, C. (1999) 'Feminist Recovery from *My Father's House*', *Feminist Review*, 61: 67–82.

Cobban, H. (2006) *Amnesty after Atrocity?* Boulder: Paradigm.

Cock, J. (1991) *Colonels and Cadres: War and Gender in South Africa.* Oxford: Oxford University Press.

Cockburn, C. (2001) 'The Gendered Dynamics of Armed Conflict and Political Violence', in F. Clark and C. Moser (eds), *Gender, Armed Conflict and Political Violence.* London: Zed Books.

Cohen, S. (2001) *States of Denial.* Cambridge: Polity Press.

Coiste na n-Iarchimi (2003) *A Museum at Long Kesh or the Maze?* Belfast: Coiste na n-Iarchimi.

Collins, R. (2004) *Interaction Ritual Chains.* Princeton: Princeton University Press.

Connerton, P. (1989) *How Societies Remember.* Cambridge: Cambridge University Press.

——— (2008) 'Seven Types of Forgetting', *Memory Studies*, 1: 59–72.

Connolly, L. (1999) 'Feminist Politics and the Peace Process', *Capital and Class*, 69: 145–59.

Conover, P., Leonard, S. and Searing, D. (1993) 'Duty is a Four-Letter Word: Democratic Citizenship in the Liberal Polity', in G. Marcus and R. Harrison (eds), *Reconsidering the Democratic Public.* Philadelphia: Penn State University Press.

Conway, B. (2003) 'Active Remembering, Selective Forgetting and Collective Identity: The Case of Bloody Sunday', *Identity*, 13: 305–23.

——— (2006) 'Foreigners, Faith and Fatherland', *Sociological Origins*, 5: 5–35.

——— (2008) 'Local Conditions, Global Environment and Transnational

Discourses in Memory Work: The Case of Bloody Sunday', *Memory Studies*, 1: 187–209.

Corcoran, F. (2000) 'Technologies of Memory', in E. Slater and M. Peillon (eds), *Memories of the Present*. Dublin: Institute of Public Administration.

Corey, A. and Joireman, S. (2004) 'Retributive Justice: The *Gacaca* Courts in Rwanda', *African Affairs*, 103: 73–89.

Cortright, D. (2008) *Peace: A History of Movements and Ideas*. Cambridge: Cambridge University Press.

Cory, P. (2005) *Cory Collusion Inquiry Report*. London: HMSO. Accessible at http://cain.ulst.ac.uk/issues/collusion/source.htm.

Coulter, Carol (1998) 'Feminism and Nationalism in Ireland', in Miller (1998).

Coulter, Colin (1999) *Contemporary Northern Irish Society*. London: Zed Books.

Courville, S. and Piper, N. (2004) 'Harnessing Hope through NGO Activism', *Annals of the American Academy of Political and Social Science*, 592: 39–61.

Crighton, E. (1998) 'Beyond Neo-Liberalism: Peacemaking in Northern Ireland', *Social Justice*, 25: 75–89.

Dagger, R. (1997) *Civic Virtues*. Oxford: Oxford University Press.

Dahrendorf, R. (2002) 'Adam Ferguson: How Civil Will Future Society Be?' Public Lecture, University of Edinburgh. Accessible at www.ed.ac.uk/events/lectures/enlightenment.

Darby, J. (ed.) (2001) *The Effects of Violence on Peace Processes*. Washington, DC: United States Institute of Peace Press.

Darby, J. and MacGinty, R. (2000) *The Management of Peace Processes*. London: Macmillan.

Davis, F. (1979) *Yearning for Yesterday*. New York: Free Press.

Deegan, M. J. (1988) *Jane Addams and the Men of the Chicago School, 1892–1920*. New Brunswick, NJ: Transaction Books.

Degnen, C. (2005) 'Relationality, Place and Absence: Dimensional Perspective in Social Memory', *Sociological Review*, 53: 729–44.

Delanty, G. (2006) 'Cosmopolitan Imagination', *British Journal of Sociology*, 57: 25–47.

Derrida, J. (1998) *An Interview with Professor Jacques Derrida*. Interviewed by Michael Naftali. Accessible at www.yadvashem.org.

——— (2002) *On Cosmopolitanism and Forgiveness*. London: Routledge.

De Silva, K. (2006) *Peace in Sri Lanka*. Accessible at www.peaceinsrilanka.org/peace2005/insidepage/background/background.asp.

Desroche, H. (1979) *The Sociology of Hope*. London: Routledge.

Destexhe, A. (1995) *Rwanda and Genocide in the Twentieth Century*. London: Pluto Press.

D'Estree, T. and Babbitt, E. (1998) 'Women and the Art of Peacemaking', *Political Psychology*, 19: 185–209.

Deutsch, M., Coleman, P. and Marcus, E. (2006) *The Handbook of Conflict Resolution: Theory and Practice*. 2nd edn. San Francisco: Jossey Bass.

Devotta, N. (2005) 'Civil Society and NGOs in Sri Lanka: Peacemakers or Parasites?' *Civil Wars*, 7: 171–82.

De Waal, A. (2007) *War in Darfur and the Search for Peace*. Cambridge, MA: Harvard University Press.

Digeser, P. (1998) 'Forgiveness and Politics', *Political Theory*, 16: 700–24.

——— (2001) *Political Forgiveness*. Ithaca, NY: Cornell University Press.

Dinnen, S., Jowitt, A. and Newton-Cain, T. (2002) *A Kind of Mending: Restorative Justice in the Pacific Islands*. Canberra: Pandanus Books.

Dobson, A. (2003) *Citizenship and the Environment*. Oxford: Oxford University Press.

——— (2006) 'Thick Cosmopolitanism', *Political Studies*, 54: 165–84.

Dougherty, B. (2004) 'Searching for Answers', *African Studies Quarterly*, 8: 39–56.

Drahos, P. (2004) 'Trading in Public Hope', *Annals of the American Academy of Political and Social Science*, 592: 18–38.

Dryzek, J. (2005) 'Deliberative Democracy in Divided Societies', *Political Theory*, 33: 218–42.

Duany, J. (2003) 'South Sudan', in Cejka and Bamat (2003).

Dunn, S. and Morgan, V. (1994) *Protestant Alienation in Northern Ireland*. Coleraine: University of Ulster.

Eberly, D. (2008) *The Rise of Global Civil Society*. New York: Encounter Books.

Edge, S. (1995) 'Women Are Trouble Did You Know That Fergus: Neil Jordan's *The Crying Game*', *Feminist Review*, 50: 173–85.

——— (1998) 'Representing Gender and National Identity', in Miller (1998).

Edwards, M. (2004) *Civil Society*. Cambridge: Polity Press.

Elbert, K (2005) *Maximizing Women's Contributions to Conflict Prevention*. Washington, DC: Hunt Alternatives Fund. Accessible at www.womenwagingpeace.net/content/articles/0417a.html.

Elster, J. (1989) *Nuts and Bolts for the Social Sciences*. Cambridge: Cambridge University Press.

——— (2004) *Closing the Books*. Cambridge: Cambridge University Press.

Eltringham, N. (2004) *Accounting for Horror: Post-Genocide Debates in Rwanda*. London: Pluto Press.

Enloe, C. (2000) *Maneuvers: The International Politics of Militarizing Women's Lives*. Berkeley: University of California Press.

Ensalaco, M. (1994) 'Truth Commissions for Chile and El Salvador', *Human Rights Quarterly*, 16: 656–75.

Eolas (2002) *Consultation Paper on Truth and Justice*. Belfast: Relatives for Justice. Accessible at www.relativesforjustice.com/downloads/eolas.pdf.

EPIC (n.d.) *Truth Recovery: A Contribution from within Loyalism*. Belfast: EPIC.

Erdelyi, M. (2008) 'Forgetting and Remembering in Psychology', *Memory Studies*, 1: 273–8.

Ericksson, M. and Wallensteen, P. (2004) 'Armed Conflict, 1989–2003', *Journal of Peace Research*, 41: 625–36.

Erikson, K. (1976) *Everything in its Path*. New York: Simon and Schuster.

Erskine, T. (2000) 'Embedded Cosmopolitanism and the Case for War', *Global Society*, 14: 569–90.

*European Journal of Social Theory* (2008) Special issue on 'Post-Traumatic Societies', 11 (3): 283–438.

Evangelista, M. (2005) *Peace Studies*. London: Taylor and Francis.

Eyerman, R. (2004) 'Cultural Trauma: Slavery and the Formation of African American Identity', in Alexander et al. (2004).

Fair, C. (2005) 'Diaspora Involvement in Insurgencies', *Nationalism and Ethnic Politics*, 11: 125–56.

Faith and Politics Group (1991) *Remembering Our Past: 1690 and 1916*. Belfast: Faith and Politics Group.

——— (1998) *Remembrance and Forgetting*. Belfast: Faith and Politics Group.

Fay, M. T., Morrissey, M. and Smyth, M. (1999) *Northern Ireland's Troubles: The Human Costs*. London: Pluto Press.

Fearon, K. (1999) *Women's Work: The Story of the Northern Ireland Women's Coalition*. Belfast: Blackstaff Press.

Fentress, J. and Wickham, C. (1992) *Social Memory*. Oxford: Blackwell.

Ferguson, A. (1966[1767]) *An Essay on the History of Civil Society*. Edinburgh: Edinburgh University Press.

Fisher, E. and McKenna, R. (1996) *Maya Cultural Activism in Guatemala*. Austin: University of Texas Press.

Fivush, R., Haden, C. and Reese, E. (1996) 'Remembering, Recounting and Reminiscing', in Rubin (1996).

Foster, C. (1989) *Women for All Seasons: The Story of the Women's International League for Peace and Freedom*. Athens: University of Georgia Press.

Fraser, T. G. (2000) *The Irish Parading Tradition*. Basingstoke: Palgrave.

Frei, N. (2002) *Adenauer's Germany and the Nazi Past*. New York: Columbia University Press.

Frost, M. (2008) 'Tragedy, Reconciliation and Reconstruction', in *European Journal of Social Theory*, 11: 351–66.

Fukuyama, F. (1992) *The End of History and the Last Man*. New York: Free Press.

Gallagher, M. (1999) 'I Married Rambo: Spectacle and Melodrama in the Hollywood Action Film', in C. Sparrett (ed.), *Mythologies of Violence in Postmodern Media*. Detroit: Wayne State University Press.

Galtung, J. (1969) 'Violence, Peace and Peace Research', *Journal of Peace Research*, 6: 167–91.
────── (1996) *Peace by Peaceful Means*. London: Sage.
Garfield, R. and Neugut, A. (2000) 'The Human Consequences of War', in B. Levy and V. Sidel (eds), *War and Public Health*. Washington, DC: American Public Health Association.
Garfinkel, H. (1956) 'Conditions of Successful Degradation Ceremonies', *American Journal of Sociology*, 61: 420–4.
Gasper, K. (2003) 'The Philippines', in Cejka and Bamat (2003).
Gawn, R. (2007) 'Truth Cohabitation: A Truth Commission for Northern Ireland?' *Irish Political Studies*, 22: 339–61.
Gellner, E. (1994) 'Adam Ferguson', in *Conditions of Liberty*. London: Hamish Hamilton.
────── (1996) 'Adam Ferguson and the Surprising Robustness of Civil Society', in E. Gellner and C. Cansino (eds), *Liberalism in Modern Times*. Budapest: Central European University Press.
Gibiro, G. (2004) 'Rwanda Genocide – Women behind Bars for Genocide', *International Criminal Tribunal for Rwanda News*. Accessible at www.hirondelle.org/hirondelle.nsf.
Gibson, J. (2004) 'Does Truth Lead to Reconciliation: Testing the Causal Assumptions of the South African Truth and Reconciliation Process', *American Journal of Political Science*, 48: 210–17.
Giddens, A. (1990) *The Consequences of Modernity*. Cambridge: Polity Press.
────── (1996) *In Defence of Sociology*. Cambridge: Polity Press.
────── (1998) *The Third Way*. Cambridge: Polity Press.
────── (2000) *The Third Way and Its Critics*. Cambridge: Polity Press.
Gobodo-Madikizela, P. (2008) 'Empathetic Repair after Mass Trauma: When Vengeance is Arrested', in *European Journal of Social Theory 11*: 331–50.
Goffman, E. (1959) *The Presentation of Self in Everyday Life*. Harmondsworth: Penguin.
Goodin, R. (2002) 'Structures of Mutual Obligation', *Journal of Social Policy*, 21: 579–96.
Govier, T. (1999) 'Forgiveness and the Unforgiveable', *American Psychological Quarterly*, 36: 59–75.
Greenhill, K. and Major, S. (2007) 'The Perils of Profiling: Civil War Spoilers and the Collapse of Intrastate Peace Accords', *International Security*, 31: 7–40.
Griffin, V. (2002) *Enough Religion to Make Us Hate*. Dublin: Columba Press.
Griswold, C. (2007) *Forgiveness: A Philosophical Exploration*. Cambridge: Cambridge University Press.
Hall, J. and Finch, F. (2005) 'Self-Forgiveness', *Journal of Social and Clinical Psychology*, 24: 621–37.

Hamber, B. (1998a) 'The Past Imperfect: Exploring Northern Ireland, South Africa and Guatemala', in Hamber (1998c).

—— (1998b) 'Remembering to Forget', in Hamber (1998c).

—— (ed.) (1998c) *Past Imperfect*. Derry: INCORE.

—— (2001) 'Does Truth Heal?' in N. Bigger (ed.) *Burying the Past*. Washington, DC: Georgetown University Press.

—— (2004) 'Public Memorials and Reconciliation Processes in Northern Ireland', paper presented at the conference on Trauma and Transitional Justice in Divided Societies, Warrington, VA, 27–29 March 2004. Accessible at www.brandonhamber.com/conferences2004.htm.

Hamber, B., Hillyard, P., Maguire, A., McWilliams, M., Robinson, G. and Russell, D. (2006) 'Discourses of Transition: Re-Imagining Women's Security', *International Relations*, 20: 487–502.

Hampson, F. O. (1996) *Nurturing Peace*. Washington, DC: United States Institute of Peace Press.

—— (2002) *Madness in the Multitude*. Oxford: Oxford University Press.

Harbom, L., Hogbladh, S. and Wallensteen, P. (2005) 'Armed Conflict and Peace Agreements', *Journal of Peace Research*, 43: 617–31.

Harland, K., Beattie, K. and McCready, S. (2005) *Young Men and the Squeeze of Masculinity*. Occasional Paper no. 1, Centre for Young Men's Studies, University of Ulster.

Hart, G. (2002) *Disabling Globalization: Places of Power in Post Apartheid South Africa*. Berkeley: University of California Press.

Harvey, D. (2000) *Spaces of Hope*. Berkeley: University of California Press.

Havel, V. (1990) *Letters to Olga*. London: Faber and Faber.

Hayes, M. A. and Tombs, D. (eds) (2001) *Truth and Memory: The Church and Human Rights in El Salvador and Guatemala*. Leominster: Gracewing.

Hayner, P. (1994) 'Fifteen Truth Commissions: A Comparative Study', *Human Rights Quarterly*, 16: 597–655.

—— (2002) *Unspeakable Truths*. London: Routledge.

Healing Through Remembering Project (2002) *Report of the Healing Through Remembering Project*. Belfast: Healing Through Remembering Project. Accessible at www.healthingthroughremembering.org/report.pdf

Held, D., McGrew, A., Goldblatt, D. and Perraton, J. (1999) *Global Transformations: Politics, Economics and Culture*. Cambridge: Polity Press.

Helms, E. (2003) 'Women as Agents of Ethnic Reconciliation? Women's NGOs and International Intervention in Postwar Bosnia-Herzegovina', *Women's Studies International Forum*, 26: 15–33.

Henderson, J. (1999) *Memory and Forgetting*. London: Routledge.

Hennessey, T. (2007) 'The Politics of Northern Ireland', in P. Addison and H. Jones (eds), *A Companion to Contemporary Britain 1939–2000*. Oxford: Blackwell.

Herbert, D. (2003) *Religion and Civil Society*. Aldershot: Ashgate.

Hird, M. (2002) *Engendering Violence*. Aldershot: Ashgate.

Hirsh, D. (2003) *Law Against Genocide: Cosmopolitan Trials*. London: Glasshouse Press.

Hitchcock, W. (2009) *Liberation*. London: Faber and Faber.

Ho, K. (2007) 'Structural Violence as a Human Rights Violation', *Essex Human Rights Review*, 4: 1–17.

Hochschild, A. (1983) *Managed Heart*. Berkeley: University of California Press.

Hodgkin, M. and Montefiore, P. (2004) 'The Rwandan Forum, 2004', *History Workshop Journal*, 60: 1–24.

Hoglund, K. (2008) 'Violence in War-To-Democracy Transitions', in A. Jarstad and T. Sisk (eds) *From War to Democracy*. Cambridge: Cambridge University Press.

Holliday, L. (1997) *Children of 'The Troubles'*. New York: Washington Square Press.

Hont, I. and Ignatieff, M. (1983) *Wealth and Virtue*. Cambridge: Cambridge University Press.

Honwana, A. (2006) *Child Soldiers in Africa*. Philadelphia: University of Pennsylvania Press.

Holton, R. (2005) *Making Globalization*. Basingstoke: Palgrave.

Howley, P. (2002) 'Restorative Justice in Bougainville', in Dinnen *et al.* (2002).

—— (2003) *Breaking Spears and Mending Hearts*. London: Zed Books.

Huddock, A. (1999) *NGOs and Civil Society*. Cambridge: Polity Press.

Human Rights Watch (1996) *Shattered Lives: Sexual Violence during the Rwandan Genocide and Its Aftermath*. New York: Human Rights Watch.

—— (2004a) *Darfur Destroyed: Ethnic Cleansing by Government and Militia Forces in West Sudan*. New York: Human Rights Watch.

—— (2004b) *Struggling to Survive: Barriers to Justice for Rape Victims in Rwanda*. New York: Human Rights Watch.

Humphrys, J. (2007) *In God We Doubt*. London: Hodder and Stoughton.

Hunt, S. (2003) 'Reconciliation Is the Basis of Rwandan *Gacaca* Justice', *Rocky Mountain News*, 8 February. Accessible at www.womenwagingpeace.net/content/articles/0118a.html.

—— (2005) *That Was Not Our War: Bosnian Women Reclaiming the Peace*. Durham, NC: Duke University Press.

—— (2006) *Half-Life of a Zealot*. Durham, NC: Duke University Press.

Huntington, S. P. (1996) *The Clash of Civilisations and the Remaking of the World Order*. New York: Simon and Schuster.

Hutchinson, E. and Bleiker, R. (2008) 'Emotional Reconciliation: Reconstituting Identity and Community after Trauma', in *European Journal of Social Theory*, 11: 385–404.

Hynes, H. P. (2004) 'On the Battlefield of Women's Bodies: An Overview of the Harm of War to Women', *Women Studies International Forum*, 27: 431–45.

Ignatieff, M. (1998) *The Warrior's Honour*. London: Chatto and Windus.

INCORE (2004) *Peace Agreements*. Accessible at www.incore.ulst.ac.uk/services/cds/agreements.

Irvin, C. and Rae, J. (2001) 'Spain and the Basque Country', in Darby (2001).

Itano, N. (2004) 'Peace Process Often Ignores Female Ex-Soldiers', *Global Policy Forum*. Accessible at www.globalpolicy.org/socecon/inequal/gender/womanwar.htm.

Itto, A. (2006) *Sudan: Guests at the Table? The Role of Women in Peace Processes*. London: Conciliation Resources. Accessible at www.c-r.org/our-work/accord/sudan/women.php.

Jankélévitch, V. (2005) *Forgiveness*. Chicago: University of Chicago Press.

Janoski, T. (1998) *Citizenship and Civil Society*. Cambridge: Cambridge University Press.

Jarman, N. (2001) 'Commemorating 1916, Celebrating Difference: Parading and Painting in Belfast', in A. Forty and S. Kuchler (eds), *The Art of Forgetting*. Oxford: Berg.

Jarymowicz, M. and Bar-Tal, D. (2006) 'The Dominance of Fear over Hope in the Life of Individuals and Collectivities', *European Journal of Social Psychology*, 36: 367–92.

Jayawardena, K. (1986) *Feminism and Nationalism in the Third World*. London: Zed Books.

Jeffrey, A. (1999) *The Truth about the Truth Commission*. Johannesburg: South African Institute of Race Relations.

Jesu-Sheriff, Y. (2000) *Sierra Leone Women and the Peace Process*. London: Conciliation Resources. Accessible at www.c-r.org/accord/s-leone/accord9/women.shtml.

Johnson, N. (2003) *Ireland, the Great War and the Geography of Remembrance*. Cambridge: Cambridge University Press.

Johnson, P. (2008) 'The Geography of Insurgent Organizations', *Security Studies*, 17: 107–37.

Johnson, R. W. and Schlemmer, L. (1996) *Launching Democracy in South Africa: The First Open Election 1994*. New Haven: Yale University Press.

Juergensmeyer, M. (2000) *Terror in the Mind of God*. Berkeley: University of California Press.

——— (ed.) (2005) *Religion in Global Civil Society*. Oxford: Oxford University Press.

Justice Network (n.d.) *Dealing with Mass Atrocities and Ethnic Violence*. Justice Network. Accessible at www.acjnet.org/docs/queen.pdf.

Justice Reconciliation Project (2007) *The Cooling of Hearts*. Gulu, Uganda: Justice Reconciliation Project.

Kagan, R. (2008) *The Return of History and the End of Dreams*. New York: Knopf.

Kagan, R. and Kristol, W. (2000) *Present Dangers*. San Francisco: Encounter Books.

Kaldor, M. (1999) *New and Old Wars: Organized Violence in a Global Era*. Cambridge: Polity Press.

―――― (2003) *Global Civil Society*. Cambridge: Polity Press.

Kaldor, M. and Muro, D. (2003) 'Religious and Nationalist Militant Groups', in Kaldor, Anheier and Glasius (2003b).

Kaldor, M., Anheier, H. and Glasius, M. (2003a) 'Global Civil Society in an Era of Regresssive Globalisation' in Kaldor, Anheier and Glasius (2003b).

―――― (eds) (2003b) *Global Civil Society 2003*. Oxford: Oxford University Press.

―――― (2005) 'Introduction', in Anheier, Glasius and Kaldor (2005).

Karl, B. and Katz, S. (1987) 'Foundations and the Ruling Class', *Daedalus*, 116: 1–40.

Karstedt, S. (2002) 'Emotions and Criminal Justice', *Theoretical Criminology*, 6: 299–317.

Katz, J. (1999) *How Emotions Work*. Chicago: University of Chicago Press.

Kaufmann, C. (1996) 'Possible and Impossible Solutions to Ethnic Civil Wars', *International Security*, 20: 13–34.

―――― (1998) 'When All Else Fails: Ethnic Population Transfers and Partitions in the Twentieth Century', *International Security*, 23: 120–56.

Kaur, K. (2003) 'Guatemala', in Cejka and Bamat (2003).

Keane, J. (1988) 'Democracy and Despotism', in J. Keane (ed.), *Civil Society and the State*. London: Verso.

―――― (2003) *Global Civil Society?* Cambridge: Cambridge University Press.

Kearns, J. and Fincham, F. (2004) 'A Prototype Analysis of Forgiveness', *Journal of Personality and Social Psychology*, 30: 838–55.

Keen, D. (1998) *The Economic Functions of Violence in Civil Wars*. Oxford: Oxford University Press.

Kelsall, T. (2005) 'Truth, Lies and Ritual', *Human Rights Quarterly*, 27: 361–91.

Kennedy, L. (1996) *Colonialism, Religion and Nationalism in Ireland*. Belfast: Institute of Irish Studies.

Kirk, J. (2003) *Promoting a Gender-Just Peace: The Role of Women Teachers in Peacebuilding and Reconstruction*. Oxford: OXFAM. Accessible at

www.oxfam.org.we/what_we_do/resources/downloads/gender_
peacebuilding_and_reconstruction_kirte.pdf.

Knox, C. and Quirk, P. (2000) *Peace Building in Northern Ireland, Israel and South Africa*. London: Macmillan.

Knudsen, T. and Laustsen, C. (2006) 'The Politics of International Trusteeship', in T. Knudsen and C. Laustsen (eds), *Kosovo Between War and Peace*. London: Routledge.

Kornhauser, W. (1959) *The Politics of Mass Society*. Glencoe, IL: Free Press.

Kriesberg. L. (2003) *Constructive Conflicts*, 2nd edn. Lanham: Rowman and Littlefield.

Kumar, K. (1998) *Postconflict Elections, Democratization and International Assistance*. London: Lynne Rienner Publishers.

Kunnie, J. (2000) *Is Apartheid Really Dead?* Boulder, CO: Westview.

Kuperman, A. (2008) 'The Moral Hazard of Humanitarian Intervention', *International Studies Quarterly*, 52: 49–80.

Lancaster, R. (1988) *Thanks to God and the Revolution*. New York: Columbia University Press.

Lane, D. (2001) 'Memory in the Service of Reconciliation and Hope', in Hayes and Tombs (2001).

Larsson, J. (2004) *Understanding Religious Violence*. Aldershot: Ashgate.

Lederach, J. P. (1997) *Building Peace*. Washington, DC: United States Institute of Peace Press.

———— (2005) *The Moral Imagination*. Oxford: Oxford University Press.

Leman-Langlois, S. and Shearing, C. (2003) 'Repairing the Future: The South African Truth and Reconciliation Commission at Work', in G. Gilligan and J. Pratt (eds), *Crime, Truth and Justice*. Cullompton, UK: Willan Publishing.

Le Mon, C. (2007) 'Rwanda's Troubled *Gacaca* Courts', *Human Rights Brief*, 14: 16–20.

Lentin, R. (ed.) (1997) *Gender and Catastrophe*. London: Zed Books.

———— (1999) 'The Rape of the Nation: Women Narrativising Genocide', *Sociological Research Online*, 4. Accessible at www.socresonline.org.uk/socresonline/4/2/lentin.html.

———— (2004) 'No Women's Law Will Rot in this State: The Israeli Racial State and Feminist Resistance', *Sociological Research Online*, 9. Accessible at www.socresonline.org.uk/9/3/lentin.html.

Leonard, J. (1997) *Memorials to the Casualties of Conflict, Northern Ireland 1969 to 1997*. Belfast: Community Relations Council. Accessible at http://cain.ulst.ac.uk/issues/commemoration/leonard/leonard97.htm.

Levy, M. (2001) 'Recovery: The Uses of Memory and History in the Guatemalan Church's REMHI Project', in Hayes and Tombs (2001).

Lewis, C. S. (1952[1942]) *Mere Christianity*. London: Collins.

Linkogle, S. (1998) 'The Revolution of the Virgin Mary: Popular Religion and Social Change in Nicaragua', *Sociological Research Online*, 3. Accessible at www.socresonline.org.uk/socresonline/3/2/8.html.

Littlewood, R. (1997) 'Military Rape', *Anthropology Today*, 13: 7–16.

Longley, E. (1994) 'From Cathleen to Anorexia', in E. Boland (ed.), *A Dozen Lips*. Dublin: Attic Press.

Lu, C. (2008) 'Shame, Guilt and Reconciliation after War', in *European Journal of Social Theory*, 11: 367–84.

Lukes, S. (2009) *Moral Relativism*. London: Profile Books.

Lundy, P. (2008) *A Critical Analysis of the Historical Enquiries Team*. Final Research Report to the British Academy, 8 January.

Lundy, P. and McGovern, M. (2001) 'The Politics of Memory in Post-Conflict Northern Ireland', *Peace Review*, 13: 27–34.

——— (2002) *Ardoyne: The Untold Story*. Belfast: Beyond the Pale.

——— (2005) *A Critical Evaluation of the Role of Community-Based Truth-Telling Processes for Post-Conflict Transition: A Case Study of the Ardoyne Commemoration Project*. Belfast: Community Relations Council. Accessible at http://cain.ulst.ac.uk/issues/victims/ardoyne/lund-ymcgovern05.htm.

——— (2006a) 'Participation, Truth and Partiality', *Sociology*, 40: 71–88.

——— (2006b) 'The Ethics of Silence', *Action Research*, 4: 49–64.

——— (2008) 'Whose Justice? Rethinking Transitional Justice from the Bottom Up', *Journal of Law and Society*, 35: 265–92.

MacInnes, J. (1998) *The End of Masculinity*. Buckingham: Open University Press.

MacIntyre, A. (1981) *After Virtue*. Notre Dame: University of Notre Dame Press.

Maley, W. (2002) 'Twelve Theses on the Impact of Humanitarian Intervention', *Security Studies*, 33: 265–78.

Maley, W., Sampford, C. and Thakur, R. (2003) *From Civil Strife to Civil Society*. New York: United Nations University Press.

Manchanda, R. (2001) *Women, War and Peace in South Asia*. London: Sage.

Mann, M. (2004) *The Dark Side of Democracy: Explaining Ethnic Cleansing*. Cambridge: Cambridge University Press.

Marks, M. (2001) *Young Warriors*. Johannesburg: University of Witwatersrand Press.

Maruna, S. (2001) *Making Good*. Washington: American Psychological Association.

Maruna, S. and Mann, R. (2006) 'A Fundamental Attribution Error? Rethinking Cognitive Distortions', *Legal and Criminological Psychology*, 11: 155–77.

Maskey, A. (2002) *Memory of the Dead: Seeking Common Ground*. Transcript of Mayoral speech, Belfast City Hall, 26 June 2002.

Mazurana, D. and Carlson, K. (2004). *From Combat to Community:*

*Women and Girls of Sierra Leone.* Washington, DC: Hunt Alternatives Fund.

McAdam, D., Tarrow, S. and Tilly, C. (2001) *Dynamics of Contention.* Cambridge: Cambridge University Press.

McCready, S., Harland, K. and Beattie, K. (2006) *Violent Victims? Young Males as Perpetrators and Victims of Violence.* Research Update No. 7, Centre for Young Man's Studies, University of Ulster.

McEvoy, K. (2003) 'Beyond the Metaphor: Political Violence, Human Rights and the New Peacemaking Criminology', *Theoretical Criminology,* 7: 319–46.

McEvoy-Levy, S. (2001) 'Youth, Violence and Conflict Transformation', *Peace Review,* 13: 89–96.

McGreal, C. (2001) 'A Pearl in Rwanda's Genocide Horror', *The Guardian,* 5 December.

McKay, S. (2004) 'Reconstructing Fragile Lives: Social Reintegration in Northern Uganda and Sierra Leone', *Gender and Development,* 12: 19–30.

McKay, S. and Maurana, D. (2004) *Where Are the Girls?* Montreal: Rights and Democracy, International Centre for Human Rights and Democratic Development.

McVeigh, K. (2006) 'Spate of Killings Obstructs Rwanda's Quest for Justice', *The Observer,* 3 December.

McWilliams, M. (1995) 'Struggling for Peace and Justice: Reflections on Women's Activism in Northern Ireland', *Journal of Women's History,* 6: 13–39.

Mead, L. (1986) *Beyond Entitlement: The Social Obligations of Citizenship.* New York: Free Press.

Meintjes, S., Pillay, A. and Turshen, M. (2001) *Women in Post-Conflict Transformation.* London: Zed Books.

Melvern, L. (2004) *A People Betrayed.* London: Zed Books.

Meyers, M. (1997) *News Coverage of Violence against Women: Engendering Blame.* London: Sage.

Miller, D. (ed.) (1998) *Rethinking Northern Ireland.* London: Longman.

Mills, C. W. (2000[1959]) *The Sociological Imagination.* Oxford: Oxford University Press.

Mindanao Commission on Women (2004) 'Mindanao Women Leaders Work on Multiculturalism', *Mindanews,* 10 August. Accessible at www.mindanews.com/ads/rage/books.html.

Misztal, B. (2003) *Theories of Social Remembering.* Buckingham: Open University Press.

Mitchell, G. (2000) *Making Peace.* Berkeley: University of California Press.

Mollering, G. (2001) 'The Nature of Trust', *Sociology,* 35: 403–20.

Moltmann, J. (1967) *Theology of Hope.* New York: Harper and Row.

Moore, B. (2000) *Moral Purity and Persecution in History*. Princeton: Princeton University Press.

Morgan, V. (2003) 'The Role of Women in Community Development in Northern Ireland', in O. Hargie and D. Dickson (eds) *Researching the Troubles*. Edinburgh: Mainstream.

Morrissey, M. and Smyth, M. (2002) *Northern Ireland after the Good Friday Agreement: Victims, Grievance and Blame*. London: Pluto Press.

Muldoon, P. (2008) 'The Moral Legitimacy of Anger', in *European Journal of Social Theory*, 11: 299–314.

Murphy, W. (2003) 'Military Patrimonialism and Child Soldier Clientalism in the Liberian and Sierra Leonean Civil Wars', *African Studies Review*, 46: 61–87.

Murtagh, C. (2008) 'A Transient Transition: The Cultural and Institutional Obstacles Impeding the Northern Ireland Women's Coalition in its Progression from Informal to Formal Politics', *Irish Political Studies*, 23: 21–40.

Nash, K. (2008) 'Global Citizenship as Show Business', *Media, Culture and Society*, 30: 3–17.

Neto, P. (2002) 'Crime, Violence and Political Uncertainty in Brazil', in Mark Shaw (2002).

Ngengahayo, F. (1997) *Report of the UNCHS (Habitat) Women in Human Settlements Development Project*. Nairobi: United Nations Center for Human Settlements.

Nilsson, D. and Kovacs, M. (2005) 'Breaking the Cycle of Violence', *Civil Wars*, 7: 396–414.

Northern Ireland Association for the Care and Resettlement of Offenders (2000) *All Truth Is Bitter: A Report of the Visit of Dr Alex Boraine*. Belfast: NIACRO and Victims Support Northern Ireland. Accessible at http://cain.ulst.ac.uk/issues/victims/docs/alltruthisbitter99.pdf.

Northern Ireland Human Rights Commission (2001) *Making a Bill of Rights for Northern Ireland: A Consultation*. Belfast: NIHRC. Accessible at www.nihrc.org/documents/pubs/bor/bor_consultation01.pdf.

Novick, P. (1999) *The Holocaust in American Life*. Boston: Houghton Mifflin.

Nussbaum, M. (1996) 'Compassion: The Basic Social Emotion', *Social Philosophy and Policy*, 13: 27–58.

—— (2002) 'Education for Citizenship in an Era of Global Connections', *Studies in Philosophy and Education*, 21: 1573–91.

Oberschall, A. (2007) *Conflict and Peace Building in Divided Societies*. London: Routledge.

OHCHR (2006) *Rule of Law Tools for Post Conflict States*. New York: Office of High Commission for Human Rights.

Onyx, J. and Bullen, P. (2000) 'Measuring Social Capital in Five Communities', *Journal of Applied Behavioural Sciences*, 36: 23–42.

Orjuela, C. (2008) *The Identity Politics of Peace Building*. London: Sage.

Oz-Salzberger, F. (1995) *Translating the Enlightenment*. Oxford: Clarendon Press.

Paris, R. (1997) 'Peace Building and the Limits of Liberal Interventionism', *International Security*, 22: 54–89.

—— (2004) *At War's End*. Cambridge: Cambridge University Press.

PEACE Foundation (1999) *Report on Bougainville for the Year 1999*. Port Moresby: PEACE Foundation Melanesia.

Penfold, P. (2005) 'Faith in Resolving Sierra Leone's Bloody Conflict', *Round Table*, 94: 549–57.

Peters, K. and Richards, P. (1998) '"Why We Fight": Voices of Youth Combatants in Sierra Leone', *Africa*, 68: 183–210.

Pingleton, J. (1989) 'The Role and Function of Forgiveness in Psychotherapy', *Journal of Psychology and Theology*, 17: 27–35.

Pinheiro, P. (2000) 'Democratic Governance, Violence and the (Un)Rule of Law', *Daedalus*, 129: 119–44.

Pocock, J. (1985) *Virtue, Commerce and History*. Cambridge: Cambridge University Press.

Porter, E. (2003) 'Women, Political Decision-Making and Peace Building', *Global Change, Peace and Security*, 15: 245–62.

Potter, M. (2008) 'Women, Civil Society and Peace-Building in Northern Ireland: Paths to Peace through Women's Empowerment', in C. Farrington (ed.), *Global Change, Civil Society and the Northern Ireland Peace Process*. Basingstoke: Palgrave.

Power, M. (2007) *From Ecumenism to Community Relations: Inter-Church Relationships in Northern Ireland 1980–2005*. Dublin: Irish Academic Press.

Powley, E. (2003) *Strengthening Governance: The Role of Women in Rwanda's Transition*. Washington, DC: Hunt Alternatives Fund. Accessible at www.un.org/womenwatch/asagi/meetings/2004/egmelectoral/ep5-powley.pdf.

Prager, J. (2008) 'Healing from History: Psychoanalytic Considerations on Traumatic Pasts and Social Repair', in *European Journal of Social Theory*, 11: 405–20.

Prozesky, M. (1990) *Christianity Amidst Apartheid*. Basingstoke: Macmillan.

Putnam, R. (2000) *Bowling Alone*. New York: Simon and Schuster.

Putzel, J. (1997) 'Accounting for the "Dark Side" of Social Capital', *Journal of International Development*, 9: 939–49.

Ramsbotham, O., Woodhouse, T. and Miall, H. (2005) *Contemporary Conflict Resolution*. Cambridge: Polity Press.

Ray, L. (1999). 'Memory, Trauma and Genocidal Nationalism', *Sociological Research Online*, 4. Accessible at www.socresonline.org.uk/socresonline/4/2/ray.html.

———— (2000) 'Memory, Violence and Identity', in J. Eldridge, J. MacInnes, S. Scott, C. Warhurst and A. Witz (eds), *For Sociology: Legacies and Prospects*. York: Sociologypress.

Reading, A. (2003) *The Social Inheritance of the Holocaust*. Basingstoke: Palgrave.

Recovery of Historical Memory Project (1999) *Guatemala: Never Again*. Maryknoll, NY: Orbis Books.

Reddy, P. (2008) 'Reconciliation in Bougainville: Civil Wars, Peacekeeping and Restorative Justice', *Contemporary Justice Review*, 11: 117–30.

Rehn, E. and Johnson-Sirleaf, E. (2002) *Women, War and Peace*. New York: United Nations Development Fund for Women. Accessible at www.unifem.undp.org.

Reilly, I. (2000) 'Legacy – People and Poets in Northern Ireland', *Australia and New Zealand Journal of Family Therapy*, 21: 162–6.

Renner, M. (1999) *Ending Violent Conflict*. Washington, DC: Worldwatch Institute.

Rex, J. (1981) *Social Conflict*. London: Longman.

Reynolds, A. (1994) *Election '94 South Africa*. Cape Town: David Philip.

Ricoeur, P. (2004a) 'The Difficulty to Forgive', in M. Junker-Kenny and P. Kenny (eds), *Memory, Narrativity, Self and the Challenge to Think God*. Munster: LIT Verlag.

———— (2004b) *Memory, History, Forgetting*. Chicago: University of Chicago Press.

Rigney, A. (2008) 'Divided Pasts: A Premature Memorial and the Dynamics of Collective Remembrance', *Memory Studies*, 1: 89–97.

Robertson, R. (1995) 'Glocalization: Time–Space and Homogeneity–Heterogeneity', in M. Featherstone, S. Lash and R. Robertson (eds), *Global Modernities*. London: Sage.

Robinson, J. (1996) 'Perspective, Meaning and Remembering', in Rubin (1996).

Roche, D. (2002) 'Restorative Justice and the Regulatory State in South African Townships', *British Journal of Criminology*, 42: 514–33.

Rolston, B. (1996) *Turning the Page Without Closing the Book*. Dublin: Irish Reporter Publications.

———— (2000) *Unfinished Business: State Killings and the Quest for Truth*. Belfast: Beyond the Pale.

Rorty, R. (1999) *Philosophy and Social Hope*. London: Penguin.

Rotberg, R. and Thompson, D. (2000) *Truth Versus Justice: The Morality of Truth Commissions*. Princeton, NJ: Princeton University Press.

Roulston, C. (1999) 'Inclusive Others: The Northern Ireland Women's Coalition in the Peace Process', *Scottish Affairs*, 26: 1–13.

Rubin, D. (ed.) (1996) *Remembering Our Past*. Cambridge: Cambridge University Press.

Rutikanga, B. (2003) 'Rwanda', in Cejka and Bamat (2003).

Sampson, S. (2003) 'From Reconciliation to Co-existence', *Public Culture*, 15: 181–6.

Sarkin, J. (2001) 'The Tension between Justice and Reconciliation in Rwanda', *Journal of African Law*, 45: 143–72.

Satha-Anand, C. (2002) 'Forgiveness in South East Asia', *Global Change, Peace and Security*, 14: 235–47.

Schaap, A. (2005) *Political Reconciliation*. London: Routledge.

Scheff, T. (1994) *Bloody Revenge*. Boulder: Westview.

—— (1997a) *Honor and Shame: Local Peacemaking through Community Conferences*. Accessible at www.soc.ucsb.edu/faculty/scheff/6.html.

—— (1997b) *Deconstructing Rage*. Accessible at www.soc.ucsb.edu/faculty/scheff/7.html.

—— (2002) Book review, *Theoretical Criminology*, 6: 361–6.

Scholz, J. and Pinney, N. (1995) 'Duty, Fear and Tax Compliance', *American Journal of Political Science*, 39: 490–512.

Schwartz, B. (2000). *Abraham Lincoln and the Forge of National Memory*. Chicago: University of Chicago Press.

Seidler, V. (1997) *Man Enough: Embodying Masculinities*. London: Sage.

—— (2006) *Transforming Masculinities*. London: Routledge.

Seligman, A. (2000) 'Trust and Civil Society', in F. Tonkiss, A. Passey and N. Fenton (eds), *Trust and Civil Society*. Basingstoke: Macmillan.

Sen, A. (1999) *Development as Freedom*. Oxford: Oxford University Press.

Shapin, S. (1994) *A Social History of Truth*. Chicago: University of Chicago Press.

Shaw, Mark (2001) *Crime and Policing in Transitional Societies*. Johannesburg: Konrad-Adenauer-Stiftung.

—— (ed.) (2002) *Democracy's Disorder*. Johannesburg: South African Institute of International Affairs.

Shaw, Martin (2003) *War and Genocide*. Cambridge: Polity Press.

—— (2007) *What is Genocide?* Cambridge: Polity Press.

Shaw, R. (2005) *Rethinking Truth and Reconciliation Commissions*. Research Report for the UN Institute for Peace, no. 130, February.

—— (2007) 'Memory Friction', *International Journal of Transitional Justice*, 1: 183–207.

Shearing, C. and Kempa, M. (2004) 'A Museum of Hope: A Story of Robben Island', *Annals of the American Academy of Political and Social Science*, 592: 62–78.

Shehadeh, L. (1999) *Women and War in Lebanon*. Gainesville: Florida University Press.

Shirlow, P. and McEvoy, K. (2008) *Beyond the Wire*. London: Pluto Press.

Shriver, D. (1995) *An Ethic for Enemies: Forgiveness and Politics*. Oxford: Oxford University Press.

Singer, J. and Conway, M. (2008) 'Should We Forget Forgetting?' *Memory Studies*, 1: 279–85.

Smith, H. (2007) 'Conflicts of Interest', *The Times Higher*, 12 October.

Smith, H. and Stares, P. (2007) *Diasporas in Conflict: Peace-Makers or Peace-Wreckers?* New York: United Nations University Press.

Smith, T. (2008) 'The Letter, the Spirit and the Future: Rudd's Apology to Australian Aboriginal Peoples', *Australian Review of Public Affairs*, March.

Smyth, G. (2004) 'A Habitable Grief: Forgiveness and Reconciliation for a People Divided', *Milltown Studies*, 53: 94–130.

Smyth, M. (1998) 'Remembering in Northern Ireland: Victims, Perpetrators and Hierarchies of Pain and Responsibility' in Hamber (1998c).

——— (2003) 'Truth, Partial Truth and Irreconcilable Truths: Reflections on the Prospects of Truth Recovery in Northern Ireland', *Smith College Studies in Social Work*, 73: 205–20.

Smyth, M. and Fay, M. T. (2000) *Personal Accounts from Northern Ireland's Troubles*. London: Zed Books.

Snells, J. and Hargrave, T. (1998) 'Forgiveness', *Journal of Family Therapy*, 20: 21–36.

Snyder, C., Harris, C., Anderson, J., et al. (1991), 'The Will and the Ways', *Journal of Personality and Social Psychology*, 60: 570–85.

Soh, S. (2009) *The Comfort Women*. Chicago: University of Chicago Press.

Soyinka, W. (2000) *The Burden of Memory, the Muse of Forgiveness*. Oxford: Oxford University Press.

Stanley, L. (2006) *Mourning Becomes: Post / Memory and the Concentration Camps of the South African War*. Basingstoke: Palgrave.

Stedman, S. (1997) 'Spoiler Problems in Peace Processes', *International Security*, 22: 5–53.

Stedman, S., Rothchild, D. and Cousens, E. (2002) *Ending Civil Wars*. Boulder, CO: Lynne Rienner.

Stevens, J. (2003) *Stevens Enquiry: Overview and Recommendations*. Accessible at www.met.police.uk/commissioner/MP-Stevens-Enquiry-3.pdf.

Stotland, E. (1969) *The Psychology of Hope*. San Francisco: Jossey-Bass.

Strangleman, T. (2004) *Work Identity at the End of the Line*. Basingstoke: Palgrave.

Strong, S. (1992) *Shining Path*. London: Fontana.

Sturken, M. (1997) *Tangled Memories*. Berkeley: University of California Press.

——— (2008) 'Memory, Consumerism and Media', *Memory Studies*, 1: 73–8.

Tavuchis, N. (1991) *Mea Culpa: A Sociology of Apology and Reconciliation*. Stanford: Stanford University Press.

Taylor, C. (2001) *Sacrifice as Terror*. Oxford: Berg.

Teegar, C. and Vinitzky-Seroussi, V. (2007) 'Controlling for Consensus:

Commemorating Apartheid in South Africa', *Symbolic Interaction*, 30: 57–78.
Tessler, M., Nachtwey, J. and Grant, A. (1999) 'Further Tests of the Women and Peace Hypothesis', *International Studies Quarterly*, 43: 519–31.
Tilly, C. (2003) *The Politics of Collective Violence*. Cambridge: Cambridge University Press.
Tombs, D. (2005) 'Truth Telling in Northern Ireland', seminar paper, Trinity College Dublin, 10 June.
Tonkiss, F. (1998) 'Civil–Political', in C. Jenks (ed.), *Core Sociological Dichotomies*. London: Sage.
Torrance, A. (2006) *The Theological Grounds for Advocating Forgiveness in the Sociopolitical Realm*. Belfast: Centre for Contemporary Christianity.
Turner, B. (1990) 'An Outline Theory of Citizenship', *Sociology*, 24: 189–217.
––––––– (2000) 'Liberal Citizenship and Cosmopolitan Virtues', in A. Vandenberg (ed.), *Citizenship and Democracy in a Global Era*. Basingstoke: Macmillan.
––––––– (2002) 'Cosmopolitan Virtues, Globalization and Patriotism', *Theory, Culture and Society*, 19: 45–63.
Tutu, D. (2001) *Dignity, Equality and Inalienable Rights*. Lecture by Archbishop Desmond Tutu, Belfast, 6 November. Belfast: Committee on the Administration of Justice.
Ungerleider, J. (2001) 'Bicommunal Youth Camps for Peace in Cyprus', *Peace Review*, 13: 583–9.
UNICEF (1997) *Children and Women of Rwarda: A Situational Analysis of Social Sectors*. New York: United Nations Children's Fund.
––––––– (2001) *An End to Violence Against Children*. New York: United Nations Children's Fund.
UNIFEM (2000) *Women at the Peace Table*. New York: United Nations Development Fund for Women.
––––––– (2005) *Securing the Peace*. New York: United Nations Development Fund for Women.
Ure, M. (2008) 'Introduction', in *European Journal of Social Theory*, 11: 283–98.
Urry, J. (1996) 'How Societies Remember the Past', in S. Macdonald and G. Fyfe (eds), *Theorizing Museums*. Oxford: Blackwell.
Uyangoda, J. (1996) 'NGOs, Hate Politics and Questions of Democracy', *Pravada*, 4–5: 6–9.
Van House, N. and Churchill, E. (2008) 'Technologies of Memory: Key Issues and Critical Perspectives', *Memory Studies*, 1: 295–310.
Villa-Vicencio, C. and Vervoerd, W. (2000) *Looking Back, Reaching Forward*. Cape Town: University of Cape Town Press.
Vinitzky-Seroussi, V. (2002) 'Commemorating a Difficult Past: Yitzak

Rabin's Memorials', *American Sociological Review*, 67: 30–51.

Vogel, A. (2006) 'Who's Making Global Civil Society: Philanthropy and US Empire in World Society', *British Journal of Sociology*, 57: 635–55.

Waghid, Y. (2004) 'Compassion, Citizenship and Education in South Africa', *International Review of Education*, 50: 525–42.

Walaza, N. (2003) 'Reconciling and Partial Truths', *Smith College Studies in Social Work*, 73: 189–204.

Wallace, C., Haerpfer, C. and Abbott, P. (2009) 'Women in Rwandan Politics and Society', *International Journal of Sociology*, 38: 111–25.

Walsh, D. (2000) *Bloody Sunday and the Rule of Law in Northern Ireland*. Dublin: Gill and Macmillan.

Walter, B. F. (2002) *Committing to Peace*. Princeton, NJ: Princeton University Press.

Ward, M. and McGivern, M. (1982) 'Images of Women in Northern Ireland', *Crane Bag*, 4: 66–72.

Ward, R. (2004) '"It's Not Tea and Buns": Women and Pro-Union Politics in Northern Ireland', *British Journal of Politics and International Relations*, 6: 494–506.

Watts, F. (2004) *Forgiveness*. London: Continuum.

Weber, M. (1947) *The Theory of Social and Economic Organization*. Ed. Talcott Parsons and trans. A. H. Henderson and Talcott Parsons. New York: The Free Press.

Weiner, E. (1998) *The Handbook of Inter-Ethnic Coexistence*. London: Continuum.

Wijesinghe, S. (2003) 'Sri Lanka', in Cejka and Bamat (2003).

Wild, L. (2006) *Strengthening Global Civil Society*. London: Institute of Public Policy Research.

Wilkinson, I. (2005) *Suffering*. Cambridge: Polity Press.

Williams, R. (2004) 'Ready for Action: GI Jane, Demi Moore's Body and the Female Combat Movie', in Y. Tasker (ed.), *Action and Adventure Cinema*. London: Routledge.

Wilmerding, J. (2002) *Restorative Justice and the Effects of War*. Accessible at http://csf.colorado.edu/forums/peace/nov02/msg00010.html

Wilson, R. (1998) 'The Politics of Remembering and Forgetting in Guatemala', in R. Sieder (ed.), *Guatemala After the Peace Accords*. London: Institute of Latin American Studies, University of London.

——— (2001) *The Politics of Truth and Reconciliation in South Africa*. Cambridge: Cambridge University Press.

Wolterstorff, N. (1983) *Until Justice and Peace Embrace*. Grand Rapids: Eerdmans.

Woodiwiss, A. (2002) 'Human Rights and the Challenge of Cosmopolitanism', *Theory, Culture and Society*, 19: 139–57.

World Bank (1998) *Rwanda Poverty Note*. World Bank Report no. 17792-RW.

Wright, S. (2001), 'Oscar Romero and Juan Gerardi: Truth, Memory and

Hope', in Hayes and Tombs (2001).

Youngs, G. (1999) 'Tampons and Cigars: (No) Escaping Sexual Difference in GI Jane', *International Journal of Politics*, 1: 479–81.

Yuval-Davis, N. (1997) *Gender and Nation*. London: Sage.

Yuval-Davis, N. and Anthias, F. (1989) *Women, Nation, State*. Basingstoke: Macmillan.

Zack-Williams, A. (2001) 'Child Soldiers in the Civil War in Sierra Leone', *Review of African Political Economy*, 87: 73–82.

Zald, M. and McCarthy, J. (1987) 'Religious Groups as the Crucible of Social Movements', in M. Zald and J. McCarthy (eds), *Social Movements in an Organizational Society*. New Brunswick: Transaction Books.

Zalewski, M. (2006) 'Intervening in Northern Ireland: Critically Re-Thinking Representations of the Conflict', *Critical Review of International Social and Political Philosophy*, 9: 479–97.

Zechmeister, J. and Romero, C. (2002) 'Victim and Offender Accounts of Inter-Personal Conflict', *Journal of Personality and Social Psychology*, 82: 675–86.

# Index